MODERN DATABASE MANAGEMENT

Dr. Bechoo Lal

Toronto Academic Press

MODERN DATABASE MANAGEMENT

Dr. Bechoo Lal

Toronto Academic Press
4164 Lakeshore Road
Burlington ON L7L 1A4
Canada
www.tap-books.com

Email: orders@arclereducation.com

ISBN: 978-1-77956-288-3

Toronto Academic Press publishes wide variety of books and eBooks. For more information about Toronto Academic Press and its products, visit our website at www.tap-books.com.

ABOUT THE AUTHOR

Bechoo Lal, PhD. became a Member (M) of IAENG: International Association of Engineers, USA with membership (108820) in 2010, a Senior Member (SM) in 2019. I am doctorate PhD in Computer Science, PhD- Information System from University of Mumbai, Master from Banaras Hindu University (BHU), PGP- Data Science from Purdue University, USA. Currently working as a Associate Professor in Department of Computer Science & Engineering, KLEF- KL University Vijayawada Campus Andhra Pradesh, India. His research areas are data science, big data analytics and Machine Learning.

Table of Contents

List of Figures

List of Tables

PREFACE

In today's rapidly evolving technological landscape, the management of data has become a critical component of virtually every aspect of business, academia, and society at large. This book, "Modern Database Management," aims to provide you with a comprehensive understanding of the principles, concepts, and technologies that underpin the effective management of data in contemporary environments. Organized into eight chapters, this book covers a wide range of topics essential for anyone seeking to navigate the complexities of modern database systems.

Chapter 1, "Introduction to Modern Database Management," serves as a foundational exploration into the fundamental concepts of database management systems, setting the stage for the subsequent chapters.

Chapter 2, "Introduction to Distributed Systems," delves into the intricacies of distributed computing and its relevance in modern database architectures.

In Chapter 3, "Computer Networks and Data Communication," we examine the essential principles of networking and communication protocols crucial for the seamless exchange of data in distributed environments.

Chapter 4, "Distributed File System," explores the design and implementation of distributed file systems, offering insights into their role in managing large-scale data storage and retrieval.

Chapter 5, "Fundamentals of Data Management," provides a comprehensive overview of data management principles, including data modeling, storage, retrieval, and manipulation.

Chapter 6, "Relational Database Constraints and Relational Data Model," delves into the foundational concepts of relational databases, constraints, and the relational model, which form the backbone of many modern database systems.

Chapter 7, "NoSQL Database," explores the emergence of non-relational database systems and their unique characteristics, offering alternatives to traditional relational databases for specific use cases.

Finally, in Chapter 8, "Cloud Databases and Big Data," we examine the transformative impact of cloud computing and big data technologies on database management, exploring their role in enabling scalability, flexibility, and accessibility of data resources.

This book aims to provide a balance of theoretical insights and practical applications, equipping readers with the knowledge and skills necessary to navigate the dynamic landscape of modern database management. Whether you are a student, a practitioner, or an enthusiast eager to explore the intricacies of database systems, we hope this book serves as a valuable resource in your journey.

–Author

CHAPTER 1

Introduction to Modern Database Management

LEARNING OBJECTIVES

After studying this chapter, you will be able to:

- Understand the fundamentals of database systems;
- Explore database models and architectures;
- Discuss the SQL and database querying;
- Understand data modeling and design;
- Discuss the role of database management in modern organizations.

"Data is the lifeblood of the modern organization, and a well-managed database is the heart that keeps it flowing, enabling businesses to thrive in an information-driven world."

INTRODUCTORY EXAMPLE

Let's talk about Mr. Smith's online bookstore. He's got a ton of books, like thousands of them. But with so many, he needs a really good way to keep track of everything, like which books are in stock, what customers are buying, and other important details.

Before, Mr. Smith might have used papers or computer files to keep track of things. But as his bookstore grows, it gets harder and harder to stay organized.

That's where modern database management comes in. It's like having a super organized filing system on a computer. With a good database, Mr. Smith can keep track of all his books, who's buying them, what's selling well, and lots more, all in one place.

Just think about how helpful it would be for Mr. Smith to quickly find any book he has, see which one's people like the most, understand what his customers are interested in, and even predict which books might be popular next. All of this is possible with a good database system.

UNIT INTRODUCTION

Modern database management represents a significant advancement in how data is handled using advanced computer systems. Today's systems have evolved from simpler past methods like basic databases and file systems to more sophisticated ones capable of managing larger volumes of data and performing diverse tasks efficiently. These modern systems stand out for their ability to scale up to accommodate growing data needs, their speed in processing data, and their flexibility to meet various requirements. They involve organizing data in structured ways, utilizing languages such as SQL for data management, and ensuring the accuracy and security of the data. Additionally, the emergence of new database types, particularly suited for handling extensive data sets, marks a notable development in this field. In an era where data is a critical asset across various sectors, understanding modern database management is essential for using the data effectively.

1.1. BASIC CONCEPTS AND DEFINITIONS

Learning Objectives

At the end of this section, readers will be able to:

- Understand the fundamentals of data;
- Differentiate between data and information;
- Understand the importance of metadata.

A database is a logically structured collection of data. It can be of any size and level of complexity for example, a salesperson may have a small database of customer contacts (a few megabytes of data) on her laptop computer. On a large mainframe computer, a large firm may develop a large database containing several terabytes (trillion bytes) of data that is utilized for decision support applications.

1.1.1. Data

Historically, the term data referred to facts about the objects and events that could be recorded and stored on computer media. For example, in a salesperson's database, the data would include facts such as customer name, address, and telephone number. This type of data is called structured data. The most important structured data types are numeric, character, and dates. Structured data are stored in tabular form (in tables, relations, arrays, spreadsheets etc.) and are most commonly found in traditional databases and data warehouses.

In addition to structured data, databases are now used to store things such as documents, e-mails, tweets, Facebook posts, GPS information, maps, photographic images, sound, and video segments. For example, the salesperson's database might include a profile image of the customer contact. It could also contain a video clip regarding the most recent product. This type of information is known as unstructured data or multimedia data. To create a real multimedia environment, structured and unstructured data are frequently integrated in the same database. For example, a car repair company can mix structured data (descriptions of customers and vehicles) with multimedia data (photos of damaged vehicles and scanned copies of insurance claim forms). One of the distinguishing features of "big data" technologies, which will be discussed further in this book, is their ability to deal with highly heterogeneous data.

1.1.2. Data versus Information

Data and information are closely related concepts that are frequently used interchangeably. It is, nevertheless, necessary to distinguish between data and information. Information is data that have been processed in such a way that the knowledge of the person who uses the data is increased. For example, consider the following list of facts:

Name	Social Security Number
Baker, Kenneth D.	324917628
Doyle, Joan E.	476193248
Finkle, Clive R.	548429344
Lewis, John C.	551742186
McFerran, Debra R	409723145

These facts justify our definition of data, but most people would agree that the data are useless in their present form. Even if you guessed that this is a list of people's names paired with their Social Security numbers, the data remain useless because you would have no idea what the entries mean. Notice what happens when you see the same data in a context, as shown in Figure 1.1.

Class Roster

Course: MGT 500 Business Policy   Semester: Spring 2010

Section: 2

Name	ID	Major	GPA
Baker, Kenneth D.	324917628	MGT	2.9
Doyle, Joan E.	476193248	MKT	3.4
Finkle, Clive R.	548429344	PRM	2.8
Lewis, John C.	551742186	MGT	3.7
McFerran, Debra R.	409723145	IS	2.9
Sisneros, Michael	392416582	ACCT	3.3

Figure 1.1. *Converting data to information (data in context).*

By adding a few additional data items and providing some structure, you are able to recognize a class roster for a particular course. Some users, such as the course teacher and the registrar's office, will find this information beneficial. However, as public awareness of the necessity of data security has grown, few companies now utilize Social Security numbers as IDs. For identifying purposes, most organizations instead utilize an internally created number.

Another way to convert data into information is to summarize it or present it for human interpretation. For example, Figure 1.2 shows summarized student enrollment data presented as graphical information. This information could be used as a basis for deciding whether to add new courses or to hire new faculty members.

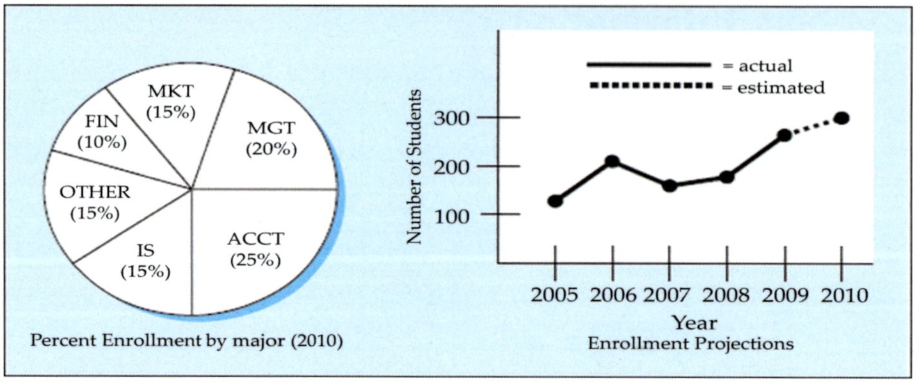

Figure 1.2. *Converting data to information (summarized data).*

1.1.3. Metadata

As discussed earlier, data become useful only when placed in some context. The primary mechanism for providing context for data is metadata. Metadata are data that describe the properties or characteristics of end-user data and the context of that data. Some of the properties that are typically described include data names, definitions, length (or size), and allowable values. Metadata describing data context include the source of the data, where the data are stored, ownership (or stewardship), and usage. Although it may seem circular, many people think of metadata as "data about data."

Some sample metadata for the Class Roster (Figure 1.1) are listed in Table 1.1. For each data item that appears in the Class Roster, the metadata show the data item name, the data type, length, minimum and maximum allowable values (where appropriate), a brief description of each data item, and the source of the data (sometimes called the system of record).

Table 1.1. *Examples Metadata for Class Roster*

Data Item		Length	Metadata		Description	Source
Name	**Type**		**Min**	**Max**		
Course	Alphanumeric	30	–	–	Course ID and name	Academic unit
Section	Integer	1	1	9	Section number	Registrar
Semester	Alphanumeric	10	–	–	Semester and year	Registrar
Name	Alphanumeric	30	–	–	Student name	Student IS
ID	Integer	9	–	–	Student ID (SSN)	Student IS
Major	Alphanumeric	4	–	–	Student major	Student IS
GPA	Decimal	3	0.0	4.0	Student grade point average	Academic unit

1.2. TRADITIONAL FILE PROCESSING SYSTEMS

Learning Objectives

At the end of this section, readers will be able to:

- Understand the traditional file processing systems;
- Learn about the drawbacks of traditional file processing systems;
- Explain the duplication of data.

When computer-based data processing was first available, there were no databases. To be useful for business applications, computers had to store, manipulate, and retrieve large files of data. Computer file processing systems were developed for this purpose. Although these systems have evolved over time, their basic structure and purpose have changed little over several decades. As business applications became more complex, it became evident that traditional file processing systems had a number of shortcomings and limitations. As a result, these systems have been replaced by database processing systems in most business applications today. Nevertheless, you should have at least some familiarity with file processing systems since understanding the problems and limitations inherent in file processing systems can help you avoid these same problems when designing database systems. It should be noted that Excel files, in general, fall into the same category as file systems and suffer from the same drawbacks/disadvantages listed below. Informal use of Excel for management of data is believed to continue to be quite widespread, although valid research results regarding this are difficult to find.

1.2.1. File Processing Systems at Pine Valley Furniture Company

Pine Valley Furniture's early computer applications employed the traditional file processing method. This approach to information system design addressed the data processing demands of particular departments rather than the organization's overall information needs. In most cases, the information systems group replied to user requests for new systems by building (or acquiring) new computer programs for specific applications such as inventory control, accounts receivable, or human resource management. There was no comprehensive map, plan, or model that governed application progress.

Three of the computer applications based on the file processing approach are shown in Figure 1.3. The systems illustrated are Order Filling, Invoicing, and Payroll.

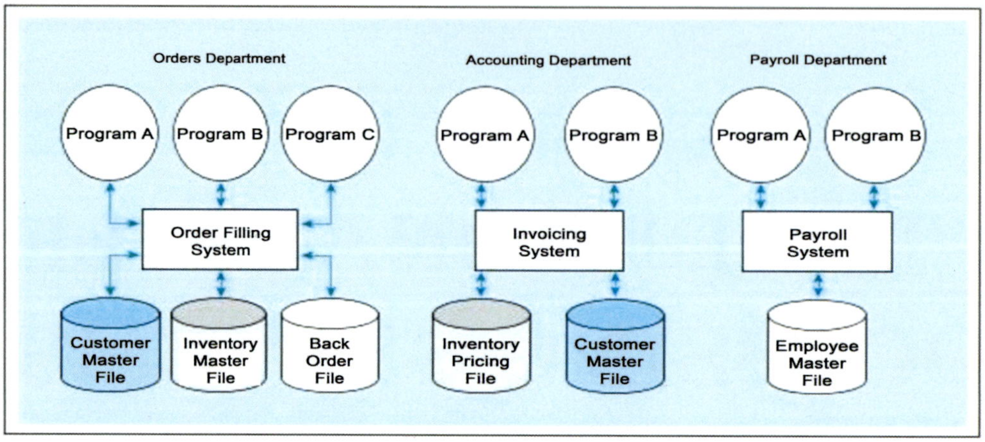

Figure 1.3. *Old file processing systems at Pine Valley Furniture Company.*

The diagram also depicts the most important data files linked with each application. A file is a grouping of connected records. The Order Filling System, for example, contains three files: Customer Master, Inventory Master, and Back Order. Some of the files used by the three applications are duplicated, which is typical of file processing systems.

Program-data dependence
Duplication of data
Limited data sharing
Lengthy development times
Excessive program maintenance

1.2.2. Drawbacks of File Processing Systems

Several disadvantages associated with conventional file processing systems are listed above and described briefly next.

1.2.2.1. Program-Data Dependence

Each database application program that accesses a specific file stores file description. In the invoicing system in Figure 1.3, for example, Program A accesses the Inventory Pricing File and the Customer Master File because the software includes a thorough file description for these files, any changes to the file structure need updates to the file descriptions for all programs that use the file. The Customer Master File is used in both the Order Filling System and the Invoicing System, as shown in Figure 1.3. Assume it is decided to increase the length of the customer address field in the records in this file from 30 to 40 characters. The file descriptions in each impacted program (up to five programs) would need to be changed. Even locating all applications affected by such modifications is frequently challenging. Worse, when making such adjustments, errors are frequently introduced.

1.2.2.2. Duplication of Data

As the applications in file processing systems are frequently built independently, unplanned duplicate data files are the rule rather than the exception. In Figure 1.4, for example, the Order Filling System has an Inventory Master File, but the Invoicing System has an Inventory Pricing File. These files provide information about Pine Valley Furniture Company's products, such as product descriptions, unit prices, and stock levels. This duplication is inefficient since it necessitates more storage space and more effort to maintain all data up to date. Data formats can be inconsistent, data values can be inconsistent, or both. In file processing systems, establishing reliable metadata is extremely challenging. The same data item, for example, may have distinct names in different files, or the same name may be used for different data items in different files.

1.2.2.3. Limited Data Sharing

Each application has its own private files in the traditional file processing system, and users have little ability to communicate data outside of their own applications. Users in the Accounting Department, for example, have access to the Invoicing System and its files, but not to the Order Filling System or the Payroll System and their files, as shown in Figure 1.4. Managers frequently discover that a required report necessitates a significant programming effort because data must be gathered from numerous incompatible files in various systems. Additional management barriers must be overcome when various organizational units own these separate files.

1.2.2.4. Lengthy Development Times

With traditional file processing systems, each new application needs the developer to design new file formats and descriptions before writing the file access logic for each new program. Long development times are incompatible with today's fast-paced business environment, where time to market is a critical corporate success factor.

1.2.2.5. Excessive Program Maintenance

All of the above factors combined to generate a significant software maintenance burden in firms that relied on traditional file processing systems. In fact, in such firms, program maintenance may consume up to 80% of the whole information system development budget. As a result, resources (money, people, and time) are not being allocated to the development of new applications.

As previously stated, these drawbacks apply even when people and organizational units store critical organizational data in Excel spreadsheets. Furthermore, many of the problems of file processing that you have talked about might also be limitations of databases if an organization does not use the database strategy correctly. For example, if an organization creates a large number of individually managed databases (say, one for each division or business function) with little or no metadata synchronization, uncontrolled data duplication, limited data exchange, delayed development time, and costly program maintenance might ensue. As a result, the database approach, as described in the next section, is as much a method of managing organizational data as it is a set of tools for defining, creating, maintaining, and accessing this data.

1.3. THE DATABASE APPROACH

Learning Objectives

At the end of this section, readers will be able to:

- Understand the database approach;
- Explain the different types of data models;
- Understand the database management;
- Explore the advantages of database approach.

So, how can you overcome file processing flaws? No, you don't reach out to Ghostbusters, but you can do better: use the database technique. You will first study some key ideas for comprehending the database approach to data management. The database strategy will then be used to overcome the constraints of the file processing approach.

1.3.1. Data Models

Designing a database effectively is critical to creating a database that fits the needs of the users. Data models capture the nature of and interactions between data and are used at various degrees of abstraction during the conceptualization and design of a database. The structure of a database has a direct relationship with its effectiveness and efficiency. There are several graphical systems that transmit this structure and are used to create data models that database designers, systems analysts, and end users can understand.

1.3.1.1. Entities

An organization maintains information regarding customers and orders as objects. They are known as "entities." In the business world, an entity is similar to a noun in that it describes a person, a location, an object, an event, or an idea for which information must be recorded and preserved. Figure 1.4 depicts the entities CUSTOMER and ORDER. An attribute is the data about the entity that you want to capture (for example, Customer Name). Many clients' data are recorded. Each customer's information is referred to as an instance of CUSTOMER.

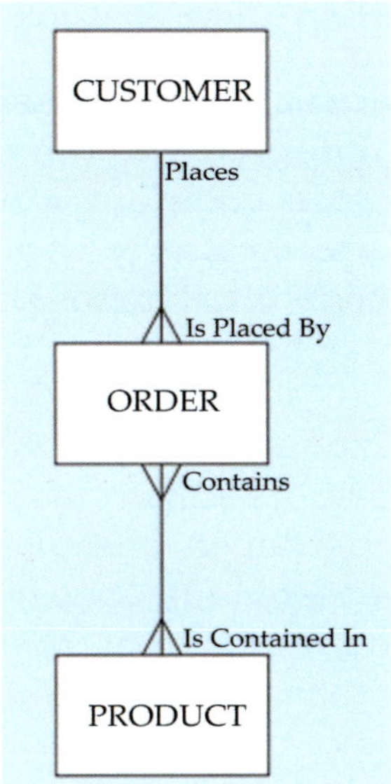

Figure 1.4. *Comparison of enterprise- and project-level data models (segment of an enterprise data model).*

1.3.1.2. Relationships

A well-structured database establishes relationships between entities in organizational data, allowing for the retrieval of necessary information. The majority of relationships are either one-to-many (1:M) or many-to-many (M:N). A client can place multiple orders with a company (the Places connection). Each order, however, is normally associated with (the Is Placed By relationship) a specific consumer. The 1:M relationship of customers who may place one or more orders is seen in Figure 1.5; the 1:M nature of the relationship is indicated by the crow's foot attached to the rectangle (entity) labeled ORDER. Figures 1.5 appear to show the same relationship. The connection between orders and products, on the other hand, is M:N. An order may include one or more products, and a product may appear on many orders. It is worth mentioning that Figure 1.5 is an enterprise-level model in which only the higher-level linkages of customers, orders, and items are included.

Figure 1.5 depicts the project-level diagram, which incorporates extra levels of detail, such as order details (Figure 1.5).

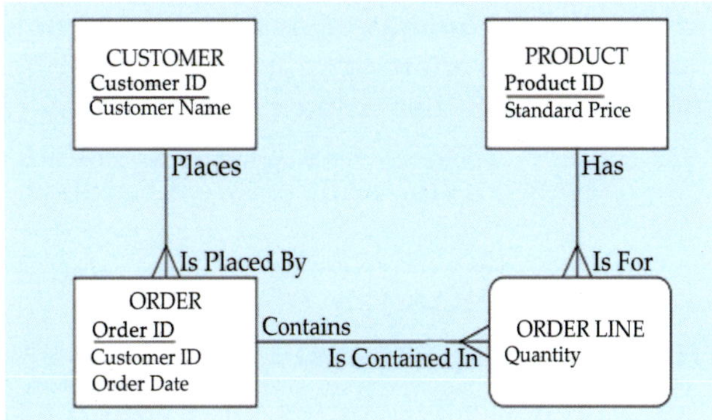

Figure 1.5. *Comparison of enterprise- and project-level data models (segment of a project data model).*

1.3.1.3. Relational Databases

Relational databases establish relationships between things by utilizing common fields included in a file, referred to as a relation. The data models in Figure 1.5 demonstrate the relationship between a customer and the customer's order by adding the customer's number with the customer's purchase. As a result, a customer's identification number is stored in the file (or relation) that contains customer information such as name, address, and so on. When a customer puts an order, his or her customer identification number is added to the relation that carries the order information. The identification number is used in relational databases to establish the relationship between the customer and the order.

1.3.2. Database Management Systems

A database management system (DBMS) is a software that allows you to use a database strategy. A DBMS's primary goal is to provide a systematic way for creating, updating, storing, and retrieving data from a database. End users and application programmers can share data, and data can be shared across numerous applications rather than propagated and stored in new files for each new application (Mullins, 2002). A DBMS also allows you to regulate data access, enforce data integrity, manage concurrency control, and restore a database.

1.3.3. Advantages of the Database Approach

The primary advantages of a database approach, enabled by DBMSs, are summarized in following list and described next.

- Program-data independence
- Planned data redundancy
- Improved data consistency
- Improved data sharing
- Increased productivity of application development
- Enforcement of standards
- Improved data quality
- Improved data accessibility and responsiveness
- Reduced program maintenance
- Improved decision support

1.3.3.1. Program-Data Independence

Data independence refers to the separation of data descriptions (metadata) from the application programs that use the data. The database approach stores data descriptions in a centralized area known as the repository. This property of database systems allows an organization's data to change and evolve (within limits) without changing the application programs that process the data.

1.3.3.2. Planned Data Redundancy

A good database design seeks to combine previously independent (and redundant) data files into a coherent structure. Each primary fact should ideally be documented in only one place in the database. For example, in the product table, which contains data about each of Pine Valley's items, facts about a product, such as the Pine Valley oak computer desk, its finish, price, and so on, are listed together in one place. Although the database technique does not completely eliminate redundancy, it does allow the designer to manage the type and degree of redundancy.

1.3.3.3. Improved Data Consistency

You can considerably reduce the chances of inconsistency by eliminating or limiting data redundancy. For example, if a customer's address is only saved once, we cannot disagree on the address. Because the address is recorded in a single location, recording the new address is substantially simpler when the customer's address changes. Finally, you avoid the waste of storage space caused by redundant data storage.

1.3.3.4. Improved Data Sharing

A database is designed to be a shared company resource. To assist this use, authorized internal and external users are granted access to use the database, and each user (or set of users) is provided with one or more user views into the database. A user view is a logical description of a section of the database that a user needs to execute a task. A user view is frequently created by identifying a form or report that a user requires on a regular basis. A human resources employee, for example, will require access to confidential employee data, whereas a customer will require access to the product catalog provided on Pine Valley's website. The views for the human resources staff and the customer come from completely separate parts of the same unified database.

1.3.3.5. Increased Productivity of Application Development

A key benefit of the database method is that it significantly reduces the cost and time required to construct new business applications. There are three major reasons why database applications can typically be designed significantly faster than traditional file apps:

- 1. Assuming that the database and associated data capture and maintenance applications have already been designed and implemented, the application developer can focus on the specific functions required for the new application without worrying about file design or low-level implementation details.
- 2. The database management system includes a variety of high-level productivity tools, such as form and report generators, as well as high-level languages for automating tasks.
- 3. Significant improvements in application developer productivity, estimated to be up to 60% (Long, 2005), are already being gained through the usage of Web services based on standard Internet protocols and a generally understood data format (XML).

1.3.3.6. Enforcement of Standards

When the database strategy is fully implemented, the database administration function should be given single-point authority and responsibility for developing and enforcing data standards. Naming conventions, data quality standards, and common methods for accessing, updating, and protecting data will all be part of these standards. The data repository gives database administrators a comprehensive set of tools for defining and enforcing these rules. Unfortunately, one of the most common causes of database failures in organizations is a failure to create a strong database administration function.

1.3.3.7. Improved Data Quality

Concerns about poor data quality are a recurrent subject in today's strategic planning and database administration. Poor data quality is estimated to have cost the US economy almost $3 trillion in 2011, nearly twice the size of the federal deficit. The database approach provides a number of tools and processes to improve data quality. Two of the more important are the following:

- i. Database designers can define integrity constraints that the DBMS will enforce. A constraint is a rule that database users must follow.
- ii. One of the objectives of a data warehouse environment is to clean up (or "scrub") operational data before it is stored in the warehouse (Jordan, 1996).

1.3.3.8. Improved Data Accessibility and Responsiveness

A relational database allows non-programming end users to easily access and present data, even when it involves multiple departments. As an illustration, a staff member can retrieve information regarding computer desks at Pine Valley

Furniture Company by executing the subsequent query:

```
SELECT *
FROM Product_T
WHERE Product Description = "Computer Desk";
```

The language used in this query is called Structured Query Language, or SQL. While the queries can be significantly more complex, the basic structure of the query is simple enough for beginners. If they grasp the structure and names of the data that aligns with their database perspective, they promptly acquire the capacity to extract solutions to novel inquiries without depending on a skilled application developer. It is important to exercise caution as this can pose a risk; queries must undergo comprehensive testing to ensure the accuracy of the data they produce before depending on their outcomes, and individuals who lack experience might not fully understand the complexity of this task.

1.3.3.9. Reduced Program Maintenance

There are numerous reasons why stored data must be modified frequently: the addition of new data item types, alterations to data formats, and so forth. An exemplary instance of this issue was the widely recognized "year 2000" problem, wherein standard two-digit year fields were expanded to four digits to account for the carryover from 1999 to 2000.

Data descriptions and the logic for accessing data are implemented within individual application programs in a file processing environment. Changes to data formats and access methods consequently necessitate the modification of application programs. Data are more independent of the application programs that utilize them in a database environment. Changes to either the data or the application programs that utilize the data do not require adjustments to the other factor, provided that they do not exceed certain limitations. Consequently, program maintenance in a contemporary database environment can be substantially diminished.

1.3.3.10. Improved Decision Support

Some databases are designed expressly for decision support applications. For example, some databases are designed to support customer relationship management, whereas others are designed to support financial analysis or supply chain management.

1.3.4. Costs and Risks of the Database Approach

A database is neither a panacea, nor does it possess the magical powers of Harry Potter. The database method, like any other business decision, has some additional expenses and risks that must be identified and managed when it is implemented.

1.3.4.1. New, Specialized Personnel

Organizations that use the database approach frequently need to hire or train people to design and deploy databases, provide database administration services, and manage a new staff. Furthermore, because technology is changing so quickly, these new employees will need to be retrained or upgraded on a frequent basis. This personnel increase may be more than offset by other productivity advantages, but a company should acknowledge the need of these specialist talents in order to maximize the potential benefits.

1.3.4.2. Integrated Data Management Framework

The database approach described above is associated with relational database technologies and used primarily as a foundation for the design and implementation of transaction processing systems (*operational systems*). Data management technologies are also increasingly often used as *informational systems*, as a foundation for analytics, or the systematic analysis and interpretation of data to improve our understanding of a real-world domain. Transactional systems are still the core of this book with a focus on relational databases and the SQL language. These technologies continue, in practice, to be a fundamental source of data for all areas of data management, and no other technology is as widely used. They form the foundation on which business activities of modern organizations are built because they enable the way in which organizations interact and do business with their stakeholders.

1.4. COMPONENTS OF DATABASE ENVIRONMENT

Learning Objectives

At the end of this section, readers will be able to:

- Identify the key components of a database environment.
- Understand the role of database management systems (DBMS) in the database environment.
- Explore the functions and responsibilities of database administrators (DBAs).
- Explain the importance of data dictionaries and metadata in database management.

Now that you've seen both the advantages and drawbacks of using a database approach to data management, let's look at the primary components of a typical database environment and their relationships. Some of these components have previously been introduced to you in previous sections. Following is a brief description of the nine components shown in Figure 1.6.

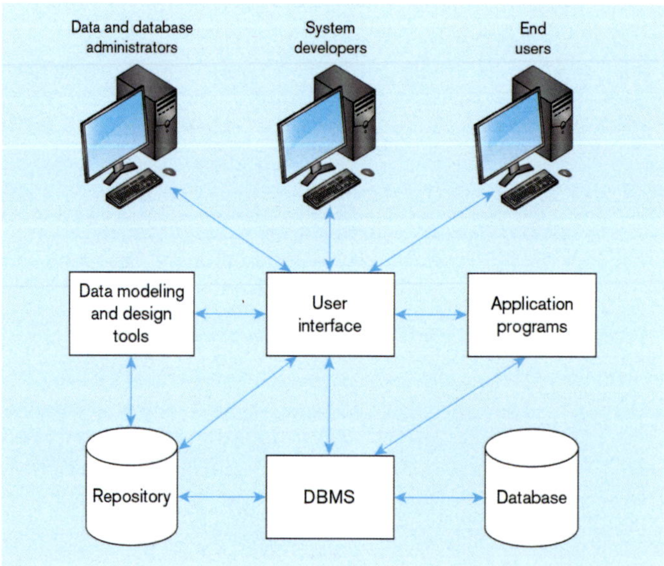

Figure 1.6. *Components of the database environment.*

1.4.1. Data Modeling and Design Tools

Data modeling and design tools are computer-aided tools for creating databases and application programs. These tools aid in the design of data models and, in some situations, can also assist in the automatic generation of the "code" required for creating the database.

1.4.2. Repository

A repository is a knowledge base that contains all data definitions, data relationships, screen and report formats, and other system components. A repository holds a large amount of metadata that is useful for managing databases and other components of an information system.

1.4.3. DBMS

A database management system (DBMS) is a software system that is used to generate, maintain, and offer controlled access to user databases.

1.4.4. Database

A database is a logically ordered collection of data that is typically intended to meet the information demands of various users in an organization. It is critical to differentiate between the database and the repository. The repository holds data definitions, whereas the database contains data occurrences.

1.4.5. Application Programs

Computer-based application applications are used for creating and updating the database, as well as to offer information to users.

1.4.6. User Interface

The user interface consists of languages, menus, and other facilities that let users to interact with various system components such as data modeling and design tools, application programs, the DBMS, and the repository.

1.4.7. Data and Database Administrators

Data administrators are persons who are responsible for the overall management of data resources in an organization. Database administrators are responsible for physical database design and for managing technical issues in the database environment.

1.4.8. System Developers

System developers are persons, such as systems analysts and programmers, who design new application programs.

1.4.9. End Users

End users are persons throughout the organization who add, delete, and modify data in the database and who request or receive information from it. All user interactions with the database must be routed through the DBMS.

In short, the database operational environment shown in Figure 1.7 is an integrated system of hardware, software, and people, designed to facilitate the storage, retrieval, and control of the information resource and to improve the productivity of the organization.

1.5. THE DATABASE DEVELOPMENT PROCESS

Learning Objectives

At the end of this section, readers will be able to:

- Identify the key components of a database environment;
- Understand the role of database management systems (DBMS) in the database environment;
- Explore the functions and responsibilities of database administrators (DBAs).

How do businesses get started with database development? Database development in many businesses begins with enterprise data modeling, which defines the scope and broad contents of organizational databases. Its goal is to generate a comprehensive image or explanation of organizational data, rather than the construction of a specific database. A specific database supplies data for one or more information systems, whereas an enterprise data model, which may include multiple databases, specifies the organization's data management strategy. Enterprise data modeling include reviewing present systems, analyzing the nature of the business areas to be serviced, describing the data required at a high degree of abstraction, and planning one or more database development projects.

Figure 1.7 depicted a part of an enterprise data model for Pine Valley Furniture Company using a simplified notation. A full enterprise data model would also include business-oriented definitions of each entity type, as well as a collection of diverse statements about how the organization functions, known as business rules that regulate the validity of data. Relationships between business objects (such as business functions, units, and applications) and data are frequently represented using matrixes, which supplement the information stored in the enterprise data model. An example of such a matrix is shown in Figure 1.7.

Business Functions \ Data Entity Types	Customer	Product	Raw Material	Order	Work Center	Work Order	Invoice	Equipment	Employee
Business Planning	X	X						X	X
Product Development		X	X		X			X	
Materials Management		X	X	X	X	X		X	
Order Fulfillment	X	X	X	X	X	X	X	X	X
Order Shipment	X	X		X	X		X		X
Sales Summarization	X	X		X			X		X
Production Operations		X	X	X	X	X		X	X
Finance and Accounting	X	X	X	X	X		X	X	X

X = data entity is used within business function

Figure 1.7. *Example business function-to-data entity matrix.*

One source of database initiatives is enterprise data modeling as part of a top-down approach to information system planning and development. Such projects frequently create new databases in order to achieve strategic organizational goals such as improved customer service, better production and inventory management, or more precise sales forecasting. Many database projects, on the other hand, emerge from the ground up. Projects are sought in this scenario by information system users who want specific information to perform their tasks or by other information systems professionals who recognize a need to improve data management in the company.

A typical bottom-up database development project revolves around the creation of a single database. Some database initiatives are solely concerned with defining, creating, and implementing a database as the foundation for future information system development. However, in most circumstances, a database and the related information processing capabilities are created as part of a larger information systems development effort.

1.5.1. Systems Development Life Cycle

The systems development life cycle (SDLC), as you may know from prior information systems courses you've attended, is a traditional process for carrying out an information systems development project. The SDLC is a comprehensive set of stages that an organization's team of information systems experts, including database designers and programmers, uses to describe, construct, manage, and replace information systems. Many versions on the life cycle are used in textbooks and organizations, with anything from 3 to 20 different phases identified.

Figure 1.8 depicts the various SDLC processes and their associated purposes (Valacich & George, 2016). The method appears circular, and it is meant to emphasize the iterative nature of system development initiatives. The phases may overlap in time, be performed in parallel, and it is possible to return to previous steps if prior decisions must be revisited.

Some believe that the most frequent approach through the development process is to cycle through the processes illustrated in Figure 1.8, but at a higher level of detail on each pass as the system's needs become more explicit.

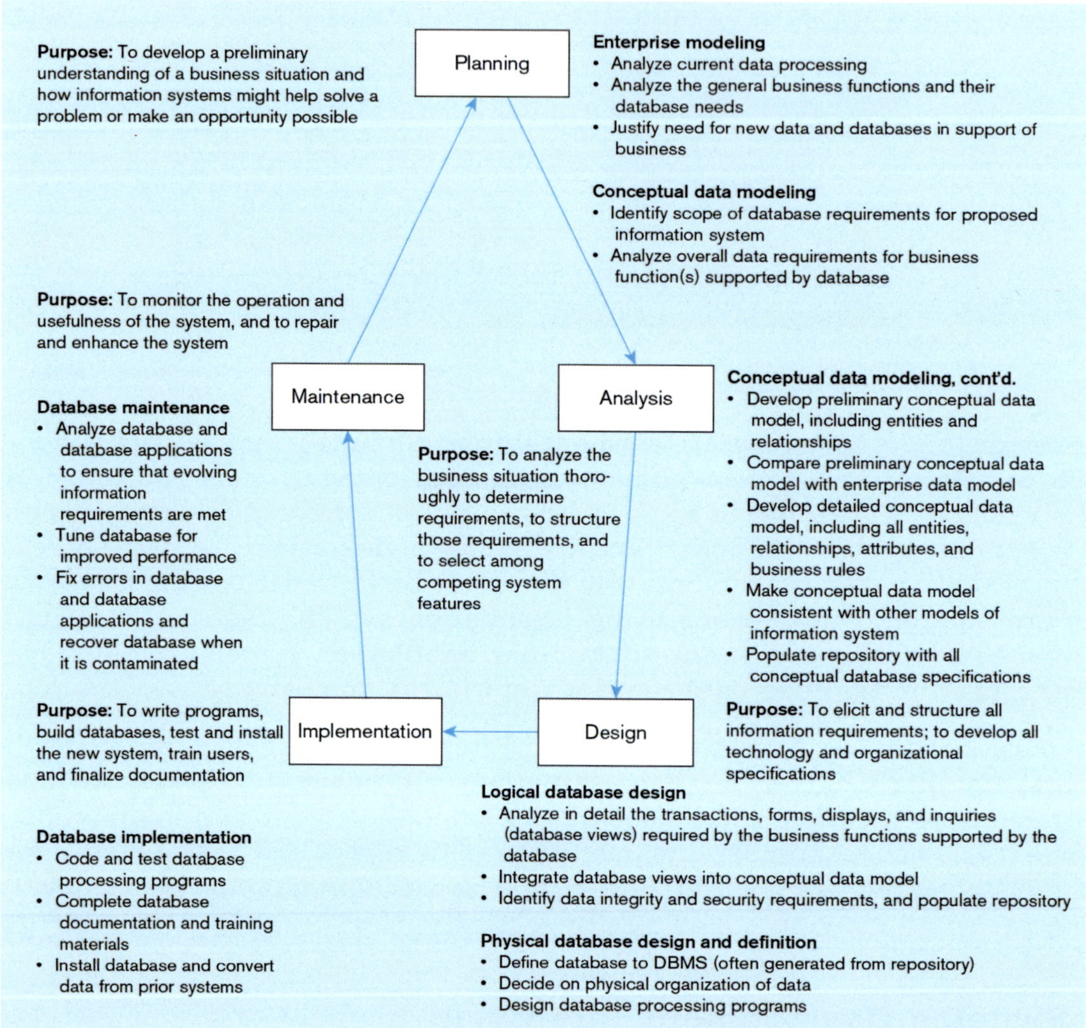

Figure 1.8. *Database development activities during the systems development life cycle (SDLC).*

Figure 1.8 also depicts the database development activities that are normally included in each phase of the SDLC. It should be noted that there is not always a one-to-one relationship between SDLC phases and database development tasks. Conceptual data modeling, for example, happens in both the Planning and Analysis phases.

1.5.1.1. Planning–Enterprise Modeling

The database creation process begins with an examination of the enterprise modeling components created during the information systems planning process. Analysts assess current databases and information systems, analyze the nature of the business area that is the topic of the development project, and explain in general terms the data required for each information system under consideration for development during this step. They determine whether data are already available in existing databases and which data must be added to support the proposed new project. Only selected initiatives go to the next step based on their predicted value to the company.

1.5.1.2. Planning–Conceptual Data Modeling

The overall data requirements of the proposed information system must be examined before starting an information systems project. This is accomplished in two stages. During the Planning phase, the analyst creates a diagram similar to Figure 1.8, as well as other documentation, to outline the extent of data involved in this specific development project without taking into account what databases already exist. At this time, only high-level data categories (entities) and important relationships are included. This SDLC stage is crucial for increasing the likelihood of a successful development process. The clearer the characterization of the organization's unique needs, the closer the conceptual model should come to addressing those needs, and the less recycling back through the SDLC should be required.

1.5.1.3. Analysis—Conceptual Data Modeling

The analyst creates a complete data model that identifies all of the organizational data that must be maintained for this information system during the Analysis phase of the SDLC. Every data property is defined, every data category is documented, every business link between data entities is represented, and every rule that governs data integrity is specified. During the Analysis phase, the conceptual data model is also examined for coherence with other types of models built to explain other aspects of the target information system, such as processing stages, data handling rules, and event scheduling. Even this detailed conceptual data model, however, is preliminary because following SDLC operations may discover missing or incorrect pieces when developing specific transactions, reports, displays, and inquiries. With expertise, the database developer develops mental models of basic business operations such as sales or financial record keeping but must always be on the lookout for deviations to an organization's standard practices. The conceptual modeling process produces a conceptual schema.

1.5.1.4. Design—Logical Database Design

From two perspectives, logical database design approaches database development. The conceptual schema must first be converted into a logical schema, which explains the data in terms of the data management technology that will be used to create the database. If relational technology is employed, the conceptual data model is translated and represented using relational model elements such as tables, columns, rows, primary keys, foreign keys, and constraints.

The analyst then performs a complete evaluation of the transactions, reports, displays, and inquiries enabled by the database as each application in the information system is built, including the program's input and output formats. During this bottom-up examination, the analyst confirms exactly what data should be kept in the database and the nature of those data as needed for each transaction, report, and so on. As each report, business transaction, and other user view is examined, the conceptual data model may need to be refined. During logical database design, one must combine or integrate the initial conceptual data model as well as these unique user perspectives into a holistic design. It is also possible that additional information processing requirements will be discovered during the design of logical information systems; in this case, these new requirements must be incorporated into the previously specified logical database design.

Following well-established guidelines for well-structured data specifications, the next stage in logical database design is to translate the combined and reconciled data requirements into basic, or atomic, elements. These rules are derived from relational database theory and a procedure known as normalization in most modern databases. The end result is a full image of the database that does not rely on a specific database management system to manage this data. After establishing a final logical database architecture, the analyst continues to specify the logic of the specific computer programs and queries required to maintain and report on the database contents.

1.5.1.5. Design—Physical Database Design

A physical schema is a set of specifications that explain how a given database management system stores data from a logical schema in a computer's secondary memory. Each logical schema has one physical schema. Physical database design necessitates familiarity with the DBMS that will be used to implement the database. An analyst decides on the organization of physical records, the choice of file organizations, the usage of indexes, and so on in physical data-base design and specification. A database designer must specify the programs that will process transactions and generate projected management information and decision support reports to do this. The goal is to create a database that can handle all data processing against it efficiently and securely. As a result, physical database design is closely coordinated with the design of all other parts of the physical information system, including programs, computer hardware, operating systems, and data communications networks.

1.5.1.6. Implementation—Database Implementation

A designer writes, tests, and installs the programs/scripts that access, create, or alter the database during database implementation. The designer may build styled reports and displays, maybe including graphs, using normal programming languages (e.g., Java, C#, or Visual Basic.NET) or special database processing languages (e.g., SQL) or special-purpose nonprocedural languages. During implementation, the designer will also complete all database documentation, train users, and establish processes for continuous support of the information system (and database) users. The final stage is to load data from existing information sources (old program files and databases, as well as new data). Loading is frequently accomplished by first unloading data from old files and databases into a neutral format (such as binary or text files), and then loading that data into the new database. Finally, the database and its accompanying apps are deployed into production to allow actual users to maintain and retrieve data. During production, the database should be backed up and recovered on a regular basis in case of contamination or destruction.

1.5.1.7. Maintenance—Database Maintenance

During database maintenance, the database evolves. The designer adds, deletes, or changes characteristics of a database's structure in this step to match changing business conditions, repair faults in database design, or increase database application processing speed. The designer may also be required to rebuild a database if it becomes tainted or deleted as a result of a software or computer system failure. This is usually the most time-consuming step in database creation because it lasts the whole life of the database and its accompanying applications. Consider each modification to the database as an abbreviated database development process in which conceptual data modeling, logical and physical database design, and database implementation take place to address requested changes.

1.5.2. Three-Schema Architecture for Database Development

The explanation earlier in this chapter of the database development process referred to several different but related models of databases developed on a systems development project. These data models and the primary phase of the SDLC in which they are developed are summarized here:

- Enterprise data model (during the information systems planning phase).
- External schema or user view (during the analysis and logical design phases).
- Conceptual schema (during the analysis phase).
- Logical schema (during the logical design phase).
- Physical schema (during the physical design phase).

An industry committee known as ANSI/SPARC released an important document in 1978 that specified three-schema architecture—external, conceptual, and internal schemas—for expressing data structure. Figure 1.10 depicts the link between the various SDLC schemas and the ANSI three-schema design. It is critical to remember that all of these schemas are simply alternative methods for different stakeholders to visualize the structure of the same database. The three ANSI-defined schemas are as discussed in subsections (Figure 1.9).

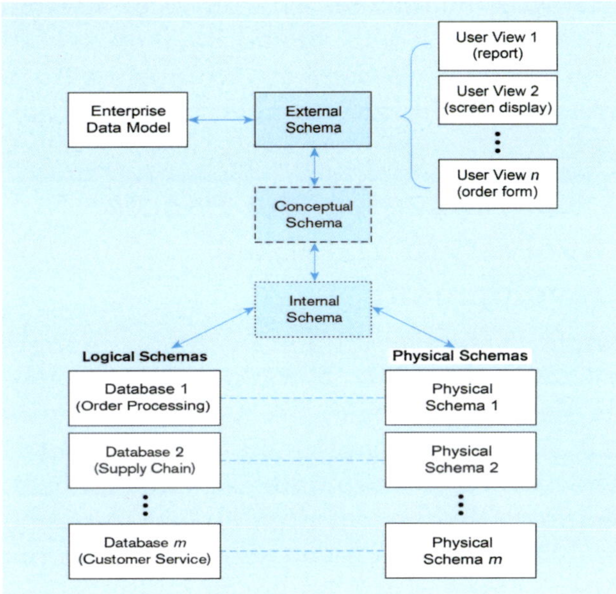

Figure 1.9. *Three-schema architecture.*

1.5.2.1. External Schema

This is the view (or points of view) of managers and other database users. The external schema can be represented as a combination of the enterprise data model (a top-down view) and a set of detailed (or bottom-up) user views, as shown in Figure 1.10.

1.5.2.2. Conceptual Schema

This schema combines the various external perspectives into a unified, logical, and all-encompassing definition of the enterprise's data. The conceptual schema represents the data architect's or data administrator's point of view.

1.5.2.3. Internal Schema

As seen in Figure 1.10, an internal schema nowadays comprises of two distinct schemas: a logical schema and a physical schema. The logical schema is a data representation for a specific sort of data management system (for example, relational). The physical schema specifies how data should be represented and saved in secondary storage using a specific DBMS (for example, Oracle).

1.5.3. Managing the People Involved in Database Development

Isn't it always ultimately about people working together? A database is created as part of a project, as shown in Figure 1.9. A project is a planned effort of related activities with a beginning and an end goal. A project begins with the Project Initiation and Planning phase and concludes with the final phases of the Implementation phase. The project will be led by a senior systems or database analyst. This individual is in charge of developing detailed project plans as well as staffing and directing the project team.

In the Planning phase, a project is launched and planned; performed during the Analysis, Logical Design, Physical Design, and execution stages; and closed down at the end of execution. The project team is constituted during the initiation phase. One or more of the following can be found on a systems or database development team:

1.5.3.1. Business Analysts

These individuals collaborate with both management and users to examine the company context and create precise system and program specifications for projects.

1.5.3.2. Systems Analysts

These individuals, who often have a greater systems development background than business analysts, may do business analyst responsibilities but also provide computer system needs.

1.5.3.3. Database Analysts and Data Modelers

These individuals concentrate on determining the requirements and design for the database component of the information system.

1.5.3.4. Users

Users provide assessments of their information needs and monitor that the developed system meets their needs.

1.5.3.5. Programmers

These individuals design and write computer programs that have commands to maintain and access data in the database embedded in them.

1.5.3.6. Database Architects

These individuals establish standards for data in business units, striving to attain optimum data location, currency, and quality.

1.5.3.7. Data Administrators

These individuals have responsibility for

existing and future databases and ensure consistency and integrity across databases, and as experts on database technology, they provide consulting and training to other project team members.

1.5.3.8. Project Managers

Project managers oversee assigned projects, including team composition, analysis, design, implementation, and support of projects.

1.5.3.9. Other Technical Experts

Other individuals are needed in areas such as networking, operating systems, testing, data warehousing, and documentation.

It is the project manager's obligation to choose and manage all of these people as an effective team. For more information on how to manage a systems development project team, see Valacich & George (2016); and Henderson et al. (2005) for a more extensive discussion of career paths and roles in data management. When agile development procedures are used, the emphasis on people rather than roles means that team members are less likely to be restricted to a specific position. They will be required to contribute and cooperate across multiple roles, making better use of their specific talents, interests, and capabilities.

1.6. EVOLUTION OF DATABASE SYSTEMS

Learning Objectives

At the end of this section, readers will be able to:

- Trace the historical development of database systems from early file-based systems to modern database management systems (DBMS).
- Understand the key challenges and limitations of early data storage and retrieval methods.
- Explore the evolution of data models, including hierarchical, network, and relational models.
- Examine the role of technological advancements and innovations in shaping the evolution of database systems.

Database management systems were originally introduced in the 1960s and have since evolved throughout the years. In most cases, the introduction period was rather protracted, with the technology first appearing during the decade preceding the one depicted in Figure 1.9. The relational model, for example, was first established by E. F. Codd, an IBM research fellow, in a paper published in 1970 (Codd, 1970). The relational paradigm, however, did not achieve widespread commercial success until the 1980s. For example, the development of SQL in the 1980s solved the difficulty of the 1970s, when programmers needed to write sophisticated algorithms to access data.

In the hierarchical model, for example, files are sorted top-down to resemble a tree or genealogical chart, whereas in the network model, each file can be associated with an arbitrary number of other files. The relational model arranges data into tables with relationships between them. The object-oriented model is built on object classes and their relationships. Object-relational databases are a cross between relational and object-oriented databases. Data warehouses are built on multidimensional databases, which allow us to see data in the form of cubes or a star structure. The diagram's last piece depicts the major aspects of the big data approach to data management while avoiding a specific modeling method (there is no one data model for big data).

Database management systems were created to address the constraints of file processing systems, which were discussed in a previous section. To conclude, the following four goals fueled the development and evolution of database technology:

- The need to provide greater independence between programs and data, thereby reducing maintenance costs.
- The desire to manage increasingly complex data types and structures.
- The desire to provide easier and faster access to data for users who have neither a background in programming languages nor a detailed understanding of how data are stored in databases.
- The need to provide ever more powerful platforms for decision support applications.

1.6.1. 1960s

During the 1960s, file processing methods remained dominant. The first database management systems, however, were established during this decade and were mostly employed for huge and sophisticated initiatives, such as the Apollo moon-landing project. This might be thought of as a "proof-of-concept" period in which the capability of managing massive volumes of data with a DBMS was demonstrated. In addition, the Data Base Task Group was formed in the late 1960s, which was the first attempt at standardization.

1.6.2. 1970s

Database management solutions became a commercial reality during this decade. Hierarchical and network database management systems were created primarily to deal with increasingly complex data structures, such as manufacturing bills of materials, which were extremely difficult to manage using traditional file processing methods. The hierarchical and network models are often considered to be first-generation DBMS. Both approaches were widely adopted, and many of these systems are still in use today. However, they shared the same major drawbacks as file processing systems: limited data independence and significant application development timeframes.

1.6.3. 1980s

During the 1970s, E. F. Codd and others developed the relational data model to solve these restrictions. During the 1980s, this paradigm, known as a second-generation DBMS, gained considerable commercial acceptability, and spread throughout the business sector. The relational model represents all data in the form of tables. SQL is typically used for data retrieval. As a result, the relational model addresses one of the primary criticisms leveled at first-generation systems: ease of access for nonprogrammers. The relational model has also demonstrated its suitability for client/server computing, parallel processing, and graphical user interfaces (Gray, 1996).

1.6.4. 1990s

The 1990s introduced a new age in computing, beginning with client/server computing and progressing to data warehousing and Internet applications. Whereas data managed by a DBMS was mostly organized (such as accounting data) in the 1980s, multimedia data (containing graphics, sound, pictures, and video) became more popular in the 1990s. Object-oriented databases (called third generation) were created in the late 1980s to deal with these more complicated data (Grimes, 1998); nevertheless, they never gained the popularity projected. Instead, in the 2000s and 2010s, new forms of data management systems were developed.

1.6.5. 2000 and Beyond

Relational databases are still the most extensively used database technology today. Because enterprises must manage massive amounts of organized and unstructured data, and because both the amount and variety of data is continually rising, the need for new technology has become obvious. As you learned earlier in this chapter in the context of the framework depicted in Figure 1.5, numerous nonrelational technologies have grown in popularity since the early 2000s. One aspect of this trend is the rise of NoSQL (Not Only SQL) databases. NoSQL is an umbrella name for a group of database technologies that are specifically built to address huge (structured and unstructured) data sets that may be stored in several locations. MongoDB and Apache Cassandra are two popular NoSQL databases. Furthermore, Hadoop is an example of a nonrelational platform built to manage massive amounts of data. The needs of social networking applications, such as blogs, wikis, and social networking sites (Facebook, Twitter, LinkedIn, and so on); the ease of generating unstructured data, such as pictures and images, from devices such as smartphones, tablets, and so on; and the data needs and opportunities of the Internet of Things fuel this search for nonrelational database technologies. Developing appropriate database techniques to cope with these many sorts of data is critical. As larger computer memory chips become more affordable, new database methods for managing in-memory databases emerge. This trend opens the door to much faster database processing.

Recent regulations such as Sarbanes-Oxley, the Health Insurance Portability and Accountability Act, and the Basel Convention have underlined the necessity of good data management methods, as has the capacity to reconstruct prior positions. This has resulted in advancements in computer forensics, with a greater emphasis and expectation placed on the detection of electronic evidence. Because effective disaster recovery and proper security are demanded by these rules, competent database management skills are becoming increasingly important.

Cloud computing is a new development that is making it easier to use database technologies (and to address some of the regulatory challenges highlighted below). Databases are one popular cloud-based technology. Relational and nonrelational databases can now be created, deployed, and managed using technology owned and managed by a service provider.

SUMMARY

A database is a logically structured collection of data. Data are stored representations of objects and events that have meaning and significance in the user's surroundings. Information is data that has been processed in such a way that the user's knowledge has increased. A database can store both data and information.

Metadata are pieces of information that explain the attributes or characteristics of end-user data as well as the context in which that data is used. A database management system (DBMS) is a software system that is used to create, maintain, and control user databases. A database management system (DBMS) maintains meta-data in a repository, which serves as a central repository for all data definitions, data linkages, screen and report formats, and other system components. Aside from databases that enable and support operational (transactional) systems, it is becoming increasingly popular for enterprises to keep databases for informative reasons (analytics) utilizing either the data warehousing strategy or the big data approach.

Early in the computer era, file processing systems were developed to allow computers to store, alter, and retrieve massive amounts of data. These systems (which are still in use today) have a number of significant shortcomings, including program and data dependency, data duplication, limited data exchange, and lengthy development cycles. To address these restrictions, the database technique was created. This strategy stresses data integration and sharing throughout the enterprise. The benefits of this method include program-data independence, improved data sharing, minimum data redundancy, and increased application development productivity.

REVIEW QUESTIONS

1. What are the main advantages of using a Database Management System (DBMS) in modern data management practices? Provide at least three key benefits.
2. Explain the concept of a primary key in a relational database. Why is it essential, and how does it differ from a foreign key?
3. Describe the purpose and functionality of a foreign key in a relational database. How does it establish relationships between tables?
4. Discuss the ACID properties in the context of database management. Why are these properties crucial for ensuring data integrity and consistency?
5. In the context of modern database management, what role does data normalization play? Provide an example of a situation where data normalization would be beneficial.

MULTIPLE CHOICE QUESTIONS

1. **Which of the following best describes a database?**
   a. A collection of tables in spreadsheet format.
   b. A structured set of data that is stored and organized for efficient retrieval and manipulation.
   c. A group of related computer programs used for data analysis.
   d. A physical device used to store data files.
2. **What is the primary purpose of a Database Management System (DBMS)?**
   a. To create attractive user interfaces for data entry.
   b. To manage and control access to data, ensuring data consistency and integrity.
   c. To generate reports and perform complex data analysis.
   d. To design data models and schemas.
3. **Which term refers to a unique identifier for each record in a relational database table?**
   a. Field
   b. Table
   c. Attribute
   d. Primary Key
4. **In a relational database, a foreign key is used to:**
   a. Identify the primary key of a different table.
   b. Store textual data.
   c. Calculate mathematical values.
   d. Define the database schema.
5. **Which of the following is NOT one of the ACID properties in database management?**
   a. Atomicity
   b. Consistency
   c. Isolation
   d. Durability

Answers to Multiple Choice Questions

1 b) 2 b) 3 d) 4 a) 5 d)

REFERENCES

1. Anderson-Lehman, R., Watson, H. J., Wixom, B., & Hoffer, J. A., (2004). Continental airlines flies high with real-time business intelligence. *MIS Quarterly Executive, 3*(4).

2. Codd, E. F., (1970). A relational model of data for large shared data banks. *Communications of the ACM, 13*(6), 377–387.

3. Fowler, M., (2005). *The New Methodology*. Available at www.martinfowler.com/articles/newMethodology.html (accessed on 02 April 2024).

4. Gray, J., (1996). Data management: Past, present, and future. *IEEE Computer, 29*(10), 38–46.

5. Grimes, S., (1998). Object/relational reality check. *Database Programming & Design, 11*(7), 26–33.

6. Groenfeldt, T., (2013). *Kroger Knows Your Shopping Patterns Better Than You Do*. Forbes Online. Available at: www.forbes.com/sites/tomgroenfeldt/2013/10/28/kroger-knowsyour-shopping-patterns-better-than-you-do (accessed on 02 April 2024).

7. Henderson, D., Champlin, B., Coleman, D., Cupoli, P., Hoffer, J., Howarth, L., et al., (2005). *Model Curriculum Framework for Post Secondary Education Programs in Data Resource Management (Vol. 1, pp. 1–20).*

8. IBM, (2011). *The Essential CIO: Insights from the 2011 IBM Global CIO Study*. Available at https://www-935.ibm.com/services/c-suite/cio/study (accessed on 02 April 2024).

9. Jordan, A., (1996). Data warehouse integrity: How long and bumpy the road? *Data Management Review, 6*(3), 35–37.

10. Laskowski, N., (2014). *Ten Big Data Case Studies in a Nutshell.* Available at http://searchcio.techtarget.com/opinion/Ten-big-data-case-studies-in-a-nutshell (accessed on 02 April 2024).

11. Long, D., (2005). *Net Overview.* Tampa Bay Technology Leadership Association.

12. Manyika, J., Chui, M., Brown, B., Bughin, J., Dobbs, R., Roxburgh, C., & Byers, A. H., (2011). *Big Data: The Next Frontier for Innovation, Competition and Productivity.* McKinsey Global Institute.

13. Mullins, C. S., (2002). *Database Administration: The Complete Guide to Practices and Procedures*. New York: Addison-Wesley.

14. Ritter, D., (1999). Don't neglect your legacy. *Intelligent Enterprise, 2*(5), 70–72.

15. Valacich, J. S., & George, J. F., (2016). *Modern Systems Analysis and Design* (8th edn.). Upper Saddle River, NJ: Prentice Hall.

CHAPTER

2 Introduction to Distributed System

LEARNING OBJECTIVES

After studying this chapter, you will be able to:

- The concept of distributed system planning and its importance;
- The features and challenges of distributed systems;
- The eight fallacies of distributed computing and their implications;
- The client/server computing model and its advantages and disadvantages;
- The world wide web as an immense distributed system;
- The advanced models of distributed systems.

"The beauty of distributed systems is that they enable us to accomplish together what would be impossible to achieve alone."

INTRODUCTORY EXAMPLE

Imagine you're the owner of a popular online store, "E-Shop Delight," known for its diverse range of products and seamless shopping experience. Your store has been growing steadily, attracting customers from around the world. However, as your customer base expands, you notice that the website's performance is starting to suffer during peak hours. Shoppers are experiencing slow page loads and occasional outages.

In an effort to address these issues, you've decided to learn about distributed systems. Distributed systems have revolutionized how modern applications and services work, allowing businesses like yours to scale efficiently, improve reliability, and enhance performance.

Before diving into the world of distributed systems, let's examine a familiar scenario. When you launched your online store, you likely started with a single web server, a centralized database, and a straightforward website. This setup worked well initially, but as your business grew, it became clear that a single server was no longer sufficient to handle the increasing load of customer requests.

Now, picture this: Instead of relying on a single server, you distribute your website's workload across multiple servers located in different data centers around the world. Each server can handle a portion of the traffic, and they work together seamlessly to provide a faster, more reliable, and scalable shopping experience for your customers, regardless of their geographical location.

This is the essence of distributed systems. They involve multiple interconnected computers and servers that collaborate to deliver a wide range of services, from e-commerce websites like yours to social media platforms, cloud computing, and more. In this chapter, we will explore the fundamental concepts, challenges, and benefits of distributed systems, setting the stage for a deeper understanding of this fascinating field.

UNIT INTRODUCTION

A distributed system is an area of computer science that deals with the study of interconnected computers functioning together to achieve shared objectives. These systems enable efficient resource and data sharing among multiple computers, often located in different places. They play a crucial role in various modern technologies, such as cloud computing, social networking, and data processing. Understanding the principles behind distributed systems is essential for developing scalable and reliable software solutions in our interconnected world.

The most significant development in information technology during the last 20 years has been the rise of networked workstations and the decline of the centralized mainframe. As a result of the redistribution of hardware resources, end users now have greater access to processing capacity. Complex tasks can be accomplished by utilizing the combined capacity of all connected computers in a network (Lamport, 2019). There are two distinct classifications of computations that occur in connections of processing nodes: centralized and distributed. A centralized solution designates a single node to perform local processing of the entire application, with all users consistently utilizing the central system. Thus, a single point of control and a single point of failure are established.

2.1. STRATEGIC PLANNING FOR DISTRIBUTED SYSTEMS

Learning Objectives

At the end of this section, readers will be able to:

- Understand hierarchical network design;
- Discuss the distributed architecture;
- Explain complete or partly connected networks.

Distributed systems are constructed on top of already installed operating and networking software. A computer network and its distribution middleware connect a group of independent computers to form a distributed system. There must be a distinct master/slave connection between two computers in a network to become autonomous. Computers can coordinate their actions and share system resources thanks to middleware, which gives users the impression that the system is one big, integrated computing facility. Therefore, middleware links distributed applications running in various physical locations and on various hardware platforms, networks, operating systems, and programming languages. The development of the middleware software complies with established standards and procedures. It offers common services like naming, tenacity, concurrency control (which ensures that accurate results are produced for concurrent processes and obtains the results as quickly as possible), event distribution, authorization (which specifies access rights to resources), security, and so on. The middleware service spans several computers (Lotero & Contreras, 2011).

The distributed architecture can be considered from the perspective of the users or the computation, as well as from the perspective of the physical components. The physical view is the first, and the logical view is the second. A distributed system is made up of a collection of nodes (computers) connected by a network of communication. The network's nodes are not tightly coupled to one another and have no shared memory (Lotero & Contreras, 2011). The system's nodes exchange information by sending messages across the communication network. Protocols for communication are used to transfer messages from a single node to another. The logical model represents the application's perception of the system. It has a number of concurrent processes as well as channels for communication between them. It is assumed that the fundamental network is fully connected. Processes communicate with one another by sending messages. A system is concurrent if, when properly executed, it consistently carries out the intended action at the predetermined time; otherwise, it is asynchronous. The failure of a synchronous system is discernible by an absence of an answer from the system. As a result, failure discovery techniques based on timeouts are used.

Complete or partly connected networks can be used to build a distributed system [HUAN05, MIN04, NELS01]. A network with all of its nodes connected to one another is called completely interconnected network. The issue in such an arrangement is that incorporating new nodes causes the number of nodes associated to the node to increase. As a result, the complexity of each node's connection implementation and the number of file descriptors are greatly increased. As a result, the scalability of such systems is constrained by each node's ability to open file descriptors and capacity to manage new connections. Scalability is the capacity of a system to keep running well when the system's size or volume changes. Because a message delivered from one computer to a different computer only travels through one link, the communication cost—the message delay—of delivering a message from its origin to the destination is minimal. Fully interconnected systems are dependable because the remaining computers remain in touch even if some links or computers fail. Direct connections exist between some computer pairs in a partially connected network, but not all of them do. Star-structured networks, multi-access bus networks, ring-structured networks, and tree-structured networks are partially connected network models. The network topology for some conventional distributed systems, like the client/server paradigm, is a star. The issue with such an arrangement is that it will collapse as a whole if the central node fails. A group of clients is linked in a multi-access bus network by a common communication channel known as a bus. When the bus link breaks, the entire system's nodes are unable to communicate with one another, making it the bottleneck. Another drawback is that performance suffers when there are more computers added or when there is a lot of traffic. Each node forms a single continuous process for signals through every link in a ring network by connecting to precisely two other nodes. The network's diameter expands as the number of points in the system does, causing a longer delay in message transmission. A node failure or cable break could isolate every node connected to the ring. The connections between the nodes form a tree-like structure in a tree-structured system (hierarchical network). Every point in the network is connected to a fixed number of other nodes at a lower level of the hierarchy. Since new nodes can be stated as the child nodes of the leaf nodes or within the nodes, the tree-structured network can scale more easily than the fully connected network. However, only messages sent between a parent node and its child node identified in such systems use a single link; all other messages sent between two nodes must pass through one or more intermediary nodes (Lavorato et al., 2010) (Figure 2.1).

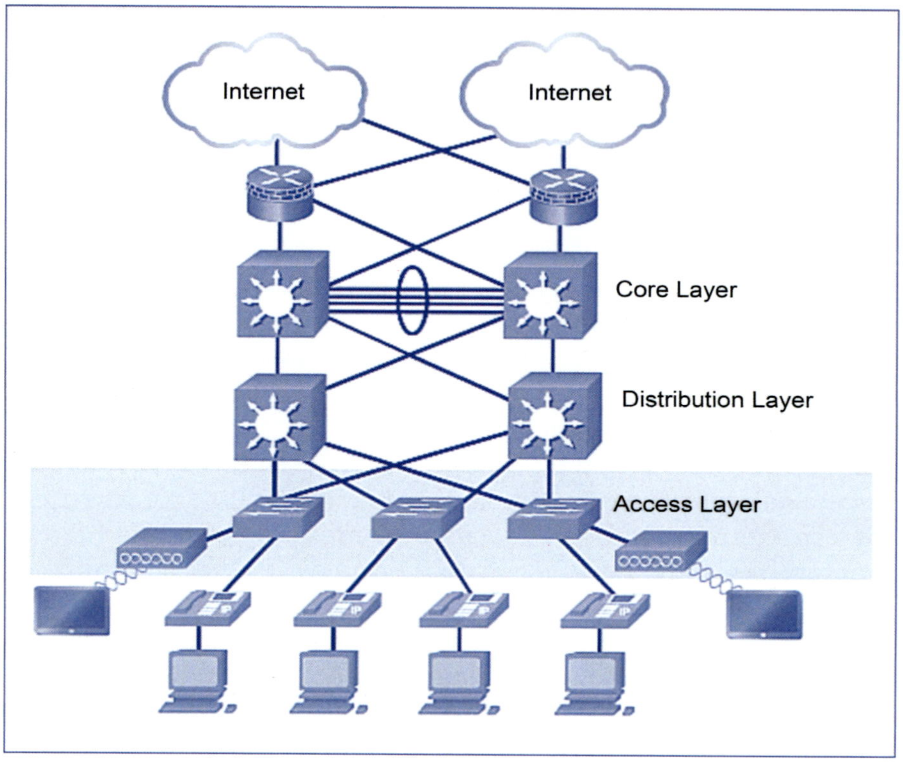

Figure 2.1. Hierarchical network design.

2.2. CHARACTERISTICS OF A DISTRIBUTED SYSTEM

Learning Objectives

At the end of this section, readers will be able to:

- Understand the characteristics of distributed system;
- Explain the fault-tolerant;
- Discuss the security and transparency.

2.2.1. Fault-Tolerant

Distributed systems are made up of numerous hardware and software components, all of which eventually fail. Such component malfunctions may lead to service interruptions. As a result, the systems ought to be capable of recovering from component failures lacking to take the wrong course of action. Fault tolerance aims to prevent system failures to maintain service even when faults are present. If a system can hide the existence of faults, it is considered to be fault tolerant. Any fault-tolerant system seeks to improve availability or reliability. The likelihood that a system will last until that point is what a system's reliability means. Even when a component fails, a reliable system avoids information loss. The percentage of time that a system is usable is known as availability. Redundancy is typically used to achieve fault tolerance. The term "redundancy" refers to unnecessary system components for the system to function properly. It comes in three varieties: time, software, and hardware. In order to achieve hardware redundancy, a system must have additional hardware components that can step in for malfunctioning ones if necessary. In order to ensure uninterrupted service in the event of a hardware component failure, software redundancy includes additional management instructions and code. The identical instruction is repeatedly carried out in time redundancy. This is utilized to address transient system errors [VIKA04] (Edwards et al., 2006).

2.2.2. Scalable

A system that is distributed can continue functioning properly even as some components are scaled up. Three factors make upscale: the total number of users and other system participants, the distance between the system's farthest nodes, and the number of organizations with administrative control over various system components. The three scale factors have a wide range of effects on distributed systems. Name resolution, identity verification, authorization, communication, use of remote resources, and user observation mechanisms are some impacted components. The three methods of replication, distribution, and caching are used to manage scale.

2.2.3. Resources Are Replicated to Produce Multiple Copies

Its application to file, naming, and authentication services lessens the burden on each server and raises the general dependability and accessibility of the services. The two most crucial replication-related issues are the locations of the versions and the methods used to maintain their consistency. Resource replication's goal determines the replicas' location within a distributed system. The replicas are dispersed throughout the system if a service is being duplicated to decrease network latency when the service is accessed. Replicas may be placed close to one another if most users are local, and the service is being replicated to increase availability or distribute the load across multiple servers. Everyone using the system should be able to tell if the object is altered. For instance, the system sends changes to any replica, and as they become available, that replica sends the updates to the others. Timestamps (the date/time the update was created) are used to distinguish the copies when across various orders.

2.2.4. Distribution

A further tool for controlling scale in distributed structures, enables the extension of a distributed service's data across multiple servers. Distributing data among several servers makes it easier for each server to maintain a smaller database, reducing the time required for searching the database. Additionally, distribution divides the workload among the servers, dividing the volume of requests that each must handle. The demand on servers can be efficiently handled if requests are distributed among servers according to their processing capacity. The upper levels can be skipped if cached copies are available from lower-level servers in a tree-structured system.

2.2.5. Another Crucial Method for Creating Scalable Systems Is Caching

The burden on servers and networks is lessened by caching. Accessing cached data is quicker than making a new request. The distinction between caching and replication is that cached data is temporary data. Consistency remains intact when consistency cannot be ensured by nullifying cached data rather than propagating updates. The client typically performs caching, which decreases the number of times the network service is requested. On the servers running those services, caching can also take place. It is quicker to read a file from the file server's memory cached copy than from the user's local disk (Francalanza et al., 2018).

2.2.5.1. Predictable Performance

Several performance metrics, including speed (the pace at which a network sends or receives data), system consumption, network capacity, and others, are used to evaluate the performance. Response time, for example, measures how long a computer system responds to an inquiry or demand. The capacity to respond as quickly as desired indicates predictable performance.

2.2.6. Openness

The attribute 'openness' guarantees that a subsystem is always available for communication with other systems. Web applications are software programs created to support interoperable networked machine-to-machine communication. These protocols make it possible to expand and scale distributed systems. An open system that can scale has an advantage over a wholly closed and independent system. The attribute of openness is attained by a distributed system that is not dependent on the heterogeneity underlying environments, such as software and hardware platforms. As a result, every client in the system, whether local or remote, has equal access to every service. Implementing, installing, and debugging novel services shouldn't be overly difficult in a system with an openness characteristic.

2.2.7. Security

By enforcing the necessary security measures, distributed systems should enable communication between applications, users, and resources on various computers. The main goals of the security features are to ensure confidentiality, integrity, and availability. Privacy and confidentiality are safeguards against disclosure to unauthorized parties. Confidentiality violations can range from unpleasant to disastrous. Integrity offers a security against corruption and alteration. The resource remains available and accessible. Numerous hacking incidents jeopardize the reliability of databases and other assets. Attacks referred to as "denial of service" target availability. Control of access and nonrepudiation are two more significant security issues. The users can access only the assets and services they are authorized by maintaining access control. Additionally, it guarantees that users won't be denied access to resources they are legally entitled to. Nonrepudiation shields a communication from being denied by one of the parties involved. The security measures implemented should ensure the proper utilization of resources by various system users.

2.2.8. Transparency

Members and application developers should view distributed systems as a whole rather than a group of interdependent parts. Users are not shown where the computer systems are located in the operations, in tandem operations, copying of data, resource discovery from various locations, failures, system recovery, etc. Transparency allows users to see the system as appearing and functioning normally, while hiding the system's distributed nature from them. A distributed system can use transparency in a variety of ways [KAZI00, PRAD02].

1. Thanks to access transparency, a distributed system's users can access local and distant assets with the same operations. (For instance, web navigation).
2. Location transparency refers to names that identify network resources (such as IP addresses) without considering the user's location or the location of the resource. Location transparency, in other words, enables a user to get to resources from any place on the network, lacking being aware of the location of the resource. The user's computer or servers located thousands of miles away from it may host the file.
3. Concurrency transparency makes it possible for multiple processes to use shared information objects concurrently without interfering

with one another (such as an ATM network). Users will only become aware of other individuals in the system if they access the same resources.

4. Replication transparency allows the system to create extra copies of files and other assets without the users noticing to improve performance and/or reliability. If a resource has been copied in multiple places, it should display to the users as one source (for example, mirroring, which offers multiple sources of identification information to ensure dependable availability for large downloads).
5. Failure transparency makes it possible for applications to finish work even when certain system components fail. The system is said to exhibit high failure transparency. For instance, if a server fails, but users receive a redirect to a different server, the user is unaware of the failure. One of the most challenging kinds of transparency to implement is failure transparency because it is difficult to tell if a server has collapsed or simply very slowly. Furthermore, because networks are unreliable, achieving complete failure transparency in a distributed system is typically impossible.
6. Migration transparency makes it easier for resources to switch between locations without changing their names. (For instance: Web Pages). Users shouldn't be aware of a resource's or a computing entity's capacity to change its logical or physical location.
7. Performance transparency guarantees that the load variation won't impair performance. Automatic reconfiguration in response to changes in the load could accomplish this. For instance, load distribution.
8. Scalability transparency enables the system to continue operating effectively even as the number of users and connected resources (such as the World Wide Web and distributed databases) increases significantly (Rodden & Blair, 1991).

2.3. EIGHT FALLACIES OF DISTRIBUTED COMPUTING

Learning Objectives

At the end of this section, readers will be able to:

- Understand fallacies of distributed systems;
- Discuss the topology of distributed system;
- Explain the transport card.

Architects and designers of distributed systems are anticipated to make 7 presumptions [ARNO06, INGR04] that turn out to be false, according to a 1994 document by Peter Deutsch. A further example of this fallacy was the eighth fallacy of distributed computing, which was added in 1997 by James Gosling, the creator of the Java computer programming language. The eight misconceptions of computer networking are the name given to the group of assumptions. The falsehoods of distributed systems are a collection of frequent but incorrect assumptions that programmers make when creating distributed applications for the first time. These assumptions led to the development of many distributed systems, many of which were unnecessarily complex due to errors that later needed to be fixed (Figure 2.2).

- The network is reliable;
- Latency is zero;
- There is infinite bandwidth;
- The networking system is secure;
- The topology doesn't change;
- There is one administrator;
- There is no transport cost;
- The network is homogenous.

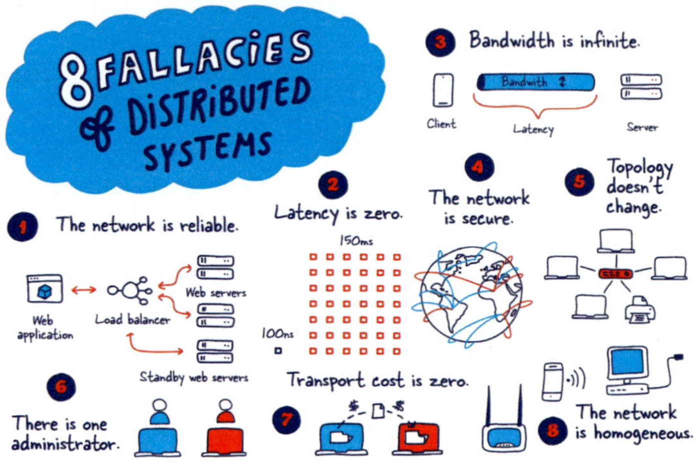

Figure 2.2. Eight fallacies of distributed system.

2.3.1. Reliability

The network will cause problems when it begins to drop packets for software developed under the assumption that the network is dependable. The autonomy of a system's nodes can frequently be increased while maintaining reliability. Replication can also increase a system's dependability.

2.3.2. Latency

The latency duration is the interval between the start of a data request and the start of the data transfer. On a LAN, latency can be reasonably good, but it quickly degrades when a user switches to WAN or internet scenarios. If latency is assumed to be zero, scalability issues will undoubtedly exist as the application expands geographically or relocates to a different type of network (Figure 2.3).

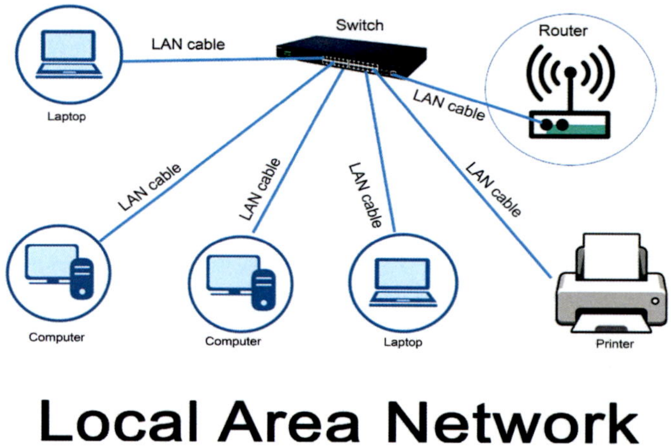

Figure 2.3. Local area network (LAN).

2.3.3. Bandwidth

A measurement of a communication channel's capacity or the amount of data we can send over it in a given period of time. A channel can carry more data the higher its bandwidth. However, this assumption continues to be false due to two factors (Kumar et al., 2015). One is that as bandwidth expands, so does the volume of data we try to fit through it. Some recent applications that use bandwidth include VoIP, videos, and IPTV. Packet loss is the additional factor causing bandwidth to be reduced along with frame size. We must make an effort to reduce the amount of information we deliver over the wire due to bandwidth restrictions (Ghosh et al., 2007).

2.3.4. Security

The network is rarely safe because the systems are constantly being attacked from many directions. Therefore, the developer must conduct threat modeling to assess the potential dangers. The next step is determining which risks must be mitigated and how (a balance between costs, risks, and their probabilities). Network, infrastructure, and software layers all play a role in modern security architectures. The software architect needs to be aware of how crucial security is and the potential effects it can have on the project (Wang et al., 2012).

2.3.5. Topology

When discussing networks, topology refers to the various possible layouts, such as a ring, bus, star, or fully connected. For instance, the physical topology of a LAN is determined by the geometric shape formed by mapping its connections and nodes onto a graph. Each LAN node can potentially have multiple outgoing links to other LAN nodes. Similarly, the network's logical topology is established by mapping the data flow between the nodes. The physical and logical layouts in some networks will be the same, but in others, they will be different. Organizational networks may undergo change whenever new applications are introduced. The operations staff will occasionally alter the network by adding or removing servers. Last but not least, server or network infrastructure disruptions can result in a routing shift. From the client's perspective, things are much worse. Moving laptops, new mobile devices, wireless ad hoc networks, etc. In short, a distributed system's topology is dynamic and constantly shifting [NELS01] (Bredon, 2013).

2.3.6. Administrator

"There is one administrator" is the sixth computer networking fallacy. Having specialists in charge of the company's databases, web servers, networks, OSes, and so on is a straightforward solution. The issue arises when the company works with third parties, such as a partner in business, or when the application is hosted on a third-party server and made available over the Internet; in both cases, it must access services provided by organizations outside the company. In such cases, the company administrators have no say over the other administrators, who may operate according to their own policies. Therefore, the idea that there is "one administrator" to oversee everything is debunked.

The administrators are usually not the ones who create the software. Therefore, developers should equip users with means of self-diagnosis and problem location. Tools for real-time monitoring of operations, such as those that help administrator's spot minor issues before they balloon into catastrophic outages, are also a practical addition. The users, assets, nodes, networks, etc., that comprise a growing distributed system will increasingly operate in different jurisdictions. This means there will be a greater diversity in the types of actors exercising administrative authority over the system. Resources, payments, security, and more can all run into trouble in an infrastructure that doesn't handle expansion well (Antamoshkin et al., 2014).

2.3.7. Transport Cost

The price of transportation will never be free. Network installation and maintenance do not come for free. Purchasing routers, investing in network security measures, leasing bandwidth for internet access, and keeping the network online all incur expenses.

2.3.8. Homogenous Network

"Network is homogeneous" is the eighth computer networking fallacy. A homogeneous network consists of nodes that do not vary in their configuration or protocol setup from one another. No network is completely uniform except for a handful of extremely simple ones. It is very challenging to incorporate proprietary protocols. To mitigate the consequences of the heterogeneity of the enterprise environment, it is recommended to use widely accepted standard technologies such as XML (extended markup language) or Web Services (Zhao et al., 2015).

2.4. CLIENT/SERVER COMPUTING

Learning Objectives

At the end of this section, readers will be able to:

- Understand the concept of client/server computing;
- Discuss the pros and cons of client/server computing.

Distributing related processing across multiple resources is gaining traction as systems of computing resources become more commonplace. Many different approaches have developed over time to make this dissemination easier. Client/server computing is a common type of distributed architecture [SILV98]. The client/server architecture develops on the modular framework. The goal of modular programming is to separate the development and testing of an application into its constituent parts. A modular program has both a core component and supplementary components. The components of a client/server model are the same as those of a modular programming model: clients and servers. Clients and servers are typically separate computers that communicate with one another over the internet. The component that makes the call is now the server, while the one that receives the call is the client (Figure 2.4).

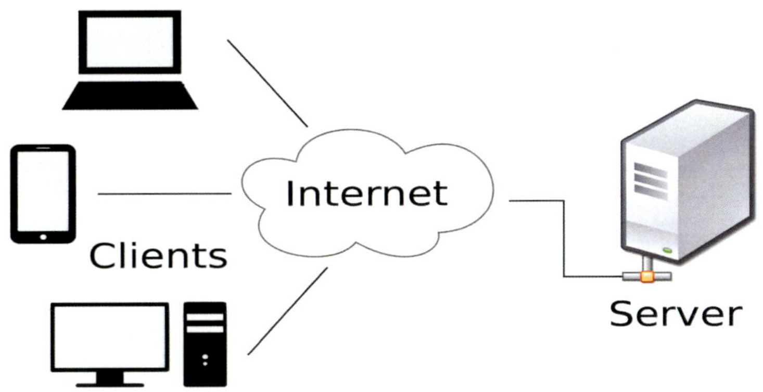

Figure 2.4. Server/client computing.

In order to get a server to do something, a client app will send it network messages. The client is responsible for managing local resources like I/O devices, disks, and other peripherals. The server application receives requests from clients over the network and processes them as they come in. In response to these requests, servers carry out operations. The client only receives the processed data and results from the server. As a result, less data is transferred between the computer's server and the client. As a result, there is a boost to the network's efficiency. The server manages the distribution of data and optimizes the use of available system resources. Whether or not a client discusses directly to the server or if an intermediary process exists in the client and the server is an essential design factor for large client/server systems. One has three levels, while the other has only two (see Figure 2.4). Web applications frequently employ N-tier architecture to route requests to additional back-end business services. The two-tier structure is more common in smaller settings due to its simplicity and ease of deployment. Nonetheless, a three-tier architecture offers more scalability than a two-tier one.

Clients and servers are linked by a third process in the structure with three levels shown in Figure 2.4. The intermediary can track which servers are used most often, leading to faster response times and greater scalability. A client machine, an application server, and a database server are the three mainstays of any database-based 3-tier client/server architecture. In this architecture, the business application is hosted on the application server, which is part of the middle tier. The data is fetched by the middle-tier a server from the database server and sent to the client. Creating a client/server application with three distinct layers requires middleware. The Database Application Programming Interface (API) is a feature of database-oriented middleware. Applets and servlets can use these classes from the popular Java Database Connectivity (JDBC) API to connect to any number of databases without knowing or caring about the specifics of each database (Adler, 1995).

Servers also need to solve the issue of authentication for security reasons. Sensitive information stored on a server may be compromised if an unauthorized client gains access in a networked environment. Public key encryption and dedicated authentication servers provide cryptographic client authentication. In order to ensure high levels of availability and fault tolerance, it is sometimes necessary to duplicate critical servers. Clients can continue to access all of the replicas, even if one of the servers hosting the replicas goes down.

Any one layer of a 3-tier architecture can be changed or updated independently of the others. Better load balancing can be achieved by decoupling database and application operations. In addition, the server tiers can be used to implement necessary security guidelines without impacting the clients.

To boost Internet retrieval performance, many organizations turn to the "proxy server model," a three-tier client/server architecture. The proxy server acts as an intermediary, distributing client requests across multiple servers for simultaneous processing. In order to access a service, such as a web page hosted on a web server, a client must first establish a connection with the proxy server. The request is evaluated by the proxy server against its filtering policies. It may restrict connections based on criteria such as IP address or protocol. If the filter verifies the request's legitimacy, the proxy will make the resource available to the client by making a request to the proper server. It's possible that a proxy server will handle your request without ever contacting the intended web server. This is made feasible by the proxy server caching the most frequently accessed pages. Proxy servers drastically improve end-user experience by caching frequently requested files on their own servers rather than making repeated requests to the original host. The term "proxy-cache server" is commonly used to refer to a proxy server that can store data for later use. Users can be verified as authorized by a proxy server by having them supply credentials like a username and password. As an added bonus, restricting the utilization of external resources to only those who need it and keeping detailed logs of their usage is a breeze. A reverse proxy can be used to distribute traffic evenly across multiple copies of the same server (Lai & Nieh., 2006).

2.4.1. Pros of Client/Server Model

- Since everything is stored in one place, the server handles the shared components used by all clients. For instance, a centralized database could be used to avoid issues brought on by duplicate and incompatible information.
- As the number of entry points providing the ability to access data is not so crucial, improved security is provided.
- Since clients play a minor function in the client/server architecture, server-level administration is sufficient.
- A scalable network allows for adding or removing clients without negatively impacting performance or necessitating extensive changes to the underlying.

2.4.2. Cones of the Client/ Server Model

- Costs skyrocketed because of the sophisticated nature of the server technology.
- If the system is not built to handle a server failure, then none of the clients will receive service.
- If the network goes down, it will be impossible to connect to any of the servers.
- If a single user generates a large amount of network traffic, it could cause delays in service for everyone else.

2.5. WORLD WIDE WEB (WWW)

Learning Objectives

At the end of this section, readers will be able to:

- Understand the origin and evolution of the web;
- Discuss the web information recovery;
- Explain the centralized architecture of distributed system.

The Internet is a global system of interconnected computer networks that enables any two computers, anywhere in the world, to exchange data and converse. The World Wide Web (WWW), often shortened to "Web," is an information retrieval system that operates over the Internet. The World Wide Web is made up of countless millions of pages housed on millions of computers around the globe. It's a system for exchanging data that's designed to work with the Web as its foundation. The computer network hosting websites is probably the most common instance of a distributed system. Words in a hypertext document link to other hypertext documents on the World Wide Web. User-selectable "links" are the highlighted words. Many other documents can be linked to from a single hypertext file (Yan & Chen, 1999).

Pages, or Web pages, are the files that make up the WWW and contain data and links to various resources on the Internet, both textual and visual. The rules established by Internet protocols govern online data exchange between computers. The HyperText Transfer Protocol (HTTP) is responsible for sending hypertext across the Internet. The Internet operates on this protocol. E-mail messages and any attached files are delivered to one or more inboxes using the Simple Mail Transport Protocol, or SMTP. VoIP (Voice over Internet Protocol) facilitates the transmission of voice calls over Internet Protocol (IP) networks. A web server is a computer that accepts requests made via HTTP from clients and returns those requests, along with any additional data (such as web pages), in the form of an HTTP response.

Hypertext serves as the primary information retrieval mechanism for the World Wide Web. User interactions can generate web pages. Hypertext Markup Language, or HTML, is a document creation language used for the creation of hypertext for the World Wide Web. Document formatting, visual characteristics like font size, italics, and bold, and the generation of hypertext links are all accomplished by inserting tags into the text using HTML. Distributed hypertext and multimedia files are jointly provided by servers implementing the Hypertext Transfer Protocol (HTTP). Clients use the computer's preexisting web browser to connect to the World Wide Web. A file's URL (uniform resource locator) is its address on the World Wide Web and can be found on any web server. The domain name system (DNS) is responsible for converting URLs into their corresponding IP addresses. The Domain Name System (DNS) is a network of computers that stores information about website addresses.

The "real" URL is the numeric address, known as the IP (Internet Protocol) address. Once the DNS has completed its translation, the browser can contact the web server and request the requested file. The file is downloaded from the server and displayed in the browser using the URL. The file is then sent to the client, the user's computer, and demonstrated on the attached screen. The web is a client-server network because of this dependency between users and service providers. Every day, millions of people worldwide use the internet to do everything from checking their email and news to listening to music, shopping, and researching topics of interest. While appearing to the user as a single, clickable resource, the web is in reality a massive, decentralized system. Standardization in content creation and distribution is essential for the continued growth and success of the World Wide Web. The World Wide Web (W3C) Consortium is a group at the forefront of efforts to standardize the web (Baentsch et al., 1997).

2.5.1. Web Information Recovery

In order to find the most pertinent results for a user's query, Web retrieval of data [AMI08, AMY04, AMY06, DIRK05, MONI03, VENK97] involves searching the largest and most linked document collection in the world: the World Wide Web. Obtaining data on the web faces many obstacles, including but not limited to since:

- Data is dispersed across many computers running different operating systems.
- Data is volatile (i.e., computers and files are added and removed constantly and are unpredictable).
- The volume of data is very large (i.e., growth is exponential).
- Data quality is inconsistent (i.e., data may be untrue, error-ridden, invalid, outdated, ambiguous, and so on due to the data's many sources and different interpretations).
- Information that is inherently diverse, including but not limited to different languages, scripts, and media formats. Therefore, it would be physically impossible for one person to examine and sort through all these pages to locate the necessary data. "Search Engine" refers to the software program most people use to look up things online. Input from a user's web browser is analyzed and utilized to query the database for incidents of specific keywords when using a search engine. Google and Yahoo! Search are just two of many available search engines that significantly speed up the process of retrieving information from the web. Centralized and decentralized search architectures are the two most common types of web search architecture.

2.5.2. Centralized Architecture

This centralized method aims to index a substantial portion of the Web without regard to specific topics or domains. Crawlers, indexers, and query handlers are the three main components of a search engine with a centralized architecture. The web pages that are retrieved by the crawler (spider or robot) are then compressed and stored in a database. Crawling (also known as robot spidering, gathering, and harvesting) describes this method. Googlebot, MSNBot, and Yahoo!'s Slurp are three of the most well-known crawlers. A crawler control module specifies a crawler's next destination URLs. The indexer processes the collected web pages, which then constructs the index, the primary data structure utilized by the search engine, which represents the crawled web pages. Each term is represented in the inverted index by a sorted list of couples, including docID and position within the document. The query engine processes user queries and returns relevant results using the index. A ranking algorithm is used to determine the order in which the results are presented to the user. Different search engines use different algorithms to determine which pages in their index contain the most relevant results for a user's query. In case the target server is down, some search engines keep a local cache copy of many popular pages indexed in their database for speed and redundancy (Singh et al., 2004).

2.5.3. Distributed Planning

Searching is a group effort involving many people who collect and trade data. The information in the documents hosted on any number of web servers is summarized and extracted using Gatherer. It's compatible with numerous documents, including HTML, PDF, Postscript, and more. The broker collects summaries from the collectors, retains them locally, and creates indexes. Data is searchable, data from other agents is fetched, and data is made accessible to user queries and other brokers. Distributed architecture's benefits include less external traffic on the server where the gatherer is running and less work repetition thanks to the gatherer not having to send the same information to multiple brokers (Rau & Wan, 1994).

2.6. ADVANCED DISTRIBUTED SYSTEM MODELS

Distributed systems save money compared to centralized ones. When redundancy is implemented, the system's availability is increased even if some components fail. A distributed system allows for the simultaneous execution of a large number of applications. Distributed systems are scalable, so adding more parts won't slow them down. In distributed computing, many different kinds of computers work together to complete a single task. As a result, distributed systems' response time and throughput are much faster than centralized ones. Distributed systems also have the advantage of being very trustworthy. The distributed systems' high availability is a great advantage. These advantages have led to the rapid development and widespread deployment of various dispersed systems and applications. Clusters, grids, P2P networks, dispersed storage systems [ANDR02, BUYY99, IAN99, POUR05], and so on are all examples of well-known distributed computing systems. In addition, distributed systems built on top of mobile computing are taking shape (Chen et al., 2017).

The idea behind clustering is that many smaller machines can be grouped together to create a computing framework that could supply all necessary processing power for much less money. Depending on the needs of the users, a grid is a type of distributed system that enables coordinated expressing and aggregation of dispersed, heterogeneous resources. Grids are typically used to support new e-Science and e-Business application developments. Grid computing typically entails geographically dispersed communities working together to solve significant problems. Sharing resources like computers, data, software, and scientific tools is necessary to accomplish this. P2P networks are distributed, decentralized systems that enable using services like high-performance computing, instant messaging, internet telephony, and file-sharing. In communities that exchange files, peer-to-peer networking serves its most well-known purpose. P2P technology is also employed in remote storage sharing and the exploitation of idle desktop PC processing power. Users of distributed storage systems are given a unified view of data that is spread across various file systems and computers that may be connected to the same network or different networks (Choi & Kim, 2001).

SUMMARY

This chapter provides an overview of the concept of distributed systems, its importance, features, and challenges. The chapter begins by highlighting the need for distributed system planning and management due to the increasing demand for more powerful and reliable computing systems. The features of distributed systems, such as scalability, fault tolerance, and transparency, are discussed along with their associated challenges. The chapter also introduces the eight fallacies of distributed computing, which are common misconceptions that can lead to faulty system design and implementation. These fallacies include assumptions about network reliability, latency, and bandwidth, among others. The client/server computing model is explained, and its advantages and disadvantages are discussed. The chapter also highlights the World Wide Web as an immense distributed system, and the challenges associated with managing such a complex system.

REVIEW QUESTIONS

1. What is a distributed system, and why is it essential to plan for one?
2. What are the primary features of distributed systems, and what are the challenges they present?
3. What are the eight fallacies of distributed computing, and how can they impact the design and operation of distributed systems?
4. What are the advantages and disadvantages of the client/server computing model in a distributed system?
5. How does the World Wide Web represent an immense distributed system, and what are the implications of its design for distributed system development?
6. What are some advanced models of distributed systems, and how do they address the challenges posed by traditional distributed systems

MULTIPLE CHOICE QUESTIONS

1. What is a distributed system?

a. A system that operates on a single machine
b. A system that operates on multiple machines
c. A system that operates on a network of machines
d. A system that operates on a cloud

2. Which of the following is a challenge in distributed systems?

a. Network latency
b. Security
c. Data consistency
d. All of the above

3. Which of the following is an example of an immense distributed system?

a. Facebook

b. Amazon

c. Google

d. All of the above

4. What are the advanced models of distributed systems?

a. Peer-to-peer systems

b. Cloud computing

c. Internet of Things (IoT)

d. All of the above

REFERENCES

1. Antamoshkin, O., Kukarcev, V., Pupkov, A., & Tsarev, R., (2014). Intellectual support system of administrative decisions in the big distributed geoinformation systems. In: 14th International Multidisciplinary Scientific GeoConference SGEM 2014 (pp. 227–232).
2. Beschastnikh, I., Wang, P., Brun, Y., & Ernst, M. D., (2016). Debugging distributed systems. Communications of the ACM, 59(8), 32–37.
3. Bigo, S., (2019). A post-5G network to break the eight fallacies of distributed computing. In: 2019 Asia Communications and Photonics Conference (ACP) (Vol. 1, pp. 1–3). IEEE.
4. Bredon, G. E., (2013). Topology and Geometry (Vol. 139, pp. 1–15). Springer Science & Business Media.
5. Chen, B., Chen, C., Wang, J., & Butler-Purry, K. L., (2017). Multi-time step service restoration for advanced distribution systems and microgrids. IEEE Transactions on Smart Grid, 9(6), 6793–6805.
6. Choi, J. H., & Kim, J. C., (2001). Advanced voltage regulation method of power distribution systems interconnected with dispersed storage and generation systems. IEEE Transactions on Power Delivery, 16(2), 329–334.
7. Chowdhury, A. A., Agarwal, S. K., & Koval, D. O., (2002). Reliability modeling of distributed generation in conventional distribution systems planning and analysis. In: Conference Record of the 2002 IEEE Industry Applications Conference. 37th IAS Annual Meeting (Cat. No. 02CH37344) (Vol. 2, pp. 1089–1094). IEEE.
8. Christofides, P. D., (2001). Control of nonlinear distributed process systems: Recent developments and challenges. AIChE Journal, 47(3), 514–518.
9. Deboosere, L., Simoens, P., De Wachter, J., Vankeirsbilck, B., De Turck, F., Dhoedt, B., & Demeester, P., (2011). Grid design for mobile thin client computing. Future Generation Computer Systems, 27(6), 681–693.
10. Doan, A., Ramakrishnan, R., & Halevy, A. Y., (2011). Crowdsourcing systems on the world-wide web. Communications of the ACM, 54(4), 86–96.

11. Dubey, A., Bose, A., Liu, M., & Ochoa, L. N., (2020). Paving the way for advanced distribution management systems applications: Making the most of models and data. IEEE Power and Energy Magazine, 18(1), 63–75.
12. Ganguly, S., Sahoo, N. C., & Das, D., (2013). Recent advances on power distribution system planning: A state-of-the-art survey. Energy Systems, 4, 165–193.
13. Ghosh, P., Basu, K., & Das, S. K., (2007). A game theory-based pricing strategy to support single/multiclass job allocation schemes for bandwidth-constrained distributed computing systems. IEEE Transactions on Parallel and Distributed Systems, 18(3), 289–306.
14. Langville, A. N., & Meyer, C. D., (2005). A survey of eigenvector methods for web information retrieval. SIAM Review, 47(1), 135–161.
15. Lavorato, M., Rider, M. J., Garcia, A. V., & Romero, R., (2010). A constructive heuristic algorithm for distribution system planning. IEEE Transactions on Power Systems, 25(3), 1734–1742.
16. Leonini, L., Rivière, É., & Felber, P., (2009). SPLAY: Distributed systems evaluation made simple. In: Proceedings of the 6th USENIX Symposium on Networked Systems Design and Implementation (Vol. 1, pp. 185–198).
17. Oluwatosin, H. S., (2014). Client-server model. IOSR Journal of Computer Engineering, 16(1), 67–71.
18. Rau, N. S., & Wan, Y. H., (1994). Optimum location of resources in distributed planning. IEEE Transactions on Power Systems, 9(4), 2014–2020.
19. Reisizadeh, A., & Pedarsani, R., (2017). Latency analysis of coded computation schemes over wireless networks. In: 2017 55th Annual Allerton Conference on Communication, Control, and Computing (Allerton) (Vol. 1, pp. 1256–1263). IEEE.
20. Rodden, T., & Blair, G., (1991). CSCW and distributed systems: The problem of control. In: ECSCW 1991: Proceedings of the Second European Conference on Computer Supported Cooperative Work (Vol. 12, pp. 77–85). Kluwer Academic Publishers, Dordrecht, The Netherlands.
21. Ruffer, S. M., Yen, D., & Lee, S., (1995). Client/server computing technology: A framework for feasibility analysis and implementation. International Journal of Information Management, 15(2), 135–150.
22. Shi, J. Y., (2016). Osi standards and the top fallacy of distributed computing. In: 2016 45th International Conference on Parallel Processing Workshops (ICPPW) (Vol. 1, pp. 356–364). IEEE.
23. Shrivastava, S. K., Ezhilchelvan, P. D., Speirs, N. A., Tao, S., & Tully, A., (1991). Principal features of the VOLTAN family of reliable node architectures for distributed systems. Computing Laboratory Technical Report Series, 1, 1–12.
24. Shukur, H., Zeebaree, S. R., Ahmed, A. J., Zebari, R. R., Ahmed, O., Tahir, B. S. A., & Sadeeq, M. A., (2020). A state of art survey for concurrent computation and clustering of parallel computing for distributed systems. Journal of Applied Science and Technology Trends, 1(4), 148–154.

25. Singh, A., Srivatsa, M., Liu, L., & Miller, T., (2004). Apoidea: A decentralized peer-to-peer architecture for crawling the world wide web. In: Distributed Multimedia Information Retrieval: SIGIR 2003 Workshop on Distributed Information Retrieval, Toronto, Canada, Revised Selected and Invited Papers (Vol. 1, pp. 126–142). Springer Berlin Heidelberg.
26. Sinha, A., (1992). Client-server computing. Communications of the ACM, 35(7), 77–98.
27. Umbrich, J., Gutierrez, C., Hogan, A., Karnstedt, M., & Parreira, J. X., (2013). Eight fallacies when querying the web of data. In: 2013 IEEE 29th International Conference on Data Engineering Workshops (ICDEW) (Vol. 1, pp. 21–22). IEEE.
28. Yang, S. J., Nieh, J., Selsky, M., & Tiwari, N., (2002). The performance of remote display mechanisms for thin-client computing. In: USENIX Annual Technical Conference, General Track (Vol. 1, pp. 131–146).
29. Zhao, L., Wang, J., & Huang, R., (2015). Immunization against the spread of rumors in homogenous networks. PloS One, 10(5), 124978.

CHAPTER

3

Computer Networks and Data Communication

LEARNING OBJECTIVES

After studying this chapter, you will be able to:

- Different data transmission modes including simplex, half-duplex, and full-duplex;
- Difference between parallel and serial transmission;
- The differences between asynchronous and synchronous transmission;
- The criteria for designing a network and the different physical structures;
- Different types of networks including LAN, MAN, and WAN;
- Different connecting devices used in computer networks.

"Computer networks are the digital highways of our interconnected world, where data communication fuels the engine of global connectivity."

INTRODUCTORY EXAMPLE

Imagine you're sitting in your cozy home office, sipping on a cup of coffee, and typing an email to a colleague halfway across the world. As you hit the "send" button, your message travels through a series of invisible highways, reaching its destination within seconds. Have you ever wondered how this seamless communication happens, or how your favorite social media updates appear instantly on your screen, regardless of where they originated? The answer lies in the world of "Computer Networks and Data Communication."

In this chapter, we will embark on a journey into the fascinating realm of computer networks, where information flows effortlessly across the globe, connecting individuals, businesses, and entire nations. We will unravel the intricacies of data communication, the backbone of our modern, interconnected world.

From the inception of the internet to the latest advancements in wireless technology, computer networks have played a pivotal role in shaping the way we live, work, and communicate. Whether you're a tech enthusiast, a business professional, or simply curious about how data travels from one point to another, this chapter will provide you with a comprehensive understanding of the principles, protocols, and technologies that underpin this global network of networks.

As we delve deeper into this chapter, you'll discover the key components of computer networks, the various types of network architectures, and the protocols that enable devices to speak the same language. You'll learn about the challenges of data transmission, including ensuring data integrity, security, and efficient routing. Moreover, we'll explore emerging trends such as the Internet of Things (IoT), cloud computing, and the ever-evolving landscape of data communication.

So, whether you're preparing for a career in networking, seeking to enhance your digital literacy, or simply intrigued by the magic behind the screens, let's embark on this exciting journey into the world of Computer Networks and Data Communication. By the end of this chapter, you'll be equipped with the knowledge to appreciate and navigate the intricacies of our interconnected world.

UNIT INTRODUCTION

In today's digital age, data communication and computer networks are essential components of modern communication systems. They enable the exchange of information and resources between computers, devices, and users across different locations and networks. Data communication refers to the transfer of data between devices or computers, while computer networks are the interconnected systems that allow these devices to communicate with each other. These networks can be local or global, wired, or wireless, and can support various applications and services such as email, web browsing, and file sharing. This chapter will provide a comprehensive introduction to data communication and computer networks. It will cover the basic concepts and principles of data communication. It will also discuss different types of computer networks, and their topologies.

In conclusion, this chapter aims to provide a foundation for understanding the concepts and technologies involved in data communication and computer networks. It will be useful for students, professionals, and anyone interested in gaining a deeper understanding of the communication systems that enable our modern digital world.

3.1. DATA COMMUNICATIONS

Learning Objectives

At the end of this section, readers will be able to:

- Understand data communications involve the transmission of digital or analog data between two or more devices or systems.
- Explain the protocols and standards are essential for ensuring reliable and efficient data communication.
- Understand the different types of transmission media, such as wired and wireless, have their own advantages and limitations in data communication.

The process of transferring data between two devices through any transmission medium is called data communications. For there to be data communications, devices that are doing the talking have to be a part of a communication system that's comprised of both software (actual computer programs) and hardware (the actual physical equipment). Jitter, delivery, accuracy, and timeliness are the four primary factors that determine how successful a data communications system will be.

3.1.1. Delivery

It is necessary for the system to transmit the data to the appropriate location. The data can only be received by device or user for which it was intended, and only by that user or device.

3.1.2. Accuracy

Data have to be sent in a correct manner by the system. It is impossible to make use of data that has been corrupted during transmission and has not been rectified.

3.1.3. Timeliness

The data must be sent by the system in timely fashion. Data given late are meaningless. When referring to the distribution of audio and video data, "timely delivery" refers to the delivery of said data as it's being created, in same order that it's being produced, and without considerable delay. This type of distribution is known as real-time transmission.

3.1.4. Jitter

This term "jitter" means arrival times of packet's variation. The term "jitter" refers to fluctuation in the times at which packets arrive (Stephens, 2004).

3.1.5. Components of Data Communication

A data transmission system consists of five parts (Figure 3.1):

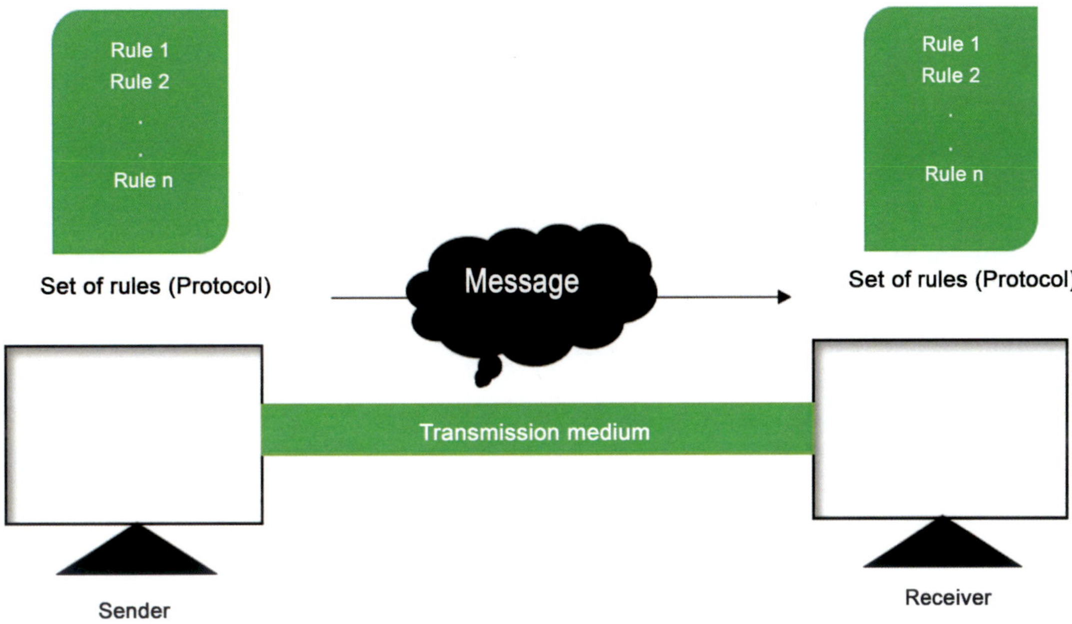

Figure 3.1. *Components of data transmission system.*

1. Message: An information (data) that has to be communicated is message. Information in popular formats of numbers, images, text, audio, and video.
2. Sender: A data message's sender is a sending device. It could be a workstation, computer, phone, video camera, and other devices.
3. Receiver: The component which's responsible for receiving the message is known as receiver. It could be a workstation, television, telephone handset, computer, or any number of other electronic devices.
4. Transmission Medium: It is the actual route a message takes to get from source to receiver. Fiber-optic cable, coaxial cable, radio waves and twisted-pair wire are some types of transmission media.
5. Protocol: Set of guidelines which controls how data is communicated is a protocol. It means that the communication devices will comprehend one another.

3.2. DATA TRANSMISSION MODES

Learning Objectives

At the end of this section, readers will be able to:

- Define data transmission modes;
- Differentiate between modes;
- Analyze the parallel and serial transmission.

Few of the modes of data transmission are as follow:

1. Simplex: Similar to a one-way street, simplex mode communication is unidirectional. When two devices are linked together, one of them can send data while other can only receive it. Keyboards and standard screens are simplex devices examples. The only function of a keyboard is to enter data, while the only function of a monitor is to display output. A simplex mode is able to convey data in only one direction while utilizing full capacity of channel (Pahlavan & Levesque, 1994).
2. Half-Duplex: In the half-duplex mode, every station is able to send and receive information, but not simultaneously. One device can only receive data when other is broadcasting, and vice versa. During transmission using a half-duplex scheme, channel's entire capacity is utilized by whichever of two devices is delivering data at any given time. CB (citizens band) and Walkie-talkies radios are examples of communication devices that use half-duplex technology. When it is not necessary to communicate in both directions at once, half-duplex mode is employed. This allows channel capacity to be utilized in its entirety by each direction (Tang & Wang, 2015) (Figure 3.2).
3. Full-Duplex: The simultaneous broadcast and receipt from both stations is possible with full-duplex communication. A full-duplex mode operates in a manner analogous to that of a road that can accommodate traffic traveling in both directions at the same time. When a link is operating in full-duplex mode, it allows signals moving in both directions to potentially share link's capacity. Full-duplex communication is typically demonstrated via telephone network. Both sides can listen and talk at same time when speaking on phone. A full-duplex mode is utilized if there's a requirement for ongoing communication in both directions. However, canal's capacity needs to be split into two directions (Bartlett et al., 1969).

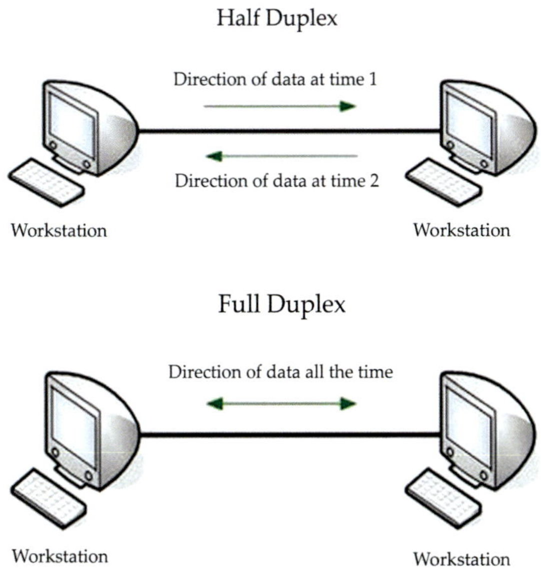

Figure 3.2. *Half duplex.*

4. Parallel Transmission: n-bit groups of binary data, which consists only of 1s and 0s, can be created. In a manner similar to how people think about and utilize spoken language, computers create and consume data in groups of bits rather than individual letters. Data can be sent n bits at a time rather than 1 by grouping. Parallel transmission is the term used for this. The parallel transmission technique is essentially straightforward: Send n bits at once using n wires. With each clock tick, all n bits of one group can be sent from one device to another because each bit has its own cable in this arrangement. Figure 3.3 demonstrates parallel transmission for n = 8 in action. Usually, a cable with connectors on both ends is made up of eight wires. Speed is a benefit of parallel transmission. When everything else is equal, parallel transmission can outperform serial transmission in terms of transfer speed by a factor of n.

Cost, however, is a serious drawback. N communication lines are needed for parallel transmission merely to send the data stream. Parallel transmission is typically only used for short distances due to its high cost (Saltzberg, 1967).

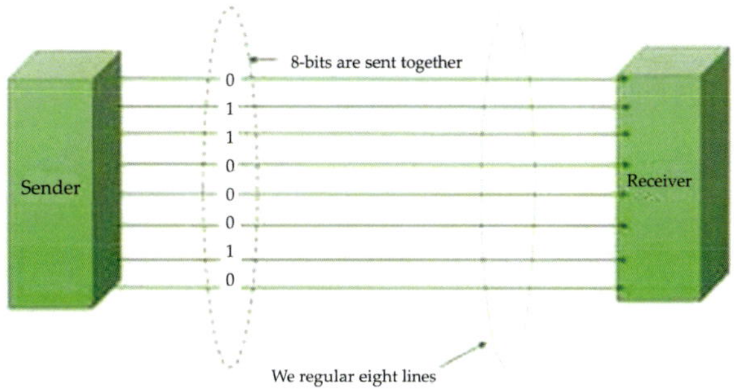

Figure 3.3. *Parallel transmission.*

5. Serial Transmission: One bit follows another when data is transmitted serially between two communicating devices, therefore we only need one communication channel instead of n.

Serial transmission, which has an advantage over parallel transmission, lowers transmission's cost by roughly factor of n with only one communication channel. Interface between transmitter and line (parallel-to-serial) as well as between line and receiver (serial-to-parallel) both require conversion devices since communication between devices is parallel.

There're 3 different ways that serial transmission can happen: asynchronous, synchronous, and isochronous (Walker, 2003) (Figure 3.4).

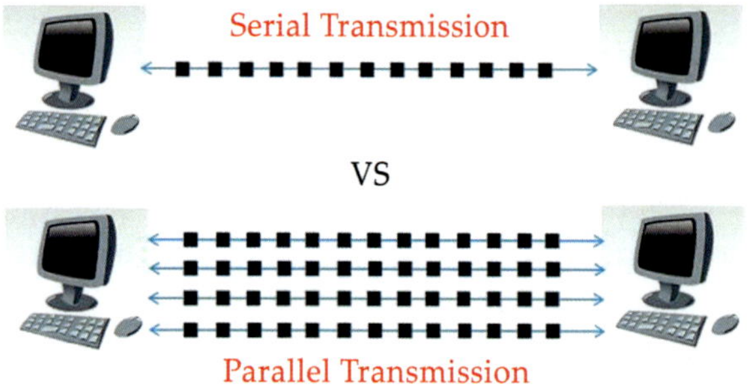

Figure 3.4. *Difference between parallel and serial transmission modes.*

6. Asynchronous Transmission: It gets its name from fact that signal timing isn't crucial. Instead, predetermined patterns are used to interpret and receive information. The information can be retrieved by the receiving device without regard to the rhythm in which it is supplied if those patterns are followed. Basis of patterns is the division of bit stream into bytes. A link transmits each group, which typically consists of 8 bits, individually. Without respect to a timer, the transmitting system manages each group independently and relays it to the connection when it is ready. The receiver cannot utilize time to anticipate when following group will arrive without synchronization. Therefore, a bit is added to beginning of every byte to notify receiver of arrival of new group. The start bit is this bit, which is often a 0. One or more extra bits are added to end of byte to signal to the receiver that the byte is complete.

By using this technique, each byte is expanded to a minimum of 10 bits, where 8 bits are used for information and 2 bits or more for signals to receiver. Transmission of each byte may subsequently be followed by gap that lasts for various amounts of time. This gap can be represented by either an empty channel or a stream of extra stop bits. A receiver is made aware of the beginning and end of each byte by start and stop bits, as well as by the gap, which also helps it synchronize with the data stream. Because the transmitter and receiver do not need to be in sync at the byte level, this method is referred to as asynchronous. However, receiver must still be synced with incoming bit stream within each byte. In other words, some synchronization is necessary, but only for a single byte. At beginning of every new byte, receiving device resynchronizes. The receiver starts a timer and starts counting bits when it notices a start bit. The receiver searches for a stop bit n bit later. It waits until it finds following start bit after detecting stop bit. As opposed to additional stop bits, an idle line is used to represent the gap in this example's start and stop bits.

Due to the need for control information and the insertion of gaps into the bit stream, asynchronous transmission is less efficient than other kinds of transmission. However, it is inexpensive and efficient, two features that make it a desirable option in circumstances like low-speed communication. An obvious application for asynchronous transmission is the connection of a keyboard to a computer. In terms of data processing, the user types slowly and randomly space out the characters.

7. Synchronous Transmission: A bit stream is merged into longer "frames," that may include several bytes, during synchronous transmission. But there is no pause between one byte and the next as they are all inserted simultaneously onto the transmission network. It's up to receiver to divide bit stream into its component bytes for decoding. To put it another way,

information is transmitted as an uninterrupted string of 1s and 0s, and the recipient breaks that string down into the bytes, or characters, which are required to reconstruct the data. The distinctions between bytes have been depicted. These distinctions are fictitious; the sender just sends its data as one single string across the line. The spaces between bursts must be filled with a particular sequence of 0s and Is that stands for idle if sender wants to deliver data in discrete bursts. As the bits come in, the receiver counts them and divides them into 8-bit chunks. There is no built-in method to assist the receiving device with adjusting its bit synchronization midstream without gaps and start and stop bits. Timing becomes crucial since the precision of the information received is entirely dependent on the receiver's capacity to maintain an accurate count of the bits as they arrive. Synchronous transmission has benefit of speed. Synchronous transmission is quicker than asynchronous transmission because there aren't any extra bits or gaps to add at sending end and remove at receiving end, and consequently, since there are less bits to transmit across the link. This makes it more advantageous for high-speed applications like data transmission between computers. Data link layer byte synchronization is completed (Luo & Südhof, 2017) (Figure 3.5).

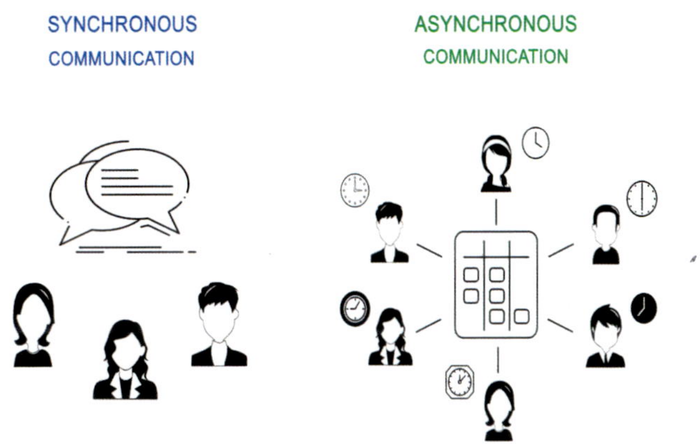

Figure 3.5. *Difference between asynchronous and synchronous transmission.*

3.3. LAYERS IN THE OSI MODEL

Learning Objectives

At the end of this section, readers will be able to:

- Define the OSI (open systems interconnection) model and its seven layers.
- Describe the specific functions and responsibilities of each OSI model layer.
- Differentiate between the OSI MODEL layers in terms of their roles in data communication.
- Evaluate the importance of the OSI model in networking and troubleshooting scenarios.

When music and video are played back in real-time, the frame delays can be unequal. The OSI model is based on a suggestion made by the International Standards Organization (ISO) as a preliminary step toward global standardization of the protocols used in the various layers (Day & Zimmermann, 1983). 1995 saw its revision (Day, 1995). Because it deals with integrating open systems—that is, systems that are accessible for communication with other systems—the model is known as the ISO-OSI (Open Systems Interconnection). The OSI model, which is a layered framework for network system design, enables communication across all types of computer systems. It consists of seven different but linked layers, each of which describes stage in transmission of data over network.

Physical (layer 1), data connection (layer 2), network (layer 3), transport (layer 4), session (layer 5), presentation (layer 6), and application (layer 7) are the seven layers that make up OSI model. The diagram below shows the layers involved in transmitting a message from device A to device B. The message may go from point A to point B via a large number of intermediate nodes. Only first three OSI model layers are typically involved in these intermediary nodes.

3.3.1. Physical Layer

The steps necessary to transport a bit stream through a physical medium are coordinated by the physical layer. The mechanical and electrical requirements of transmission medium interface are covered. It also describes actions and responsibilities that physical equipment and interfaces must take in order for transmission to occur.

The following issues are likewise of relevance to the physical layer:

1. Physical Characteristics of Interfaces and Medium: An interface property between devices and transmission media are determined by physical layer. Furthermore, it specifies kind of transmission media.
2. Representation of Bits: A data in physical layer is just a stream of bits (a series of Os or 1s) without any meaning. Before being delivered, bits must first be encoded into electrical or optical signals. The physical layer determines type of encoding.
3. Data Rate: Additionally, transmission rate, or number of bits that are transferred per second, is established at physical layer. In other words, duration of a bit, or how long it lasts, is defined by physical layer.
4. Synchronization of Bits: In addition to using the same bit rate, the transmitter and receiver both need to be in sync at the bit level. To put it another way, the clocks of the sender and the recipient must match.
5. Line Configuration: The physical layer deals with how devices are connected to media. Two devices are connected point-to-point using dedicated link. A multipoint configuration has multiple devices sharing a link.
6. Physical Topology: It describes connections between network components. A mesh topology connects every device to every other device, and a hybrid topology, which mixes two or more topologies, connects every device to every other device. Each device is connected to the next to form a ring in a bus topology.
7. Transmission Mode: Simplex, half-duplex, or full-duplex transmission between two devices are all defined by the physical layer. In simplex mode, only one device can send, while the other can only receive. A one-way communication technique is simplex. In half-duplex mode, two devices can send and receive, but not simultaneously. Two devices can send and receive simultaneously while operating in full-duplex (or just duplex) mode (Mabrouk et al., 2016).

3.3.2. Data Link Layer

The data link layer converts the physical layer, a fundamental transmission facility, into a reliable link. It creates an illusion that physical layer is error-free at network layer, layer above.

A data link layer also performs following extra tasks: A frame. Data link layer receives a stream of bits from network layer and converts them into frames, which are small, manageable data units:

1. Physical Addressing: If frames must be dispersed among numerous computers on the network, to identify sender and/or recipient of frame, data link layer adds header to frame. Address of device which connects network of sender to system for which frame is intended is known as receiver address of frame.
2. Flow Control: If the rate at which data are produced in the sender is lower than the rate at which data are absorbed by the receiver,

a data connection layer applies flow control to prevent overloading the receiver.

3. Error Control: A data link layer improves physical layer dependability by introducing methods to detect and retransmit corrupted or missing frames. It also makes use of technique to find duplicate frames. To achieve error control, a trailer is often introduced at end of frame.
4. Access Control: When multiple devices are sharing the same link, data link layer protocols are required to determine which device is in charge at any one time.

3.3.3. Network Layer

Sending packet from source to destination—and occasionally over many networks (links)—is responsibility of network layer. Data link layer controls packet delivery between two systems connected by same network (links), whereas network layer ensures every packet arrives at its intended destination from the point of origin. In most cases, if two systems are connected by same link, a network layer isn't necessary. However, network layer will typically require source-to-destination delivery if two systems are linked to distinct networks (links) using devices (Njoh, 2010).

Following are some additional duties of the network layer:

1. Logical Addressing: The data link layer's physical addressing solution addresses the addressing issue locally. When a packet crosses a network boundary, a different addressing scheme is needed to help identify source and destination systems. The network layer adds a header, among other things, logical addresses of sender and receiver, to the packet originating from the top layer.
2. Routing: When two separate links or networks are connected to create a larger network or a network of networks, the connecting devices, which are known as routers or switches, are responsible for directing data packets to the appropriate destination. It is one of the network layer's duties to offer this mechanism.

3.3.4. Transport Layer

From one operation to another, the complete message must be transmitted over the transport layer. A process is a running application program on a host. Although network layer regulates packet delivery from source to destination, it has no knowledge of how the packets are related. It treats each element independently, regardless of whether it is part of another message. Assuring that complete message arrives intact and in right order is responsibility of transport layer, which also controls flow from source to destination.

The transport layer also has the following requirements:

1. Service-Point Addressing: Nowadays, computers typically have several programs active at once. As a result, transmission of data between two computers is referred to as source-to-destination delivery, as well as between one specific processes (running program) on one computer and another specific process (running program) on another computer. Therefore, a service-point address (sometimes called port address) must be included in transport

layer header. Following delivery of each packet by network layer to appropriate computer, transport layer transfers full message to that computer's relevant process (LaMagna et al., 2016).

2. Segmentation and Reassembly: A message is separated into sendable sections, each with its own sequence number. When message arrives at its destination, transport layer may accurately rebuild it by utilizing these numbers to identify and replace any missing packets during transmission.
3. Connection Control: A transport layer might be either connection-oriented or connection-free. A connectionless transport layer is used to transfer each segment to the target machine's transport layer, which interprets each one as a single packet. A connection-oriented transport layer connects to transport layer at destination computer before sending packets. Once all of data has been sent, the connection is terminated.
4. Flow Control: It is handled by transport layer, which is also responsible for data connection layer. But at this layer, flow regulation takes place over multiple links rather than just one.
5. Error Control: It is handled by transport layer, as well as the data connection layer. However, at this layer, error handling is done process-to-process rather than across a single link. While being sent to receiving transport layer, sending transport layer ensures that no part of the message is lost, duplicated, or destroyed. Retransmission is frequently used to correct errors (Moon & Kim, 2007) (Figure 3.6).

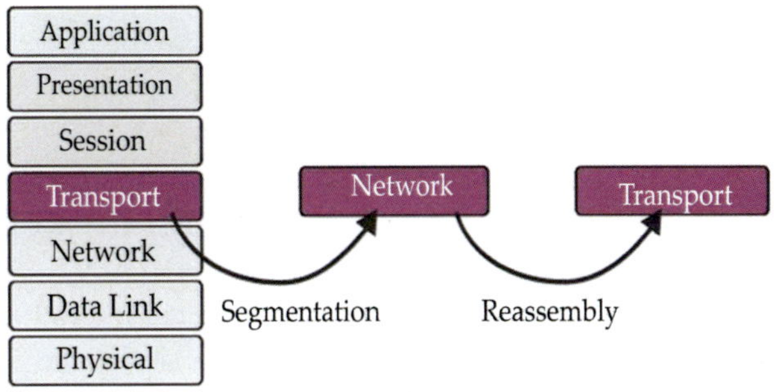

Figure 3.6. *Transport layer.*

3.3.5. Session Layer

There are some tasks that need for greater assistance than what first 3 layers (physical, data link, and network) can provide. Network dialog controller is located at session layer. It's responsible for establishing, maintaining, and synchronizing system communication.

The session layer is required to perform the following specialized duties:

1. Dialog Control: Two separate systems are able to communicate with one another in session layer. It allows two processes to communicate either in half-duplex (only one direction at a time) or full-duplex (both ways at once).
2. Synchronization: A process can use the session layer to insert synchronization and checkpoint points into a data stream.

3.3.6. Presentation Layer

Between two systems, the presentation layer controls syntax and semantics of the information communicated. The following are some specific responsibilities for the presentation layer:

1. Translation: Character strings, integers, and other data types

are widely used to communicate between two processes (running programs). The information must be transformed into bit streams before it can be transmitted. In light of the fact that diverse computers employ distinct encoding schemes, it falls on the presentation layer to guarantee compatibility. At sender, the presentation layer converts the data from the format that is unique to the sender to a more universal one. A receiving device's presentation layer converts common format into the receiver-specific format (Fiala et al., 2004).

2. Encryption: When dealing with sensitive information, a system needs to be able to maintain users' privacy. Encryption is used by sender to convert the original data into a new format before sending the new message through network. Decryption reverses first procedure of returning message's original format.
3. Compression: Data compression reduces an amount of bits required to hold data. When transmitting multimedia elements such as music, text, and video, data compression is critical.

3.3.7. Application Layer

The application layer provides network connectivity to both software and human users. Email, shared database administration, remote file access and transfer and variety of other distributed information services are available, as are user interfaces and support.

The application layer provides the services listed below:

1. Network Virtual Terminal: Users can connect to far-off hosts using network virtual terminal, software that replicates genuine terminal.
2. File Transfer, Access, and Management: A user can download files to their local workstation using this program, manage or control those files locally, and access files on a remote host (to make changes or read data) all at same time.
3. Directory Services: This program provides information about numerous items and services, as well as worldwide access to external database sources (Engler et al., 1995).

3.4. NETWORKS

Learning Objectives

At the end of this section, readers will be able to:

- Explain the concept of computer networks and their significance in modern computing.
- Discuss the key components and architecture of a typical network, including nodes, routers, switches, and cables.
- Analyze different types of network topologies, such as star, bus, ring, and mesh, highlighting their advantages and disadvantages.

Nodes are the individual components that make up a network. They are connected to one another through communication lines. Any machine, like a computer or printer that can send or receive data created by other nodes on network is referred to as a node.

3.4.1. Network Criteria

Network needs to be able to fulfill variety of needs. Performance, dependability, and security are the three that are most important.

3.4.1.1. Performance

You can measure performance in different ways, such as reaction and transit times. Transit time is amount of time it takes for message to travel between two devices. Response time is period of time between request and a response. Network performance is determined by multitude of elements, some of which are number of users, transmission channel's kind, linked equipment's capabilities, and software effectiveness (Stoilova et al., 2020).

3.4.1.2. Reliability

Network dependability can be assessed using frequency of failure, time it takes for link to recover from failure, and network's resilience in case of disaster.

3.4.1.3. Security

Examples of network security problems are protecting data from unauthorized access, preventing data loss and development, and creating guidelines and methods for recovering from breaches and data loss (Figure 3.7).

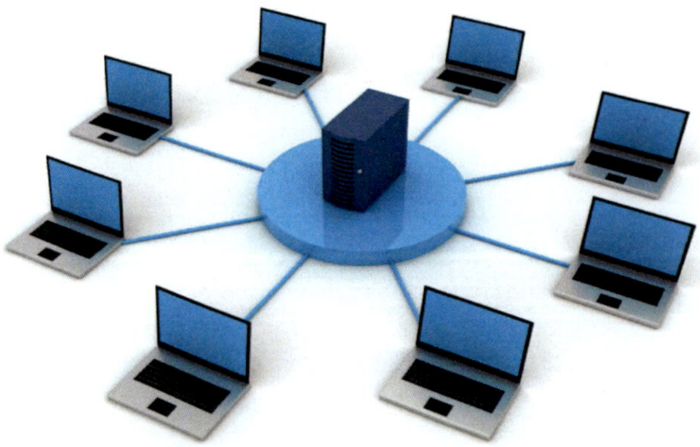

Figure 3.7. *Computer networking.*

3.4.2. Physical Structures

3.4.2.1. Types of Connections

Network is made up of two or more devices connected by connections. Connection enables data flow between two devices, which is a communications channel. Connections that are both point-to-point and multipoint are possible.

1. Point-to-Point: A point-to-point connection establishes direct link between two devices. Only these two gadgets are permitted to use the link's maximum transmission speed. Point-to-point connections frequently include a physical wire or cable going between two ends, although alternative options, such satellite connectivity or as microwave, are also possible. To change channel on a television, use an infrared remote control, which establishes point-to-point connection with television's control system.
2. Multipoint: More than two devices can be linked together through a single connection in a multipoint setup. In a multipoint setting, channel capacity is split between multiple users over either space or time. If several different devices are able to use same connection at same time, then we call that a spatially shared connection. When users must alternate using a connection, it's deemed timeshared (Modarressi et al., 2010).

3.4.2.2. Physical Topology

This term "physical topology" refers to network's physical topology. A topology is made up of two or more links, and a link connects one or more devices. The topology of a network is represented geometrically to highlight the relationships between each of the connections and links, also known as nodes. There are four primary topologies that could exist: mesh, ring, bus, and star (Bejerano et al., 2003) (Figure 3.8).

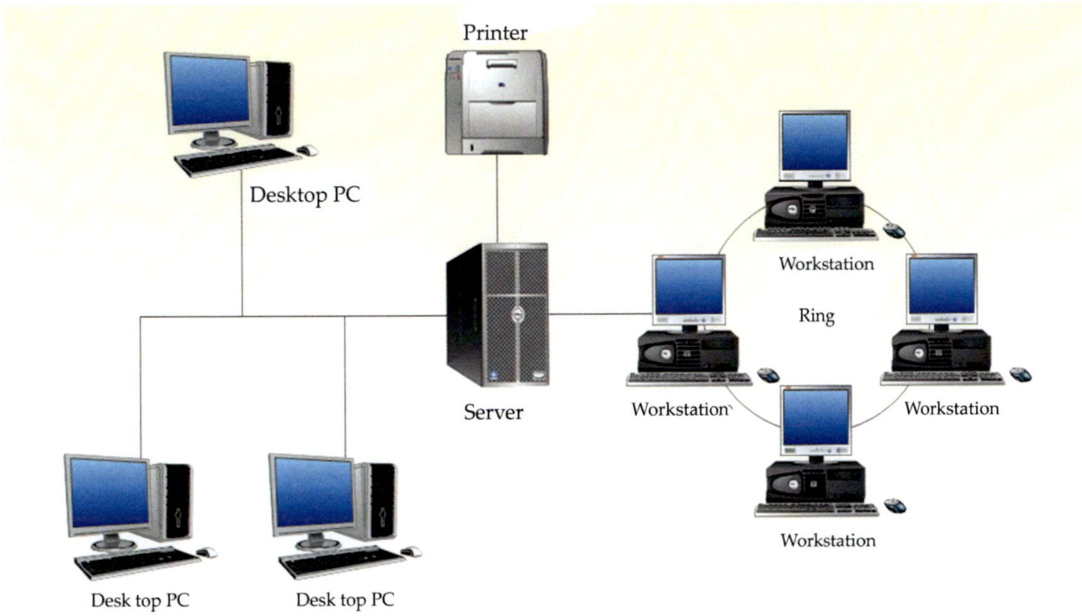

Figure 3.8. *Physical topology.*

1. Mesh: Each device has distinct point-to-point connection with other device, in mesh topology. According to definition of the phrase, a dedicated link only sends data between two devices it connects. In order to determine mesh network with n node's total number of physical links, we first address requirement that every node should be connected to every other node. Nodes in n-I group should be connected to node 1, nodes in the n-I group must be connected to node 2, and nodes in the n-I group must be connected to node n. There should be n(n–1) physical connections. On the other hand, if each physical link supports two-way communication (duplex mode), number of links can be divided by two. In other words, a mesh topology requires n(n–1)/2 duplex-mode links. To support those many links, each network device should've n–1 input/output ports in order to communicate with other n–1 station (Mubeen & Kumar, 2010).

Advantages:

- Since each connection can support its own data load when using dedicated links, traffic issues which arise when links are shared by many devices are avoided.
- Mesh topology is trustworthy. One broken link does not render the system useless.
- The advantages of security or privacy exist. When a message is sent over a dedicated line, only intended recipient can see it. Other users are prevented from viewing messages by physical obstacles.
- Identification and isolation of faults are made simple by point-to-point connections. Traffic can be rerouted to avoid links that might have

issues. This feature helps the network manager to locate fault precisely and assists in determining its source and resolution (Bianchi et al., 2003).

Disadvantages:

- A mesh's drawbacks are linked quantity of cabling required for each device to communicate with each other.
- Installation and reconnecting might be challenging.
- There may not be enough room (in the form of ceilings, floors, or walls) to accommodate sheer weight of the wiring.
- The cost of the cable and I/O ports required to connect each link may be unaffordable (Maxemchuk, 1985).

2. Star Topology: In star topology, the hub, which serves as the central controller, is the sole dedicated point-to-point link that each device has. Devices are not connected to one another directly. A star topology, on the other hand, does not provide direct traffic between devices, in contrast to a mesh topology. The controller performs the role of a market: A device must transfer data to controller before controller may pass data to other connected device in order for the two devices to communicate (Zhu et al., 2019) (Figure 3.9).

Advantages:

- The cost of star topology is lower than that of mesh topology. For any device in a star to connect to any number of other devices, only one connection and one I/O port are needed.
- Simple to install and modify.
- The amount of wiring required is significantly reduced, and adding, moving, or removing devices only requires one connection: that between the device and hub.
- Strongness is another benefit. If only one of the links is broken, only that connection will be disrupted. The remaining connections are active. This element also makes fault isolation and fault identification simple. As long as hub is operational, it can be used to track link issues and avoid broken links (Barranco et al., 2009).

Disadvantages

- The dependence of star topology on a single point, hub, is one of its major drawbacks. If the hub breaks, the system is useless. When compared to mesh, a star requires a far lower number of wires; nonetheless, each node must still be connected to the central hub. Because of this, a star topology frequently requires more cabling than certain other topologies (such as bus or ring) (Balabanov et al., 2016).

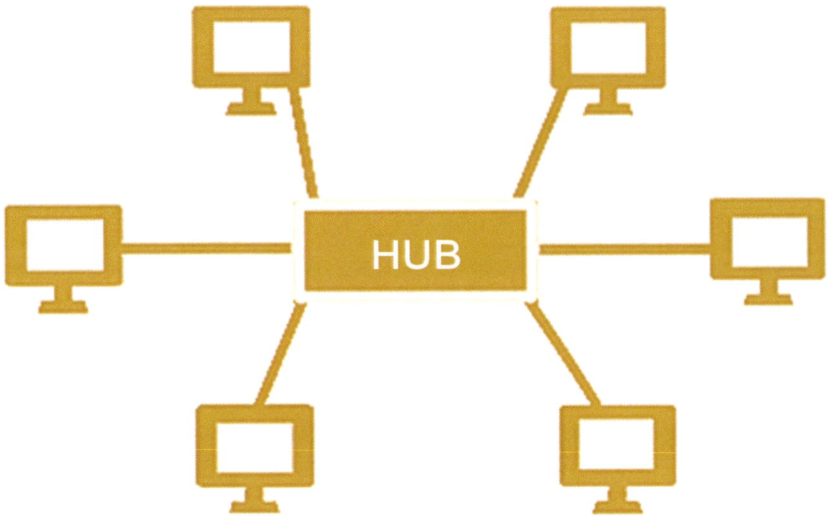

Figure 3.9. *Star topology.*

3. Bus: The topology of bus is multipoint. The backbone of a network is the main connection between all of the nodes. To connect nodes to bus cable, drop lines and taps are used. Drop lines are connections between devices and main cables. A tap is connector which makes a connection with the metallic core of a cable by either splicing into main cable or cutting through cable's wrapping. Some of an energy of a signal is converted into heat as it moves along the backbone. As a result, as it moves farther and farther, it gets weaker and weaker. As a result, there are restrictions on the amount of taps and the spacing between them that a bus can sustain.

- Ø Advantages: A bus topology has the benefit of being simple to implement. The most effective route for laying backbone cable can be chosen and drop lines of various lengths can be used to connect it to the nodes. In this regard, the cabling demands of a bus topology are lower than those of a mesh or star topology. For instance, four lengths of cable that reach the hub are needed if there are four network devices configured in a star pattern in the same room. This redundancy is removed in a bus. Only the backbone wire traverses entire construction. Each drop line simply needs to extend as far as closest bone point.
- Ø Disadvantages: Inconvenient reconnecting and fault separation are two drawbacks. Typically, a bus is built to be installed as efficiently as possible. Therefore, adding more devices may be challenging. Quality reduction may result from signal reflection at the taps. This deterioration can be avoided by limiting number and closeness of devices connected to particular cable length. The backbone might consequently need to be changed or replaced to accommodate additional devices. Additionally, even communication between devices on same side of the issue is halted by failure or break in bus cable. Noise is produced in both directions as a result of damaged area reflecting signals in direction of origin (Lafata & Vodrazka, 2011).

4. Ring: The only other two devices are on either side of each point-to-point link that each device in ring topology has. Until it reaches its destination, signal is delivered along a ring in a single direction from one device to the next. Each component of ring contains a repeater. A device's repeater regenerates bits and sends them on when it receives a signal meant for another device.

- Advantages: Installing and rearranging a ring is not that difficult. Only the immediate neighbors of each device are connected, either physically or logically. Adding or removing device simply requires two connections to be changed. The only limitations are those related to media and traffic (such as the number of devices and the maximum ring length). Fault isolation is also made simpler. In a ring, a signal typically circulates constantly. One device can sound an alarm if it doesn't get a signal within a predetermined time frame.
- Disadvantages: Traffic that is only going one way can be problematic. The entire network might go down in one ring if there is break in ring (e.g., station that is disabled). Using a secondary ring or a switch that can turn the break off can remedy this problem. Ring topologies were widespread when IBM debuted their local-area network Token Ring. Today, this topology is less common due to the demand for faster LANs.

3.5. NETWORK CATEGORIES

Learning Objectives

At the end of this section, readers will be able to:

- Explain the concept of network categories;
- Discuss the different types of network categories;
- Identify the key components and technologies associated with network categories;
- Evaluate the advantages and disadvantages of different network categories.

3.5.1. Local Area Networks (LAN)

Local area networks, commonly known as LANs, are privately owned networks that can cover huge areas on a campus or in a building. In corporate offices and manufacturing facilities, personal computers and workstations are frequently connected in order to share resources (such printers) and transmit information. LANs differ from other networks in three ways:

- Their transmission technology;
- Their size; and
- Their topology.

Due to LAN size limitations, the worst-case transmission time is constrained and known ahead. It is possible to use specific types of designs that would not be feasible without knowledge of this bond. It also makes network administration simpler. LANs may employ a transmission technique similar to the party lines historically employed by telephone companies in rural regions, which consists of a cable to which all the devices are connected. Traditional LANs feature rates between 10 and 100 Mbps, a delay of a few microseconds or nanoseconds, and a low error rate.

3.5.2. Metropolitan Area Network (MAN)

The city is surrounded by a MAN, or metropolitan area network. The most well-known MAN is the cable television network, which may be found in many different locations. Communities without sufficient over-the-air television coverage formerly relied on communal antenna installations. In these early systems, massive antenna was installed on a nearby hill, and signal was then sent to clients' residences. These were initially ad hoc, locally developed systems. Then businesses started to enter the market, winning contracts from local governments to wire a full city. Next phase was television content, including entire channels made only for cable. These channels frequently have a narrow focus, such as all sports, all cuisine, all gardening, etc. But from the time they were developed until late 1990s, they were solely made for receiving television. The MAN is not limited to cable television. Another MAN, known as IEEE 802.16, has been developed recently in connection with high-speed wireless Internet access (Green et al., 1993) (Figure 3.10).

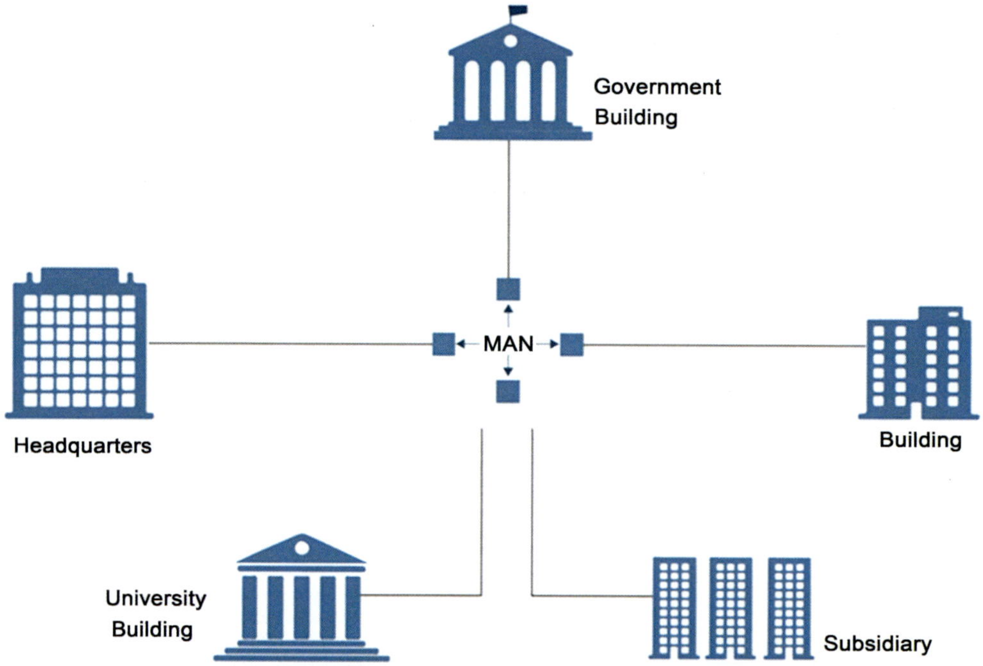

Figure 3.10. *Metropolitan area network (MAN).*

3.5.3. Wide Area Network (WAN)

Wide area networks, or WANs, typically cover whole continent or country. It has a number of computers designed to run user (or application) programs. These devices are referred to as hosts. A communication subnet, or simply subnet, connects the hosts. Hosts, such as people's personal computers, are owned and controlled by the consumers, as opposed to communication subnets, which are frequently operated and owned by telephone companies or Internet service providers. Similar to how the telephone system transmits speech from speaker to listener, the function of subnet is to transport messages from host to host. An entire network design is significantly simplified by separating the network's purely communication-related components—the subnet—from its application-related components—the hosts (Yang et al., 2019). Transmission lines and switching equipment make up the subnet in the majority of wide area networks. Between machines, bits are moved using transmission lines. Optical fiber, copper wire, or even radio links can be used to construct them. In the majority of WANs, the network has a large number of transmission lines, each of which connects two routers. Without a common transmission line, two routers can only talk to one another via going through a third router. For a packet to be transmitted from one router to another, it must first be received by all of the intermediate routers along the path, stored until the appropriate output line becomes available, and then forwarded. A store-and-forward or packet-switched subnet is one that is set up using this technique (Kandula et al., 2014). Store-and-forward subnets are present in almost all wide area networks, with the exception of satellite-based ones. Cells are frequently used to describe small, uniformly sized packets. The idea behind a packet-switched WAN is crucial. In most cases, when a process on one host has to transmit a message to a process on another computer, sending host first divides message into packets, each of which bears its own sequential number. A network is then rapidly bombarded with these packets, one at a time. The packets are transmitted to the receiving host individually through the network, where they're combined back into original message and sent to receiving process. Not all WANs use packet switching. Satellite network is an additional option. Every router has an antenna that it uses to transmit and receive data. Every router can hear the satellite's output, and in some situations, they may also hear each other's upward transmissions to the satellite. When just some of the routers have a satellite antenna, they may be connected to a sizable point-to-point subnet. Satellite networks are broadcast by nature and perform best when that characteristic is significant (Wang et al., 1998) (Figure 3.11).

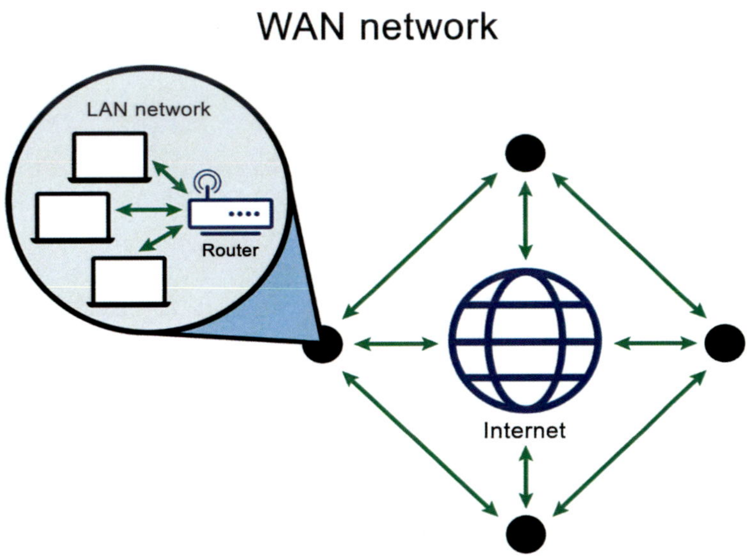

Figure 3.11. *Wide area network (WAN).*

3.6. CONNECTING DEVICES

Learning Objectives

At the end of this section, readers will be able to:

- Explain the concept of device connectivity;
- Discuss different methods of device connectivity;
- Demonstrate the process of setting up device connections;
- Analyze the challenges and security considerations in device connectivity.

3.6.1. Repeaters

A device that solely functions at physical layer is called repeater. Within a network, signals that contain information can only travel so far before attenuation compromises integrity of data. Before the signal deteriorates or becomes corrupted, a repeater receives it and recreates the original bit pattern. A signal is then sent by the repeater. A repeater joins two segments of the same LAN, not two separate LANs. The connected segments continue to be a part of a single LAN. A repeater cannot connect two LANs that use different protocols. Although it's tempting, it is incorrect to equate repeater to an amplifier. An amplifier amplifies anything that is supplied into it without being able to distinguish between intended signal and background noise. A repeater regenerates the signal rather than amplifying it. It makes a copy, bit for bit, at original strength of signal that's weak or corrupted (Lucamarini et al., 2018).

3.6.2. Bridges or Link Layer Switches

Both physical layer and data connection layer are utilized by bridge or link layer switch (also known as a switch). As a component of the physical layer, it is responsible for regenerating the signal that it is given. Due to fact that the bridge operates at data link layer, it's possible for it to investigate physical (MAC) addresses that are contained within frame. A bridge has the ability to filter. It has the ability to examine a frame's destination address and determine whether it should be forwarded or dropped. The decision must state the port if the frame is to be forwarded. A table on a bridge links addresses to ports. Let's use an illustration. In Figure 3.11, a bridge links two LANs together. A bridge analyzes its table to determine departure port when a frame with the destination station 712B13456142 arrives at port 1. Its table indicates that since frames for 712B13456142 depart from port 1, there is no requirement for forwarding and the frame can be deleted. On other hand, if a frame for the address 712B13456141 arrives at port 2, frame is forwarded, and the departure port is port 1. In the first scenario, LAN 2 is left without any traffic; in second scenario, both LANs are active. In our illustration, two-port bridge is shown; in practice, bridge typically includes more ports (Ortiz et al., 2012).

3.6.3. Hubs

A hub is a piece of equipment which only works at physical layer. Within a network, signals which contain information can only travel so far before attenuation compromises integrity of data. When a signal is received, a repeater regenerates and retimes original bit pattern before it is too weak or corrupted. After then, the signal will be sent via the repeater. A repeater is a multiport device, frequently referred to as a hub, which may act as both a repeater and a connecting point in a star architecture. Upon arrival at the hub, a packet from station A to station B has its frame's signal regenerated to eliminate any potential corrupting noise. However, the hub forwards packets from all outgoing terminals except one that received signal. In other words, frame is broadcasted. Every station in LAN receives it, but only station B saves it and other station discard it. A physical layer device is a hub. They lack a link layer address and don't look at the receiving frame's link layer address. They just regenerate damaged bits and release them through every port (Goldenberg et al., 2009).

3.6.4. Routers

Using host-to-host addressing, router is 3-layer device which routes packets according to their logical addresses. When linking local area networks (LANs) and wide area networks (WANs) to internet, a router will consult its routing table to determine the best route to take. To update routing tables routing protocols are used, which are usually dynamic in nature. A three-layer device is a router. It functions at the network, data connection, and physical layers. As a device operating at the physical layer, it recreates signal that it receives. The router examines packet's physical addresses as link layer device. A router examines network layer addresses in its capacity as network layer device. Networks can be linked through a router. To put it another way, a router is an internetworking tool that joins separate networks to create an internetwork. A router differs significantly from a repeater or switch in three ways.

- Each interface on a router is assigned both physical and logical address;
- A router only responds to packets whose link layer destination address coincides with interface's address at which packet arrives; and
- When a router forwards a packet, it modifies the link layer address of the packet (Chao, 2002).

3.6.5. Gateways

Gateway is often a computer which performs operations on all seven OSI model layers or all five Internet layers. An application message is received, read, and evaluated by a gateway. As a consequence of this, it is possible to utilize it in the role of a connecting device between two distinct forms of internetworks. For example, a network built using the OSI model can be linked to another network built using the Internet model. A frame received from first system may be moved up to OSI application layer and deleted by gateway bridging the two systems (Gong, 2001).

3.7. ANALOG AND DIGITAL

Learning Objectives

At the end of this section, readers will be able to:

- Explain the fundamental differences between analog and digital signals.
- Discuss the advantages and disadvantages of analog and digital technologies in various applications.
- Describe the process of analog-to-digital conversion and digital-to-analog conversion, including their importance in modern communication systems.

3.7.1. Analog Data

Continuous information is referred to as "analog data." For example, a continuous type of information is provided by an analog clock with minute, second, and hour hands. Analog data, such as sounds produced by a human voice, can use continuous values. An analog wave is generated in air whenever someone speaks. A microphone may record this, and the analog signal it produces can then be transformed to a digital signal by sampling (Lguensat et al., 2017).

3.7.2. Digital Data

Information with discrete states is referred to as digital data. For instance, a digital clock that displays the minutes and hours will abruptly shift from 8:05 to 8:06. Discrete values can be found in digital data. As an illustration, data are stored in computer memory as Os and 1s. For transmission via a media, they can be modulated into an analog signal or turned into digital signal (Selwyn, 2015).

Signals can be digital or/and analog, much like data they represent. An analog signal can have an infinite number of levels of intensity over time. There are an endless number of values along the wave's path as it travels from value A to value B. On other hand, there are finite number of defined values for a digital signal. While each value might be any integer, it's frequently as straightforward as 1 and O. Plotting signals on two perpendicular axes is the most basic technique to display them. Strength or value of a signal is shown on vertical axis. Time is represented via horizontal axis. A digital signal and analog signal are shown in Figure 3.12. There is infinity of points that the curve that represents the analog signal travels through. However, the digital signal's vertical lines show how the signal abruptly switches from one value to another (Petrova et al., 2010).

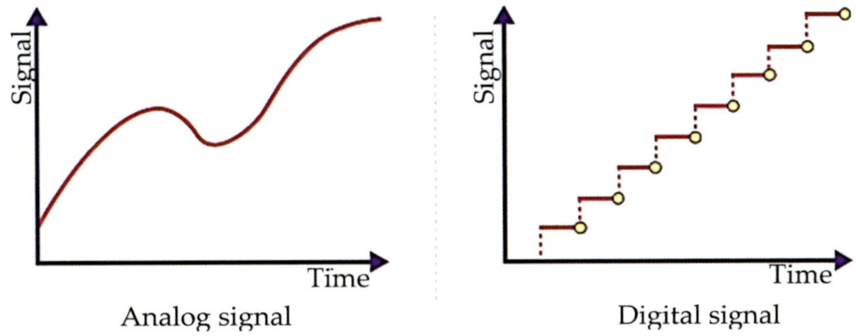

Figure 3.12. *Graphical representation of analog and digital signals.*

3.7.3. Periodic and Nonperiodic Signals

In a defined amount of time, known as a period, a periodic signal completes a pattern and then repeats that pattern across consecutive similar periods. A cycle is result of one whole pattern being completed. Nonperiodic signal swings without showing a pattern or cycle that repeats over time (Gregory & Loredo, 1993).

3.7.4. Periodic Analog Signals

There are 2 types of periodic analog signals: basic and composite. Sine waves and other similarly simple periodic analog signals cannot be decomposed into their component parts. The sine waves that make up a composite periodic analog signal are individually identifiable.

3.8. SINE WAVE

Most basic type of periodic analog signal is the sine wave. The change that takes place over the course of a cycle is consistent and unchanging, taking the form of a continuous, rolling flow when we think of it as simple oscillating curve. You can see the sine wave in Figure 3.12. A single arc above time axis and single arc below it make up each cycle (Dorman et al., 1997).

3.8.1. Characteristics of Signals

3.8.1.1. Peak Amplitude

Absolute value of signal's peak intensity is its peak amplitude, which is proportional to energy it contains. Electric signal peak amplitude is frequently expressed in volts (Hartmann, 1978).

3.8.1.2. Period and Frequency

The term "period" describes how many seconds it takes for a signal to go through one cycle. The quantity of periods in I s is referred to as frequency. Remember that period and frequency are just two different ways to define the same thing. The calculations below demonstrate that period is inverse of frequency and frequency is inverse of period.

$f = 1/T$ and $T = 1/f$

Duration is formally measured in seconds. The official frequency measurement unit is Hertz (Hz), or cycle per second (Jha et al., 2014).

3.8.1.3. Phase

The waveform's location in relation to time O is indicated by the word phase. Phase specifies the amount of the movement if we consider the wave to be something that may move either backward or forward along time axis. It shows situation of the first cycle right now. Degrees or radians are used to express phase [1° is 2n/360 rad, and 1 rad is 360/(2n)]. A phase shift of 360° is equivalent to shift of full period, phase shift of 180° is equivalent to change of half period, and phase shift of 90° is equivalent to shift of a quarter period.

- A sine wave with phase of 0° and zero amplitude starts at time 0. The size is expanding.

- A sine wave with a 90° phase has its maximum amplitude at time 0. Less amplitude is being seen.
- A sine wave having zero amplitude and phase of 0° starts at 0 time. The magnitude is increasing (Haider et al., 2012).

3.8.1.4. Wavelength

Another feature of signal passing across transmission medium is its wavelength. The wavelength of a fundamental sine wave links its period or frequency to the medium's transmission speed. The wavelength of a signal depends on both medium and frequency, whereas signal frequency is independent of medium. Every signal has a characteristic called wavelength. The term wavelength is frequently used in data communications to describe how light travels through an optical cable. A simple signal can reach a maximum distance in one wavelength. If one knows the signal's duration and propagation speed (speed of light), one may compute wavelength. However, because period and frequency are connected to one another, if we express wavelength by λ, frequency by f, and propagation speed by c (speed of light), we get:

Wavelength = Propagation speed × Period = propagation speed/frequency

$$\lambda = c/f$$

Typically, wavelength is measured in micrometers (microns) rather than meters (Roy et al., 2009).

3.8.1.5. Bandwidth

The bandwidth of a composite signal is the range of frequencies that it contains. In most cases, bandwidth simply the difference between two numbers. A composite signal's bandwidth, for instance, is 5,000–1,000, or 4,000, if its frequencies range from 1,000 to 5,000. All integer frequencies between 1,000 and 5,000 are included in the periodic signal's bandwidth (for example, 1,000, 100 I, 1002,). The nonperiodic signals' bandwidth is similar to that of periodic signals, but their frequencies are continuous (Lai & Baker, 1999).

3.9. COMMON NETWORK APPLICATIONS

Learning Objectives

At the end of this section, readers will be able to:

- Explain the concept of network applications and their role in modern communication systems.
- Discuss the various categories of common network applications, such as web browsing, email, and instant messaging, and their respective protocols.
- Analyze the key characteristics and features of popular network applications, including file sharing, video conferencing, and online gaming.
- Evaluate the security risks associated with common network applications and propose measures to mitigate potential threats and vulnerabilities.

3.9.1. TELNET

TErminaL NETwork is referred to by the acronym TELNET. It follows International Organization for Standards' (ISO) recommended standard TCP/IP protocol for virtual terminal service. Through use of TELNET, it is possible to connect to a remote system so that local terminal seems to be one at remote system. When TELNET was developed, timesharing was the norm for most operating systems, including UNIX. Multiple users can access a huge computer in this setting. A terminal, which typically consists of a keyboard, monitor, and mouse, is how a user interacts with a computer. With the aid of a terminal emulator, even a microcomputer may emulate a terminal (Marx et al., 2022).

3.9.1.1. Logging

Users who participate in timesharing have some access rights to certain resources. Every authorized user has a username and, most likely, a password. The user is identified as a system component by the user identification. With a user ID or log-in name, user logs into system to gain access. To stop unauthorized users from accessing the resources, the system also has password checking.

Local log-in is the process of logging into a local timesharing system. The terminal driver accepts the keystrokes entered by the user at terminal or on computer running terminal emulator. An operating system receives the characters from terminal driver. Following the operating system's interpretation of character combination, desired application program or utility is called. A user logs in remotely when she wishes to use an application software or utility that is hosted on another computer. TELNET client and server programs are utilized here. The user's keystrokes are acknowledged by the local operating system but are not translated by the terminal driver. TELNET client receives characters and transforms them into the international character set known as network virtual terminal (NVT) characters before sending them to the local TCP/IP protocol stack. Instructions or text, in NVT format, are transmitted over the Internet and reach the remote machine's TCP/IP stack. Here, the operating system receives the characters and sends them along to TELNET server, which converts them into equivalent characters that the distant computer can comprehend. The remote operating system, however, isn't made to accept characters from TELNET server; rather, it's made to receive characters from terminal driver, thus characters cannot be delivered directly to an operating system. Answer is to include software known as a pseudoterminal driver that makes it appear as though characters are coming from a terminal. An appropriate application program is then sent the characters by the operating system (Pallen, 1995).

3.9.2. Electronic Mail

Email is one of a most widely used Internet services. The success of this application program was probably never anticipated by the Internet's creators. Early electronic mail messages were brief and text-only; they allowed users to communicate quickly, such as exchanging memoranda. Electronic mail is significantly more complicated now. It permits the use of text, audio, and video in messages. Additionally, it permits sending a single message to one or more receivers (Markus, 1994).

3.9.2.1. User Agent

First element of an electronic mail system is a user agent. It offers assistance to user to make sending as well as receiving messages simpler.

- Services Provided by User Agent: A software application (user agent) composes, reads, responds to, and forwards messages. Moreover, this manages mailboxes.

3.9.2.2. Composing Messages

The user is assisted in writing the email message that will be sent by a user agent. The majority of user agents display a template for the user to fill out on the screen. Some even have an editor that can perform duties like grammar and spell checking as well as other advanced word processing functions. Of course, a user might also construct the message in their own text editor or word processor and import it, or paste or cut it, into user agent template (Malone et al., 1987).

3.9.2.3. Reading Messages

Reading incoming messages is the user agent's second responsibility. When a user activates it, a user agent first confirms mail in an incoming inbox. Most user agents display a one-line summary of each piece of mail they have received. Here are the fields included in each email:

- A flag field which displays mail's state, such as whether it's new, already read but unanswered, or read and responded to;

- A number field;
- The message's size;
- A sender;
- An optional subject field.

3.9.2.4. Replying to Messages

User can respond to a message using user agent after reading it. User agent often enables user to reply to message's original sender or to every recipient. Original message and revised message could both be included in the reply message.

3.9.2.5. Forwarding Messages

It's called "replying" when you send a message back to original sender or to people who received the copy. Sending a communication to a third party is referred to as forwarding. A user agent enables the recipient to transmit message to a third party with or without additional comments.

1. Handling Mailboxes: An inbox and outbox are the two mailboxes that a user agent typically produces. Each box is file with unique format which only user agent can handle. All received emails are kept in the inbox until user deletes them. All sent emails are stored in outbox until user deletes them. Today's user agents can usually create personalized mailboxes (Khare et al., 2022).
2. User Agent Types: There are two types of user agents: command-driven and GUI-based.
3. Command-Driven: This user agents have existed since early days of electronic mail. They continue to exist in servers as an underlying user agent. In order to do its duty, a keyboard command of one character is often accepted by a command-driven user agent. For instance, at the command prompt, a user can write letter R to reply to message's sender or letter R to reply to all recipients and sender. Pine, Elm, and Mail, are command-driven user agent's examples.
4. GUI-based: This user agents are common today. They have graphical user interface (GUI) elements which let user utilize keyboard and mouse to interact with the software. They feature visual elements like menu bars, panels, and icons that make it simple to access the services. User agents with GUIs include Microsoft Outlook, Eudora, and Netscape (Levi & Güder, 2009).

3.9.2.6. Addresses

In order to distribute mail a mail handling system should use a unique addressing system. A @ symbol separates the local element of the address from domain name on the Internet.

1. Local Part: All mail received for a user is saved in the user mailbox, a distinct file defined in the local part, for subsequent retrieval by message access agent.
2. Domain Name: The domain name is 2nd component of address. A company often chooses one or more hosts, also known as mail servers or exchangers, to receive and deliver email. Each mail exchanger's allocated domain name either originates from DNS database or is a logical name (company's name).

3.9.2.7. SMTP

Message transfer agents handle the actual mail transfer. A system needs a server MTA in order to receive mail, and a client MTA in order to send mail. A Simple Mail Transfer Protocol (SMTP) is an official protocol which describes MTA client and server on Internet.

The sender and mail server of sender, as well as two mail servers, both use SMTP. SMTP only outlines the requirements for sending commands and responses back and forth (Moore, 2003).

3.9.2.8. Commands and Responses

SMTP transfers messages between an MTA server and an MTA client using commands and responses.

1. Commands: The client sends commands to server. It is made up of a keyword and one to many arguments. Around 14 commands are included in SMTP. Every implementation must support the first five instructions, which are requirements. The following three are quite useful and advised. The latter six are rarely used (Bazydło et al., 2017).
2. Responses: The server sends responses to client. A three-digit code which represents a response maybe followed by more textual data.

3.9.2.9. Mail Transfer Phases

There are three steps involved in moving a mail message: connection formation, mail transfer, and connection termination.

3.9.3. POP3

POP3 is a straightforward protocol with constrained functionality. The receiver computer has client POP3 software installed, while mail server has server POP3 software. When a user needs to download email from a mailbox hosted on a mail server, the client is the first step in the mail access process. On TCP port 110, the client and server create a connection. Then, in order to access the mailbox, it submits its username and password. Following that, a user can list and get each individual mail message.

The delete mode and keep mode are POP3's 2 operating modes. After each retrieval in delete mode, mail is removed from mailbox. After recovery, mail stays in mailbox when in keep mode. When a user is seated at her desk-based computer and able to store and organize incoming mail after reading or responding, delete mode is typically employed. When a user accesses her email from a device other than her primary computer (such a laptop, for example), user will frequently switch to retain mode. Message is read, but it's preserved in system so you can find it and organize it later (Tzerefos et al., 1997).

3.9.4. IMAP

Internet Mail Access Protocol, version 4 (IMAP4) is another mail access protocol. POP3 and IMAP4 are comparable, however IMAP4 offers additional functions and is more capable and sophisticated.

POP3 has a number of deficiencies. It prevents the user from organizing her mail on server and prevents user from having several folders on server. Additionally, POP3 does not permit the user to scan a portion of mail before downloading it. IMAP4 offers the following additional features:

- Before downloading, a user can examine email header.
- Before downloading, a user can scan email's contents for a certain string of characters.

- Email can be partially downloaded by the user. This is especially helpful if the email has multimedia that requires a lot of bandwidth, and your bandwidth is constrained.
- On the mail server, a user has the option to create, delete, or rename mailboxes.
- A user's folder for storing emails can have a hierarchy of mailboxes (Crispin, 1996).

3.9.5. Web-Based Mail

Since email is used so often these days, several websites offer this function to all visitors. Hotmail and Yahoo are two popular web pages. The concept is extremely basic. Through HTTP, mail is transferred from Alice's browser to her mail server. SMTP is still used for message transfer from originating mail server to receiving mail server. Finally, message is sent from transmitting server (Web server) to Bob's browser using HTTP. The final stage is quite fascinating. The most common protocol used is HTTP, not POP3 or IMAP4. Bob sends a message to website (such as Hotmail) asking for ability to recover his emails. The website sends Bob form to complete, along with the login name and password. The email is transmitted in HTML format from Web server to Bob's browser if login name and password match (Cobanoglu et al., 2001).

3.9.6. FTP

The TCP/IP standard mechanism for moving file from one host to another is called File Transfer Protocol (FTP). Although this may seem easy and uncomplicated to transfer information between systems, there are a few issues that must be resolved beforehand. For instance, two systems might employ various file naming standards. Text and data may be represented by two distinct systems in two different ways.

On two separate computers, distinct directory structures could occur. FTP has provided an incredibly straightforward and elegant solution to all of these issues.

FTP creates two connections between the hosts, which sets it apart from other client/server programs. Data transfer occurs over one link, while control information (commands and responses) occurs over the other. FTP is more effective when commands and data transport are separated. Simple communication protocols are used by control connection. Only one line of command or one line of response has to be transferred at a time. On the other hand, the data connection requires more complicated regulations because it transfers a wide variety of data kinds. However, rather than TCP, FTP has a higher level of sophistication. Both connections are handled equally by TCP. FTP uses the well-known TCP ports 20 and 21 for control and data connections, respectively.

The fundamental model of FTP is shown in Figure 3.13. Client control process, user interface, and client data transmission process are the three parts of the client. The server's control process and data transfer procedure are its two main parts. The means of control connect the control processes. And data is connected to processes of data transfer.

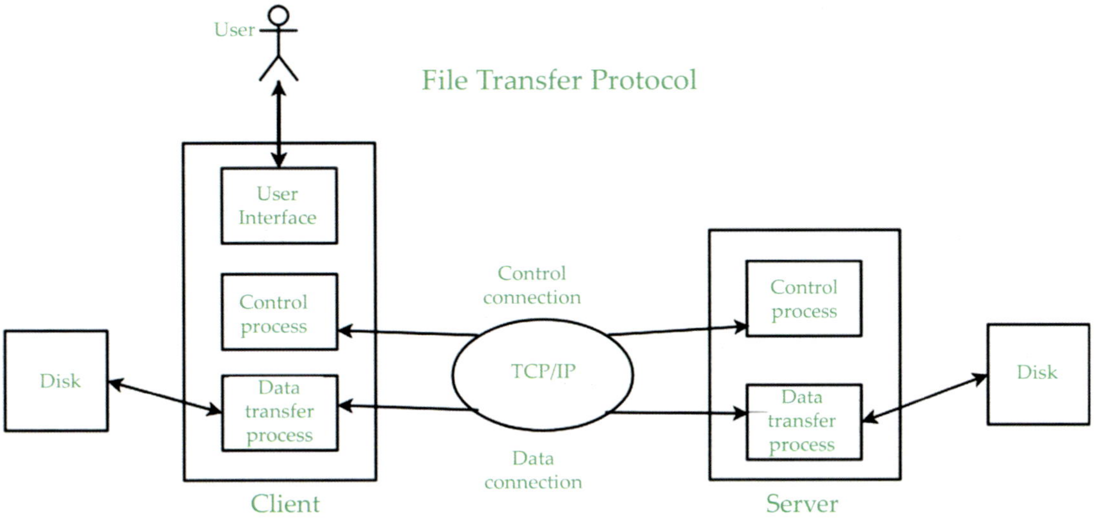

Figure 3.13. *Illustration of fundamental model of file transfer protocol.*

The control connection is active, throughout whole interactive FTP session. Each file transmission involves opening and closing the data connection. It opens each time a command involving file transfers is executed and shuts once the file has been transmitted. In other words, control connection opens when user initiates an FTP session. Data connection may close and open several times if many files are transferred while control connection is active.

3.9.6.1. Transmission Mode

Block mode, Stream mode, and compressed mode are three transmission modes that FTP might use to send a file through data connection. A default mode is stream mode. A steady stream of bytes is sent from FTP to TCP carrying data. Data is divided into segments of the correct size by TCP. There is no requirement for an end-of-file if data are only a stream of bytes (file structure). In this instance, the sender's termination of data connection signifies the end of the file. A 1-byte end-of-record (EOR) character and 1-byte end-of-file (EOF) character are both present at the end of a file if data are broken up into records (record structure). While in block mode, data can be sent from FTP to TCP in blocks. Each block in this example has a 3-byte header before it. The block descriptor is the first byte, and the next two bytes specify the block's size in bytes. If file is large, data can be compressed in the compressed mode. Run-length encoding is the often-employed compression technique. This approach replaces a data unit's repeated appearances with a single occurrence and the number of repetitions. This typically consists of blank spaces in text files. Null characters are typically compressed in binary files (Circiumarescu et al., 2015).

3.9.7. HTTP

The World Wide Web's Hypertext Transfer Protocol (HTTP) is a protocol mostly used to access data there. FTP and SMTP are combined to form HTTP. Because it transports files and makes use of TCP, it's comparable to FTP. However, because it only makes use of one TCP connection, it is easier to use than FTP. There is no separate connection for control; all communication that takes place between client and server is limited to the transfer of data. HTTP is comparable to SMTP because data transmitted between client and server looks like SMTP messages. Additionally, MIME-like headers are used to govern how the messages are formatted. In contrast to SMTP, HTTP communications are understood and read by HTTP server and HTTP client (browser), not by humans. HTTP messages are delivered instantly, whereas SMTP messages are archived and forwarded. The request message contains commands that client sends to server. A response message includes contents of downloaded file or other data. TCP services are used by HTTP on the well-known port 80 (Jestratjew & Kwiecien, 2012).

3.9.7.1. HTTP Transaction

HTTP is a stateless protocol, despite the fact that it makes use of TCP's services. The transaction is started by the client sending request message. A server responds by sending the response.

1. Messages: Request lines, headers, and occasionally bodies make up a request message. There are three parts to a response message: status line, header, and occasionally body (Naik, 2017).
2. Request and Status Lines: First line of request message is known as the request line, while first line of a response message is known as status line. One common field is present (Hadi & Ali, 2019).
   - i. Request Type: In the request message, this field is utilized. There are various defined request types in HTTP version 1.1. Request type is divided into categories called methods.
   - ii. URL: It means Uniform Resource Locator
   - iii. Version: A current version of HTTP
   - iv. Status Code: In response message, it's utilized. Similar fields exist in SMTP and FTP protocols as well as the status code field. There are three digits in it. The values in 200 range signify successful request, as opposed to codes in 100 range, which are only informative. A client site error is indicated by codes in the 400 range and a client site redirection code in the 300 range. The codes in the 500 range, lastly, denote a server-side problem.
   - v. Status Phrase: It functions as a reply signal. Status phrase provides a text explanation of the status code. (Kockelman, 2007).

SUMMARY

The chapter "Data Communication and Computer Networks" provides an overview of the basics of data communication and computer networks. It covers the different modes of data transmission, including simplex, half-duplex, and full-duplex, as well as the differences between parallel and serial transmission and asynchronous and synchronous transmission. The chapter also explains the seven layers of the OSI model and their functions in network communication. It discusses the criteria for designing a network and the different physical structures that can be used to build a network. Additionally, the chapter covers different types of networks such as LAN, MAN, and WAN, and the connecting devices used in computer networks. Furthermore, the chapter explains the differences between analog and digital data, periodic and non-periodic signals, and the characteristics of signals such as amplitude, frequency, and phase. This information is important in understanding how data is transmitted across a network.

Overall, the chapter provides a foundational understanding of data communication and computer networks, which is essential for anyone interested in working in the field of information technology.

REVIEW QUESTIONS

1. What is the importance of data communication in computer networks and why is it essential?
2. What are the different modes of data transmission, and how do they differ from each other? Give examples of scenarios where each mode is useful.
3. What is the difference between parallel and serial transmission, and what are the advantages and disadvantages of each?
4. Explain the difference between asynchronous and synchronous transmission and provide examples of when each would be used.
5. What are the seven layers of the OSI model, and how do they relate to data communication and computer networks?
6. What are the criteria for designing a network, and what are the different physical structures that can be used to implement a network?
7. Describe the different types of networks, including LAN, MAN, and WAN, and how they differ from each other.
8. What are some examples of connecting devices used in computer networks, and what are their roles in network communication?
9. Explain the differences between analog and digital data, periodic and non-periodic signals, and the characteristics of signals such as amplitude, frequency, and phase. How are these concepts related to data communication and computer networks?

MULTIPLE CHOICE QUESTIONS

1. **What is the importance of data communication in computer networks?**
   a. To save data
   b. To transmit data
   c. To delete data
   d. To encrypt data
2. **What is simplex transmission?**
   a. Communication in both directions simultaneously
   b. Communication in one direction only
   c. Communication in both directions but not simultaneously
   d. Communication through a single medium
3. **What is the difference between parallel and serial transmission?**
   a. Parallel transmission uses multiple channels while serial transmission uses a single channel.
   b. Parallel transmission is faster than serial transmission.
   c. Parallel transmission is used for short distances while serial transmission is used for long distances.
   d. Parallel transmission sends multiple bits at once while serial transmission sends one bit at a time.
4. **What is synchronous transmission?**
   a. Data transmission without a clock signal
   b. Data transmission with a clock signal
   c. Data transmission in both directions simultaneously
   d. Data transmission through multiple channels
5. **How many layers are there in the OSI model?**
   a. 5
   b. 6
   c. 7
   d. 8

Answers to Multiple Choice Questions

1. (b); 2. (b); 3. (d); 4. (b); 5. (c)

REFERENCES

1. Balabanov, T., Zankinski, I., & Barova, M., (2016). Strategy for individuals distribution by incident nodes participation in star topology of distributed evolutionary algorithms. Cybernetics and Information Technologies, 16(1), 80–88.
2. Barranco, M., Proenza, J., & Almeida, L., (2009). Quantitative comparison of the error-containment capabilities of a bus and a star topology in CAN networks. IEEE Transactions on Industrial Electronics, 58(3), 802–813.
3. Bujas, G., Vuković, M., Vasić, V., & Mikuc, M., (2015). Smart detection and classification of application-layer intrusions in web directories. SmartCR, 5(6), 510–519.
4. Burdin, V., Gubareva, O., Gureev, V., & Masyuk, S., (2020). Simulation of data transmission in a simplex acousto-optical channel on dual-mode optical fiber. In: 2020 International Conference on Information Technology and Nanotechnology (ITNT) (Vol. 1, pp. 1–4). IEEE.
5. Cerutti, I., Behredin, A. M., Andriolli, N., Ladouceur, O. L., & Castoldi, P., (2016). Ring versus bus topology: A network performance comparison of photonic integrated NoC. In: 2016 18th International Conference on Transparent Optical Networks (ICTON) (Vol. 1, pp. 1–4). IEEE.
6. Chao, H. J., (2002). Next generation routers. Proceedings of the IEEE, 90(9), 1518–1558.
7. Circiumarescu, L. D., Predusca, G., Angelescu, N., & Puchianu, D., (2015). Comparative analysis of protocol RIP, OSPF, RIGRP and IGRP for service video conferencing, E-mail, FTP, HTTP. In: 2015 20th International Conference on Control Systems and Computer Science (Vol. 1, pp. 584–589). IEEE.
8. Clark, D. D., Pogran, K. T., & Reed, D. P., (1978). An introduction to local area networks. Proceedings of the IEEE, 66(11), 1497–1517.
9. Cobanoglu, C., Moreo, P. J., & Warde, B., (2001). A comparison of mail, fax and web-based survey methods. International Journal of Market Research, 43(4), 1–15.
10. Crispin, M., (1996). RFC2060: Internet Message Access Protocol-Version 4rev1, 1(2), 213.
11. Crochiere, R. E., & Rabiner, L. R., (1981). Interpolation and decimation of digital signals—A tutorial review. Proceedings of the IEEE, 69(3), 300–331.
12. Dorman, M. F., Loizou, P. C., & Rainey, D., (1997). Speech intelligibility as a function of the number of channels of stimulation for signal processors using sine-wave and noise-band outputs. The Journal of the Acoustical Society of America, 102(4), 2403–2411.
13. Gruen, L. C., & Woods, E. F., (1983). Structural studies on the microfibrillar proteins of wool. Interaction between α-helical segments and reassembly of a four-chain structure. Biochemical Journal, 209(3), 587–595.
14. Guan, J. F., Yang, H., & Wirasinghe, S. C., (2006). Simultaneous optimization of transit line configuration and passenger line assignment. Transportation Research Part B: Methodological, 40(10), 885–902.

15. Guangyong, L., & Ruolan, L., (2021). Analysis and design of graduation design management system based on des encryption algorithm. In: 2021 4th International Conference on Advanced Electronic Materials, Computers and Software Engineering (AEMCSE) (Vol. 1, pp. 682–685). IEEE.
16. Hadi, A. S., & Ali, S. H., (2019). Resource description framework representation for transaction log file. Journal of Computational and Theoretical Nanoscience, 16(3), 1093–1099.
17. Haider, R., Alam, R., Yousuf, N. B., & Salim, K. M., (2012). Design and construction of single phase pure sine wave inverter for photovoltaic application. In: 2012 International Conference on Informatics, Electronics & Vision (ICIEV) (Vol. 1, pp. 190–194). IEEE.
18. Handa, T., Shoji, S., Ike, S., Takeda, S., & Sekiguchi, T., (1997). A very low-power consumption wireless ECG monitoring system using body as a signal transmission medium. In: Proceedings of International Solid State Sensors and Actuators Conference (Transducers' 97) (Vol. 2, pp. 1003–1006). IEEE.
19. Hartmann, W. M., (1978). The effect of amplitude envelope on the pitch of sine wave tones. The Journal of the Acoustical Society of America, 63(4), 1105–1113.
20. Iren, S., Amer, P. D., & Conrad, P. T., (1999). The transport layer: Tutorial and survey. ACM Computing Surveys (CSUR), 31(4), 360–404.
21. Jebamalai, J. M., Marlein, K., & Laverge, J., (2022). Design and cost comparison of district heating and cooling (DHC) network configurations using ring topology–A case study. Energy, 258, 124777.
22. Jestratjew, A., & Kwiecien, A., (2012). Performance of HTTP protocol in networked control systems. IEEE Transactions on Industrial Informatics, 9(1), 271–276.
23. Jha, K., Mishra, S., & Joshi, A., (2014). High-quality sine wave generation using a differential boost inverter at higher operating frequency. IEEE Transactions on Industry Applications, 51(1), 373–384.
24. Kandula, S., Menache, I., Schwartz, R., & Babbula, S. R., (2014). Calendaring for wide area networks. In: Proceedings of the 2014 ACM Conference on SIGCOMM (Vol. 1, pp. 515–526).
25. Khare, A., Singh, S., Mishra, R., Prakash, S., & Dixit, P., (2022). E-mail assistant–automation of e-mail handling and management using robotic process automation. In: 2022 International Conference on Decision Aid Sciences and Applications (DASA) (Vol. 1, pp. 511–516). IEEE.
26. Kim, H., Oh, S., & Viswanath, P., (2020). Physical layer communication via deep learning. IEEE Journal on Selected Areas in Information Theory, 1(1), 5–18.
27. Kockelman, P., (2007). From status to contract revisited: Value, temporality, circulation, and subjectivity. Anthropological Theory, 7(2), 151–176.
28. Lafata, P., & Vodrazka, J., (2011). Application of passive optical network with optimized bus topology for local backbone data network. Microwave and Optical Technology Letters, 53(10), 2351–2355.

29. Lai, K., & Baker, M., (1999). Measuring bandwidth. In: IEEE INFOCOM'99. Conference on Computer Communications; Proceedings Eighteenth Annual Joint Conference of the IEEE Computer and Communications Societies; The Future is Now (Cat. No. 99CH36320) (Vol. 1, pp. 235–245). IEEE.
30. LaMagna, M., Hartman-Caverly, S., & Marchetti, L., (2016). Redefining roles and responsibilities: Implementing a triage reference model at a single service point. Journal of Access Services, 13(2), 53–65.
31. Landfeldt, B., Larsson, T., Ismailov, Y., & Seneviratne, A., (1999). SLM, a framework for session layer mobility management. In: Proceedings Eight International Conference on Computer Communications and Networks (Cat. No. 99EX370) (Vol. 1, pp. 452–456). IEEE.
32. Larkins, D. B., & Dinan, J., (2016). Extending a message passing runtime to support partitioned, global logical address spaces. In: 2016 First International Workshop on Communication Optimizations in HPC (COMHPC) (Vol. 1, pp. 11–16). IEEE.
33. Levi, A., & Güder, C. B., (2009). Understanding the limitations of S/MIME digital signatures for e-mails: A GUI based approach. Computers & Security, 28(3, 4), 105–120.
34. Lguensat, R., Tandeo, P., Ailliot, P., Pulido, M., & Fablet, R., (2017). The analog data assimilation. Monthly Weather Review, 145(10), 4093–4107.
35. Lucamarini, M., Yuan, Z. L., Dynes, J. F., & Shields, A. J., (2018). Overcoming the rate–distance limit of quantum key distribution without quantum repeaters. Nature, 557(7705), 400–403.
36. Luo, F., & Südhof, T. C., (2017). Synaptotagmin-7-mediated asynchronous release boosts high-fidelity synchronous transmission at a central synapse. Neuron, 94(4), 826–839.
37. Lynch, N. A., Mansour, Y., & Fekete, A., (1988). Data link layer: Two impossibility results. In: Proceedings of the Seventh Annual ACM Symposium on Principles of Distributed Computing (Vol. 1, pp. 149–170).
38. Mabrouk, A., Tourki, K., & Hamdi, N., (2016). Transmission mode selection scheme for physical layer security in multi-user multi-relay systems. In: 2016 IEEE 27th Annual International Symposium on Personal, Indoor, and Mobile Radio Communications (PIMRC) (Vol. 1, pp. 1–6). IEEE.
39. Maihofer, C., (2004). A survey of geocast routing protocols. IEEE Communications Surveys & Tutorials, 6(2), 32–42.
40. Malone, T. W., Grant, K. R., Lai, K. Y., Rao, R., & Rosenblitt, D., (1987). Semistructured messages are surprisingly useful for computer-supported coordination. ACM Transactions on Information Systems (TOIS), 5(2), 115–131.
41. Markus, M. L., (1994). Electronic mail as the medium of managerial choice. Organization Science, 5(4), 502–527.
42. Marx, G., Greiner, W., Juhra, C., Elkenkamp, S., Gensorowsky, D., Lemmen, S., & Deisz, R., (2022). An innovative telemedical network to improve infectious disease management in critically ill patients and outpatients (TELnet@ NRW): Stepped-

wedge cluster randomized controlled trial. Journal of Medical Internet Research, 24(3), 34098.

43. Maxemchuk, N. F., (1985). Regular mesh topologies in local and metropolitan area networks. AT&T Technical Journal, 64(7), 1659–1685.
44. Modarressi, M., Tavakkol, A., & Sarbazi-Azad, H., (2010). Virtual point-to-point connections for NoCs. IEEE Transactions on Computer-Aided Design of Integrated Circuits and Systems, 29(6), 855–868.
45. Moon, S., & Kim, J., (2007). Network-adaptive selection of transport error control (NASTE) for video streaming over WLAN. IEEE Transactions on Consumer Electronics, 53(4), 1440–1448.
46. Moore, K., (2003). Simple Mail Transfer Protocol (SMTP) Service Extension for Delivery Status Notifications (DSNs) (Vol. 1, pp. 3461).
47. Mubeen, S., & Kumar, S., (2010). Designing efficient source routing for mesh topology network on chip platforms. In: 2010 13th Euromicro Conference on Digital System Design: Architectures, Methods, and Tools (Vol. 1, pp. 181–188). IEEE.
48. Naik, N., (2017). Choice of effective messaging protocols for IoT systems: MQTT, CoAP, AMQP and HTTP. In: 2017 IEEE International Systems Engineering Symposium (ISSE) (Vol. 1, pp. 1–7). IEEE.
49. Njoh, A. J., (2010). Toponymic inscription, physical addressing, and the challenge of urban management in an era of globalization in Cameroon. Habitat International, 34(4), 427–435.
50. OConnor, T. J., (2010). Detecting and responding to data link layer attacks. SANS Institute InfoSec Reading Room, 13, 125.
51. Oh, H., & Ngo, C. T., (2018). A slotted sense multiple access protocol for timely and reliable data transmission in dynamic wireless sensor networks. IEEE Sensors Journal, 18(5), 2184–2194.
52. Oostvogels, J., Yang, F., Michiels, S., & Hughes, D., (2020). Zero-wire: A deterministic and low-latency wireless bus through symbol-synchronous transmission of optical signals. In: Proceedings of the 18th Conference on Embedded Networked Sensor Systems (Vol. 1, pp. 164–178).
53. Ortiz, G., Uemura, H., Bortis, D., Kolar, J. W., & Apeldoorn, O., (2012). Modeling of soft-switching losses of IGBTs in high-power high-efficiency dual-active-bridge DC/DC converters. IEEE Transactions on Electron Devices, 60(2), 587–597.
54. Pahlavan, K., & Levesque, A. H., (1994). Wireless data communications. Proceedings of the IEEE, 82(9), 1398–1430.
55. Pallen, M., (1995). Guide to the Internet: Logging in, fetching files, reading news. BMJ, 311(7020), 1626–1630.
56. Pavel, L., (2015). Novel protection strategies for passive optical networks based on ring and bus topologies. Transactions on Emerging Telecommunications Technologies, 26(9), 1131–1153.

57. Petrova, M., Mähönen, P., & Osuna, A., (2010). Multi-class classification of analog and digital signals in cognitive radios using support vector machines. In: 2010 7th International Symposium on Wireless Communication Systems (Vol. 1, pp. 986–990). IEEE.
58. Qureshi, S. U. H. H., & Newhall, E., (1973). Adaptive receiver for data transmission over time-dispersive channels. IEEE Transactions on Information Theory, 19(4), 448–457.
59. Ross, F. E., (1987). Rings are' round for good! IEEE Network, 1(1), 31–39.
60. Saltzberg, B., (1967). Performance of an efficient parallel data transmission system. IEEE Transactions on Communication Technology, 15(6), 805–811.
61. Seemkooei, A. A., (2001). Comparison of reliability and geometrical strength criteria in geodetic networks. Journal of Geodesy, 75, 227–233.
62. Selwyn, N., (2015). Data entry: Towards the critical study of digital data and education. Learning, Media, and Technology, 40(1), 64–82.
63. Sinha, P., Jha, V. K., Rai, A. K., & Bhushan, B., (2017). Security vulnerabilities, attacks, and countermeasures in wireless sensor networks at various layers of OSI reference model: A survey. In: 2017 International Conference on Signal Processing and Communication (ICSPC) (Vol. 1, pp. 288–293). IEEE.
64. Śmiałek, M., Jarzębowski, N., & Nowakowski, W., (2012). Translation of use case scenarios to Java code. Computer Science, 13, 35–52.
65. Soni, A., Upadhyay, R., & Jain, A., (2017). Internet of things and wireless physical layer security: A survey. In: Computer Communication, Networking, and Internet Security: Proceedings of IC3T 2016 (Vol. 3, pp. 115–123). Springer Singapore.
66. Stephens, R., (2004). Analyzing jitter at high data rates. IEEE Communications Magazine, 42(2), S6–10.
67. Stoilova, S., Munier, N., Kendra, M., & Skrúcaný, T., (2020). Multi-criteria evaluation of railway network performance in countries of the TEN-T orient–east med corridor. Sustainability, 12(4), 1482.
68. Tang, A., & Wang, X., (2015). A-duplex: Medium access control for efficient coexistence between full-duplex and half-duplex communications. IEEE Transactions on Wireless Communications, 14(10), 5871–5885.
69. Tang, Y., Moon, K., & Lee, H. J., (2009). Write synchronization in bit-patterned media. IEEE Transactions on Magnetics, 45(2), 822–827.
70. Tassiulas, L., & Papavassiliou, S., (1995). Optimal anticipative scheduling with asynchronous transmission opportunities. IEEE Transactions on Automatic Control, 40(12), 2052–2062.
71. Wang, Y., Zhang, Z. L., Du, D. H. C., & Su, D., (1998). A network-conscious approach to end-to-end video delivery over wide area networks using proxy servers. In: Proceedings IEEE INFOCOM'98, the Conference on Computer Communications; Seventeenth Annual Joint Conference of the IEEE Computer and Communications Societies; Gateway to the 21st Century (Cat. No. 98) (Vol. 2, pp. 660–667). IEEE.
72. Wilkov, R., (1972). Analysis and design of reliable computer networks. IEEE Transactions on Communications, 20(3), 660–678.

73. Yang, Z., Cui, Y., Li, B., Liu, Y., & Xu, Y., (2019). Software-defined wide area network (SD-WAN): Architecture, advances, and opportunities. In: 2019 28th International Conference on Computer Communication and Networks (ICCCN) (Vol. 1, pp. 1–9). IEEE.
74. Yoon, G., Kwon, D. H., Kwon, S. C., Park, Y. O., & Lee, Y. J., (2006). Ring topology-based redundancy ethernet for industrial network. In: 2006 SICE-ICASE International Joint Conference (Vol. 1, pp. 1404–1407). IEEE.
75. Zhao, W., Ammar, M., & Zegura, E., (2004). A message ferrying approach for data delivery in sparse mobile ad hoc networks. In: Proceedings of the 5th ACM International Symposium on Mobile ad Hoc Networking and Computing (Vol. 1, pp. 187–198).
76. Zhu, Y., Qian, D., Ren, D., & Xia, H., (2019). StarNet: Pedestrian trajectory prediction using deep neural network in star topology. In: 2019 IEEE/RSJ International Conference on Intelligent Robots and Systems (IROS) (Vol. 1, pp. 8075–8080). IEEE.

CHAPTER 4

Distributed File System

LEARNING OBJECTIVES

After studying this chapter, you will be able to:

- The importance and benefits of distributed file systems;
- The different types of distributed file systems and their characteristics;
- The architecture of distributed file systems and their components;
- The challenges in implementing distributed File Systems and strategies for overcoming them;
- The case studies of distributed file system implementations;
- The applications and use cases of distributed file systems, such as big data analytics and cloud computing.

"Distributed File Systems transform the concept of data storage from a single point of vulnerability into a network of resilience, were information flows seamlessly, adapting to the demands of modern computing."

INTRODUCTORY EXAMPLE

Imagine you are part of a large multinational corporation with offices spread across the globe. Your company relies heavily on data, from customer information and financial records to research documents and multimedia files. Storing and accessing this vast amount of data efficiently and reliably is crucial for your business operations.

In the past, traditional file systems would have you grappling with challenges like data redundancy, limited scalability, and the risk of data loss due to hardware failures. However, with the advent of distributed file systems, these challenges are addressed in a revolutionary way.

Picture a scenario where your colleague in a different continent needs access to a critical report for an upcoming meeting. In a distributed file system, this file isn't limited to a single server or location. Instead, it's seamlessly distributed across multiple servers, possibly in data centers across the world. When your colleague requests the file, the system intelligently retrieves it from the nearest and most accessible server, ensuring lightning-fast access and minimal latency, regardless of their geographical location.

Distributed file systems are at the core of modern cloud storage, data sharing platforms, and many cutting-edge technologies. They have transformed the way organizations manage, store, and access their data, offering unparalleled scalability, fault tolerance, and data availability.

UNIT INTRODUCTION

A distributed file system is a system that enables multiple computers or nodes to share and access files and data across a network. It is a type of file system that allows multiple users to access and store data in a transparent and coordinated manner, irrespective of the location of the data or the users. The distributed file system provides a unified view of data and files that can be accessed and managed by users from multiple locations. The distributed file system is an essential component of modern computing systems, especially in environments where data is shared across multiple nodes or servers. It offers several advantages over traditional file systems, including increased scalability, reliability, and fault tolerance. It is integral to cloud computing, big data analytics, content delivery networks, and scientific data management. (Howard et al., 1988).

Remember

A distributed file system can improve the availability and reliability of data storage but must also address challenges such as consistency and scalability.

4.1. IMPORTANCE OF DISTRIBUTED FILE SYSTEM

Learning Objectives

At the end of this section, readers will be able to:

- Explain the concept of a distributed file system (DFS) and its fundamental characteristics.
- Discuss the advantages and disadvantages of using a distributed file system compared to a traditional centralized file system.
- Explore the key components and technologies commonly used in building distributed file systems, including distributed data storage and access protocols.

The distributed file system is an essential component of modern computing systems, especially in environments where data is shared across multiple nodes or servers. It offers several benefits over traditional file systems, including the subsections.

4.1.1. Scalability

The distributed file system can be easily scaled up or down to meet the changing demands of the users. It can handle large volumes of data and can support multiple users simultaneously.

4.1.2. Fault Tolerance

Distributed file systems are designed to be fault tolerant. They can recover from failures and continue to operate without any interruption. They use various techniques such as redundancy, replication, and backup to ensure that data is always available (Gray & Cheriton, 1989).

4.1.3. Reliability

Distributed file systems are designed to be reliable. They use various techniques such as data checksums and error detection to ensure that data is not corrupted or lost.

4.1.4. Performance

Distributed file systems are designed to provide high-performance access to data. They use various caching and replication techniques to reduce latency and improve performance (Sur et al., 2010).

4.1.5. Transparency

Distributed file systems provide a transparent and coordinated view of data and files. They enable users to access data from any location and provide a unified view of data and files, irrespective of their location.

In conclusion, the distributed file system is an essential component of modern computing systems. It provides a scalable, fault-tolerant, and reliable way to access and share data across multiple nodes or servers. It is a critical component of cloud computing, big data analytics, content delivery networks, and scientific data management (Stroud, 1992).

4.2. TYPES OF DISTRIBUTED FILE SYSTEM

Learning Objectives

At the end of this section, readers will be able to:

- Understand the different types of distributed file system (DFS);
- Discuss the key benefits and challenges of distributed file systems;
- Compare and contrast different types of distributed file systems.

There are various types of distributed file systems that are widely used in different computing environments. Here are some of the most popular types of distributed file systems:

4.2.1. Network File System (NFS)

NFS is a distributed file system that enables users to access and share files across a network. It was initially developed by Sun Microsystems in the 1980s and is widely used in Unix and Linux environments. NFS uses the client-server model, where the client requests data from the server, and the server responds with the requested data. NFS provides a transparent view of data and files across multiple platforms and operating systems. It allows users to access files as if they were stored locally, even if they are stored on remote servers. NFS supports multiple file-sharing protocols, including TCP/IP, UDP/IP, and Remote Procedure Call (RPC). One of the primary benefits of NFS is its simplicity and ease of use. It is a well-established protocol that is widely supported in various operating systems and platforms. It also provides reliable data sharing and access over a network, which is essential for collaboration and productivity (Butt et al., 2006) (Figure 4.1).

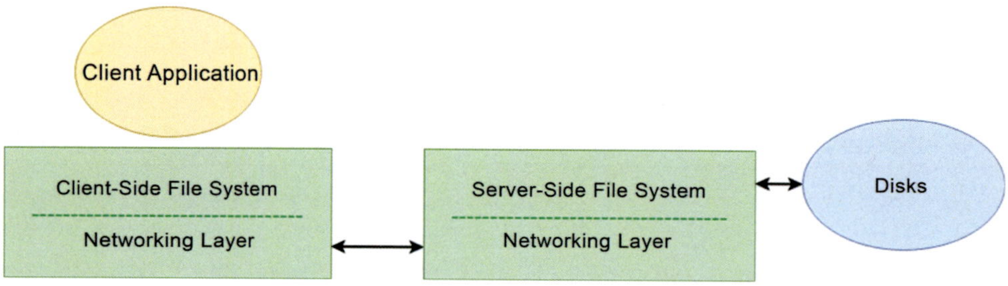

Figure 4.1. *Network file system (NFS).*

4.2.2. Andrew File System (AFS)

AFS is a distributed file system that was developed at Carnegie Mellon University in the 1980s. AFS is designed to provide a transparent and coordinated view of data and files across multiple nodes or servers. AFS uses caching and replication techniques to improve performance and reduce latency.

AFS is known for its scalability and reliability. It can handle large volumes of data and is designed to be fault tolerant. It uses a client-server model, where the client requests data from the server, and the server responds with the requested data. AFS uses a directory-based naming convention to organize and access files. The file names are hierarchical, and users can access files by navigating the directory structure. AFS also supports access control, where administrators can define permissions and access rights for different users and groups.

AFS is widely used in scientific research, education, and corporate environments. It provides a reliable and efficient way to access and share data across multiple nodes or servers (Tobbicke, 1994).

4.2.3. Hadoop Distributed File System (HDFS)

HDFS is a distributed file system that is designed for big data analytics and processing. HDFS is a part of the Apache Hadoop project and is widely used in big data environments. HDFS uses a master-slave architecture, where the master node manages the file system's metadata, and the slave nodes store the data. HDFS is designed to be fault-tolerant and scalable. It uses replication to ensure that data is always available, even if some nodes fail. HDFS is optimized for large data sets and can handle terabytes or even petabytes of data. HDFS supports various data access models, including read, write, and append. It also supports distributed processing frameworks such as MapReduce and Spark, which enables parallel processing of data across multiple nodes.

HDFS is widely used in big data environments such as data warehousing, analytics, and machine learning. It provides a scalable and efficient way to store and process large data sets (Shvachko et al., 2010).

4.2.4. Google File System (GFS)

GFS is a distributed file system that was developed by Google in the early 2000s. GFS is designed to handle large volumes of data and is widely used in big data environments. GFS uses a master-slave architecture, where the master node manages the file system's metadata, and the slave nodes store the data. GFS is optimized for read-intensive workloads and supports large file sizes. It is designed to be fault-tolerant and uses replication to ensure that data is always available, even if some nodes fail. GFS also uses a distributed lock service to ensure that data is consistent across multiple nodes.

GFS supports various data access models, including read, write, and append. It also supports distributed processing frameworks such as MapReduce and Bigtable, which enables parallel processing of data across multiple nodes. GFS is widely used in big data environments such as data warehousing, analytics, and machine learning. It provides a scalable and efficient way to store and process large data sets (Ghemawat et al., 2003).

4.2.5. Luster File System

Luster is a distributed file system that is designed for high-performance computing environments. Luster is an open-source file system and is widely used in scientific research and engineering environments. Luster uses a distributed architecture, where the file system is spread across multiple nodes or servers. It uses a metadata server to manage the file system's metadata and multiple object storage targets to store the data. Luster is designed to be scalable and can handle large volumes of data.

Luster supports various data access models, including read, write, and append. It also supports distributed processing frameworks such as MPI, which enables parallel processing of data across multiple nodes. Luster is known for its high-performance capabilities and is optimized for large file sizes and high-throughput workloads. It is widely used in scientific research and engineering environments, where high-performance computing is essential (Schwan, 2003).

4.2.6. Ceph File System

Ceph is a distributed file system that is designed for cloud environments. Ceph is an open-source file system and is widely used in cloud computing environments. Ceph uses a distributed architecture, where the file system is spread across multiple nodes or servers. It uses a metadata server to manage the file system's metadata and multiple object storage targets to store the data. Ceph is designed to be scalable and can handle large volumes of data.

Ceph supports various data access models, including read, write, and append. It also supports distributed processing frameworks such as Hadoop, which enables parallel processing of data across multiple nodes. Ceph is known for its flexibility and scalability. It can be deployed on commodity hardware and can scale to handle petabytes of data. It is widely used in cloud computing environments, where flexibility and scalability are essential (Maltzahn et al., 2010).

4.2.7. Gluster File System

Gluster is a distributed file system that is designed for scale-out NAS environments. Gluster is an open-source file system and is widely used in storage and virtualization environments. Gluster uses a distributed architecture, where the file system is spread across multiple nodes or servers. It uses a metadata server to manage the file system's metadata and multiple storage bricks to store the data. Gluster is designed to be scalable and can handle large volumes of data. Gluster supports various data access models, including read, write, and append. It also supports distributed processing frameworks such as Hadoop and Spark, which enables parallel processing of data across multiple nodes.

Gluster is known for its simplicity and flexibility. It can be deployed on commodity hardware and can scale to handle petabytes of data. It is widely used in storage and virtualization environments, where flexibility and scalability are essential (Donvito et al., 2014).

4.3. ARCHITECTURE OF DISTRIBUTED FILE SYSTEM

Learning Objectives

At the end of this section, readers will be able to:

- Explain the concept of a Distributed File System (DFS), highlighting its key characteristics and the need for such systems in modern computing environments.
- Discuss the architectural components of a typical Distributed File System, including the roles of client, server, and metadata servers, and how they collaborate to provide a seamless file-sharing experience.
- Analyze the various distributed file system architectures, such as the centralized, decentralized, and hybrid models, and compare their advantages and disadvantages in terms of scalability, fault tolerance, and performance.

A distributed file system (DFS) is a file system that is designed to provide access to files and directories that are stored on multiple networked computers. The architecture of a DFS is designed to allow files to be accessed and shared by users across multiple machines and locations. The architecture of a distributed file system typically consists of several components that work together to provide a unified file system interface (Lin et al., 2017) (Figure 4.2).

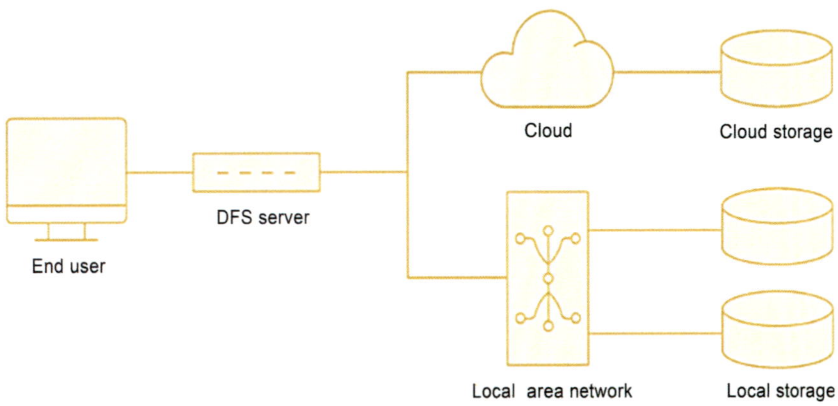

Figure 4.2. *Schematic of distributed file system architecture.*

These components are discussed in subsections.

4.3.1. Components of Distributed File System

The components of a distributed file system include:

1. Clients: These are machines that access files in the distributed file system. They use standardized interfaces to access files and directories, just like a local file system.
2. Servers: These are machines that store files in the distributed file system. They are responsible for managing the file system metadata, handling file requests from clients, and providing data access mechanisms to clients.
3. Communication Protocols and Interfaces: These are the standardized methods that clients and servers use to communicate with each other. They define how clients and servers send and receive data and how they interact with the file system metadata.
4. Name and Metadata Services: These are responsible for managing the file system metadata. They use a distributed database to store metadata information, which allows them to scale and handle large volumes of data.
5. Data Storage and Access Mechanisms: These are responsible for storing and retrieving data from the distributed file system. They can use a variety of storage technologies, including local disks, network-attached storage (NAS), or object storage systems.
6. Caching and Replication Techniques: These are used to improve file system performance and reliability. Caching is used to store frequently accessed data in local memory, while replication is used to make copies of data on multiple servers to ensure data availability and reduce the impact of server failures (Sivaraman & Manickachezian, 2014).

4.3.2. Communication Protocols and Interfaces

Communication protocols and interfaces are standardized methods that clients and servers use to communicate with each other. The most commonly used protocols and interfaces in distributed file systems include:

1. Network File System (NFS): It is a widely used protocol that allows clients to access files on remote servers as if they were local files.
2. Common Internet File System (CIFS): It is a protocol that is used by Windows clients to access files on remote servers.
3. Remote Procedure Call (RPC): It is a protocol that is used to enable clients and servers to communicate with each other.
4. Simple Network Management Protocol (SNMP): It is a protocol that is used for monitoring and managing network devices (Gifford et al., 1991).

4.3.3. Name and Metadata Services

Name and metadata services are responsible for managing the file system metadata, which includes information such as file names, file sizes, and file permissions. The most commonly used name and metadata services in distributed file systems include:

4.3.3.1. Network Information Service (NIS)

NIS is a directory service that is used to provide centralized authentication, authorization, and configuration information to networked computers.

4.3.3.2. Lightweight Directory Access Protocol (LDAP)

LDAP is a protocol that is used to provide access to directory services, such as NIS (Salim et al., 2009).

4.3.3.3. Common Internet File System Distributed Namespace (CIFSDN)

CIFSDN is a namespace service that is used to manage the file system metadata in Windows environments.

4.3.4. Data Storage and Access Mechanisms

Data storage and access mechanisms are responsible for storing and retrieving data from the distributed file system. The most commonly used data storage and access mechanisms in distributed file systems include:

4.3.4.1. Network-Attached Storage (NAS)

NAS is a storage technology that is used to provide file-level storage to networked computers (Kumar, 2013).

4.3.4.2. Object Storage

Object storage is a storage technology that is used to store data as objects, rather than as files.

4.3.4.3. Distributed Block Storage

Distributed block storage is a storage technology that is used to provide block-level storage to networked computers.

4.3.5. Caching and Replication Techniques

Caching and replication techniques are used to improve file system performance and reliability. The most commonly used caching and replication techniques in distributed file systems include:

4.3.5.1. Distributed File System Replication (DFSR)

DFSR is a replication technology that is used to synchronize data across multiple servers in a distributed file system (Sumirat et al., 2023).

4.3.5.2. File Caching

File caching is a technique that is used to store frequently accessed data in local memory, so that it can be accessed more quickly.

4.3.5.3. Server Load Balancing

Server load balancing is a technique that is used to distribute file system requests across multiple servers, to ensure that no single server becomes overloaded.

4.4. DISTRIBUTED FILE SYSTEM IMPLEMENTATION

Learning Objectives

At the end of this section, readers will be able to:

- Explain the concept of a distributed file system and its significance in modern computing environments.
- Discuss the key challenges and design considerations involved in implementing a distributed file system, such as data consistency, fault tolerance, and scalability.
- Describe the architectural components and key technologies commonly used in distributed file system implementations, including distributed storage, naming services, and data replication.

The implementation of a distributed file system involves designing and deploying the architecture, components, communication protocols, and services required to support the file system's functionality. The implementation process typically involves the following steps:

- Designing the architecture and selecting the appropriate components for the file system.
- Developing the communication protocols and interfaces that allow clients and servers to interact with each other.
- Implementing the name and metadata services that manage the file system metadata.
- Implementing the data storage and access mechanisms that store and retrieve data from the file system.
- Implementing caching and replication techniques to improve file system performance and reliability.
- Testing and optimizing the file system to ensure that it meets the performance and reliability requirements (Cheng & Sheu, 1991).

4.4.1. Challenges in Implementing Distributed File System

Implementing a distributed file system can be challenging due to the following reasons:

1. Network Latency: Distributed file systems typically involve the transfer of large

amounts of data over a network, which can result in network latency issues that affect performance.

2. Network Security: Distributing data across multiple servers increases the risk of data breaches and other security threats, which must be addressed by implementing appropriate security measures.
3. System Complexity: Distributed file systems involve multiple components and services, which can make them complex to design, implement, and manage.
4. Synchronization: Synchronizing data across multiple servers can be challenging, as it requires coordination between the servers to ensure that the data remains consistent (Huang et al., 2020).

4.4.2. Strategies for Implementing Distributed File System

To overcome the challenges involved in implementing a distributed file system, the following strategies can be adopted:

1. Use of Distributed File System Software: Various distributed file system software, such as NFS, AFS, HDFS, GFS, Luster, Ceph, and Gluster, provide a ready-made solution to implementing a distributed file system.
2. Use of Cloud-based Storage Services: Cloud-based storage services, such as Amazon S3, Azure Blob Storage, and Google Cloud Storage, provide an easy-to-use solution to implementing distributed file storage.
3. Use of Distributed File System Architecture: By adopting a distributed file system architecture, the system can be designed to handle the challenges of network latency, network security, system complexity, and synchronization (Devulapalli & Wyckoff, 2007).

4.4.3. Case Studies of Distributed File System Implementation

There are many examples of successful distributed file system implementations, including:

1. Facebook's Haystack: Haystack is Facebook's distributed file system that is used to store and serve billions of images to its users. It uses HDFS as its underlying storage system and relies on custom metadata management to optimize the retrieval of images.
2. Google's File System (GFS): It is a distributed file system that is used to store and serve the company's massive data sets. It uses a master-slave architecture and a custom file access protocol to optimize data retrieval.
3. CERN's Ceph File System: CERN, the European Organization for Nuclear Research, uses Ceph as its distributed file system to store and manage the vast amounts of data generated by its particle physics experiments. Ceph provides a scalable and fault-tolerant storage solution that can handle the large data volumes generated by the experiments (Levy & Silberschatz, 1990).

4.5. APPLICATIONS AND USE CASES OF DISTRIBUTED FILE SYSTEM

Learning Objectives

At the end of this section, readers will be able to:

- Explore real-world applications and use cases of distributed file systems across various industries, such as cloud computing, data analytics, content delivery networks (CDNs), and scientific research.
- Evaluate the specific challenges and considerations associated with implementing distributed file systems in different scenarios, including security concerns, data consistency, and performance optimization.

Distributed file systems are widely used in various applications and use cases that require the storage, management, and sharing of large volumes of data across multiple servers. Some of the common applications and use cases of distributed file systems include:

4.5.1. Big Data Analytics

Big data analytics involves processing and analyzing large datasets to extract insights and value. Distributed file systems such as HDFS, GFS, Luster, and Ceph are commonly used in big data analytics to store and manage the massive amounts of data generated by organizations. Distributed file systems provide a scalable and fault-tolerant storage solution for big data, enabling organizations to store and manage petabytes or even exabytes of data across multiple servers. By distributing data across multiple servers, distributed file systems also enable high-speed data access and processing, which is critical for big data analytics (Mahmoud et al., 2018).

4.5.2. Cloud Computing

Cloud computing involves delivering computing resources over the internet. Cloud storage services, such as Amazon S3, Azure Blob Storage, and Google Cloud Storage, use distributed file systems to store and manage the data of their clients. Distributed file systems enable cloud storage providers to provide a scalable and fault-tolerant storage solution for their clients' data, while also ensuring high-speed data access and processing. By distributing data across multiple servers, distributed file systems also enable cloud storage providers to achieve high levels of scalability and fault tolerance, which are critical for cloud computing.

4.5.3. Content Delivery Networks

Content Delivery Networks (CDNs) use distributed file systems to store and deliver content to users across the globe. CDNs, such as Akamai, Cloudflare, and Fastly, rely on distributed file systems to ensure that content is delivered quickly and reliably to users, regardless of their location. Distributed file systems enable CDNs to store and manage large volumes of content, such as videos, images, and web pages, across multiple servers, which ensures high-speed content delivery and reduces latency (Borst et al., 2010)

4.5.4. High-Performance Computing

High-performance computing (HPC) systems require high-speed data access and processing to handle complex computations and simulations. Distributed file systems such as Luster, Ceph, and Gluster are commonly used in HPC systems to store and manage large datasets. Distributed file systems provide a scalable and fault-tolerant storage solution for HPC systems, enabling them to store and manage large datasets across multiple servers. By distributing data across multiple servers, distributed file systems also enable HPC systems to achieve high-speed data access and processing, which is critical for complex computations and simulations.

4.5.5. Multimedia Streaming

Multimedia streaming applications require a scalable and reliable storage solution for large media files, such as videos and music. Distributed file systems such as HDFS, GFS, and Ceph are commonly used in multimedia streaming applications to ensure that media files are delivered quickly and reliably to users. Distributed file systems enable media streaming providers to store and manage large volumes of media files across multiple servers, which ensures high-speed media delivery and reduces latency.

4.5.6. Scientific Data Management

Scientific experiments generate large volumes of data that need to be stored and managed efficiently. Distributed file systems such as Ceph, Gluster, and Luster are commonly used in scientific data management to provide a scalable and fault-tolerant storage solution. By distributing data across multiple servers, distributed file systems enable scientists to store and manage large datasets across multiple servers, which ensures high-speed data access and processing. Distributed file systems also provide fault tolerance, ensuring that data is not lost in the event of server failure (Lee et al., 2021).

SUMMARY

The chapter "Distributed File System" discusses the importance and benefits of using a distributed file system, which allows multiple computers to share data across a network. Different types of distributed file systems are presented, including Network File System (NFS), Common Internet File System (CIFS), and Google File System (GFS), each with its own characteristics and features. The architecture and components of distributed file systems, such as metadata servers, data servers, and clients, are also explained.

The challenges in implementing distributed file systems, such as data consistency and fault tolerance, are identified and strategies for overcoming them are discussed. Case studies of distributed file system implementations, including Hadoop Distributed File System (HDFS) and Microsoft Azure File Storage, are presented to illustrate how these systems are used in real-world scenarios.

Finally, the chapter explores the various applications and use cases of distributed file systems, such as big data analytics and cloud computing. Overall, the chapter provides a comprehensive overview of distributed file systems, their benefits, challenges, and real-world applications.

REVIEW QUESTIONS

1. What are the benefits of using a Distributed File System?
2. What are the different types of Distributed File Systems and what are their characteristics?
3. Describe the architecture of a Distributed File System and its components.
4. What are some challenges associated with implementing a Distributed File System, and what are some strategies for overcoming them?
5. Can you provide examples of case studies of Distributed File System implementations?
6. What are some common applications and use cases of Distributed File Systems, such as Big Data Analytics and Cloud Computing?

MULTIPLE CHOICE QUESTIONS

1. What is the importance of Distributed File Systems?

a. They enable users to access and share files from anywhere in the network.

b. They provide a centralized storage system for all network users.

c. They increase data security and reliability.

d. All of the above.

2. Which of the following is not a characteristic of Distributed File Systems?

a. Scalability

b. Fault tolerance

c. Centralized storage
d. High performance

3. **What are the components of a Distributed File System?**
   a. Client, server, file metadata, and data storage
   b. Client, server, file system cache, and backup storage
   c. Client, server, file system cache, and data storage
   d. Client, server, file metadata, and backup storage
4. **What is a challenge in implementing Distributed File Systems?**
   a. Limited storage capacity
   b. Difficulty in maintaining data consistency
   c. Lack of security features
   d. All of the above
5. **Which Distributed File System is commonly used in cloud computing?**
   a. Hadoop Distributed File System (HDFS)
   b. Network File System (NFS)
   c. Andrew File System (AFS)
   d. None of the above
6. **Which application uses Distributed File Systems for large-scale data analysis?**
   a. Social media platforms
   b. E-commerce websites
   c. Big data analytics
   d. Gaming platforms

Answers to Multiple Choice Questions

1. (d); 2. (c); 3. (c); 4. (b); 5. (a); 6. (c)

REFERENCES

1. Borst, S., Gupta, V., & Walid, A., (2010). Distributed caching algorithms for content distribution networks. In: 2010 Proceedings IEEE INFOCOM (Vol. 1, pp. 1–9). IEEE.
2. Butt, A. R., Johnson, T. A., Zheng, Y., & Hu, Y. C., (2006). Kosha: A peer-to-peer enhancement for the network file system. Journal of Grid Computing, 4(3), 323–341.
3. Cheng, H. C., & Sheu, J. P., (1991). Design and implementation of a distributed file system. Software: Practice and Experience, 21(7), 657–675.
4. Devulapalli, A., & Wyckoff, P., (2007). File creation strategies in a distributed metadata file system. In: 2007 IEEE International Parallel and Distributed Processing Symposium (Vol. 1, pp. 1–10). IEEE.

5. Donvito, G., Marzulli, G., & Diacono, D., (2014). Testing of several distributed file-systems (HDFS, Ceph and GlusterFS) for supporting the HEP experiments analysis. In: Journal of Physics: Conference Series (Vol. 513, pp. 42014). IOP Publishing.
6. Ghemawat, S., Gobioff, H., & Leung, S. T., (2003). The Google file system. In: Proceedings of the Nineteenth ACM Symposium on Operating Systems Principles (pp. 29–43).
7. Gifford, D. K., Jouvelot, P., Sheldon, M. A., & O'Toole, Jr. J. W., (1991). Semantic file systems. ACM SIGOPS Operating Systems Review, 25(5), 16–25.
8. Gray, C., & Cheriton, D., (1989). Leases: An efficient fault-tolerant mechanism for distributed file cache consistency. ACM SIGOPS Operating Systems Review, 23(5), 202–210.
9. Howard, J. H., Kazar, M. L., Menees, S. G., Nichols, D. A., Satyanarayanan, M., Sidebotham, R. N., & West, M. J., (1988). Scale and performance in a distributed file system. ACM Transactions on Computer Systems (TOCS), 6(1), 51–81.
10. Huang, H., Lin, J., Zheng, B., Zheng, Z., & Bian, J., (2020). When blockchain meets distributed file systems: An overview, challenges, and open issues. IEEE Access, 8, 50574–50586.
11. Kumar, K. L., (2013). Implementing network file system protocol for highly available clustered applications on network attached storage. In: 2013 5th International Conference and Computational Intelligence and Communication Networks (Vol. 1, pp. 496–499). IEEE.
12. Lee, J. Y., Kim, M. H., Raza, S. S. A., Ahn, S. U., Yoon, H., & Noh, S. Y., (2021). Performance evaluations of distributed file systems for scientific big data in FUSE environment. Electronics, 10(12), 1471.
13. Levy, E., & Silberschatz, A., (1990). Distributed file systems: Concepts and examples. ACM Computing Surveys (CSUR), 22(4), 321–374.
14. Lin, Z., Li, K., Hou, H., Yang, X., & Li, H., (2017). MDFS: A mimic defense theory based architecture for distributed file system. In: 2017 IEEE International Conference on Big Data (Big Data) (Vol. 1, pp. 2670–2675). IEEE.
15. Mahmoud, H., Hegazy, A., & Khafagy, M. H., (2018). An approach for big data security based on Hadoop distributed file system. In: 2018 International Conference on Innovative Trends in Computer Engineering (ITC) (Vol. 1, pp. 109–114). IEEE.
16. Maltzahn, C., Molina-Estolano, E., Khurana, A., Nelson, A. J., Brandt, S. A., & Weil, S., (2010). Ceph as a scalable alternative to the Hadoop distributed file system. Login: The USENIX Magazine, 35, 38–49.
17. Salim, M., Akhtar, M. S., & Qadeer, M. A., (2009). Data retrieval and security using lightweight directory access protocol. In: 2009 Second International Workshop on Knowledge Discovery and Data Mining (Vol. 1, pp. 685–688). IEEE.
18. Satyanarayanan, M., Howard, J. H., Nichols, D. A., Sidebotham, R. N., Spector, A. Z., & West, M. J., (1985). The ITC distributed file system: Principles and design. ACM SIGOPS Operating Systems Review, 19(5), 35–50.

19. Schwan, P., (2003). Lustre: Building a file system for 1000-node clusters. In: Proceedings of the 2003 Linux Symposium (Vol. 2003, pp. 380–386).
20. Shvachko, K., Kuang, H., Radia, S., & Chansler, R., (2010). The Hadoop distributed file system. In: 2010 IEEE 26th Symposium on Mass Storage Systems and Technologies (MSST) (Vol. 1, pp. 1–10). IEEE.
21. Sivaraman, E., & Manickachezian, R., (2014). High performance and fault tolerant distributed file system for big data storage and processing using Hadoop. In: 2014 International Conference on Intelligent Computing Applications (Vol. 1, pp. 32–36). IEEE.
22. Stroud, R., (1992). Transparency and reflection in distributed systems. In: Proceedings of the 5th Workshop on ACM SIGOPS European Workshop: Models and Paradigms for Distributed Systems Structuring (Vol. 1, pp. 1–5).
23. Sumirat, U., Setiawan, A., Wilyanti, S., & Al-Hakim, R., (2023). Analysis of distributed file system replication using the NDLC method with hyper-V virtual simulation machine. SaNa: Journal of Blockchain, NFTs and Metaverse Technology, 1(1), 11–23.
24. Sur, S., Wang, H., Huang, J., Ouyang, X., & Panda, D. K., (2010). Can high-performance interconnects benefit Hadoop distributed file system. In: Workshop on Micro Architectural Support for Virtualization, Data Center Computing, and Clouds (MASVDC). Held in Conjunction with MICRO (Vol. 1, p. 10).
25. Tobbicke, R., (1994). Distributed file systems: Focus on Andrew file system/ distributed file service (AFS/DFS). In: Proceedings Thirteenth IEEE Symposium on Mass Storage Systems; Toward Distributed Storage and Data Management Systems (Vol. 1, pp. 23–26). IEEE.

CHAPTER 5

Fundamentals of Data Management

LEARNING OBJECTIVES

After studying this chapter, you will be able to:

- The importance and benefits of rational databases
- The characteristics of Structured Query Language
- The concept of Normalization and Database
- The query optimization and Performance Tuning

"Data management is the cornerstone upon which valuable insights and informed decisions are built, making the fundamentals of data management the bedrock of progress in the digital age."

INTRODUCTORY EXAMPLE

In a hospital, managing patient information efficiently is critical for providing high-quality healthcare services. A Hospital Information System (HIS) is a comprehensive database management system designed to handle various aspects of hospital operations, from patient records to inventory management. Here's how it works:

- **Patient Records Management:** The HIS maintains a central database containing detailed records of each patient's medical history, including diagnoses, treatments, medications, and lab results. Each patient is assigned a unique identifier, such as a medical record number, to ensure accurate and secure data retrieval.
- **Appointment Scheduling:** The HIS includes a scheduling module that allows hospital staff to book appointments for patients with doctors, specialists, or diagnostic services. This module ensures efficient allocation of resources and minimizes wait times for patients.
- **Clinical Decision Support:** The HIS may incorporate clinical decision support tools that provide healthcare professionals with real-time guidance based on evidence-based medicine and best practices. For example, when prescribing medications, the system can alert physicians to potential drug interactions or allergies, helping to prevent medical errors.
- **Billing and Insurance Management:** The HIS integrates with billing and insurance systems to streamline the financial aspects of healthcare services. It tracks services rendered to patients, generates invoices, and submits claims to insurance providers electronically, reducing administrative overhead and improving revenue cycle management.
- **Inventory Control**: In addition to patient-related data, the HIS manages inventory for medical supplies, equipment, and pharmaceuticals. It tracks inventory levels, alerts staff to low stock or expiring items, and facilitates seamless replenishment through automated ordering processes.
- **Reporting and Analytics**: The HIS generates various reports and analytics to monitor hospital performance, track outcomes, and identify areas for improvement. Administrators can analyze data on patient demographics, treatment outcomes, resource utilization, and financial metrics to make informed decisions and optimize operations.

By leveraging a robust HIS, hospitals can enhance patient care, streamline workflows, improve efficiency, and ensure compliance with regulatory requirements. This example illustrates how a database management system plays a pivotal role in modern healthcare delivery, empowering providers to deliver timely, personalized, and effective care to patients.

UNIT INTRODUCTION

Efficient data management is crucial for the success of technology companies across all industries in modern times. Data management implementation ensures the systematic organization, accessibility, and security of data, enabling businesses to make educated decisions, extract valuable insights, and gain a competitive edge. This chapter offers a comprehensive examination of the fundamental principles of managing information in SQL and NoSQL, as well as the evolving advancements in cloud computing and data architectures.

Relational Database Management Systems (RDBMS) are often regarded as the primary foundation for modern data management. Data storage follows an organized methodology that utilizes tables, rows, and columns to methodically organize data. Databases that incorporate relationships offer a multitude of advantages, including the assurance of accuracy and consistency, as well as the provision of powerful query capabilities. This chapter explores the core principles of database systems, their defining characteristics, and the relational model that forms the basis for their development (Berry & Linoff, 2000).

SQL is a widely recognized language that enables efficient communication with relational database systems. The software enables users to construct and manage information, conduct queries, and supervise database administration. SQL is a computer language that consists of two primary components: DDL (Data Definition Language) and DML (Data Manipulation Language) statements. These components facilitate the effective creation, modifications, and retrieval of information. This chapter examines the essential components of SQL, including data types, managers, commands, and the syntax used for common operations (Figure 5.1).

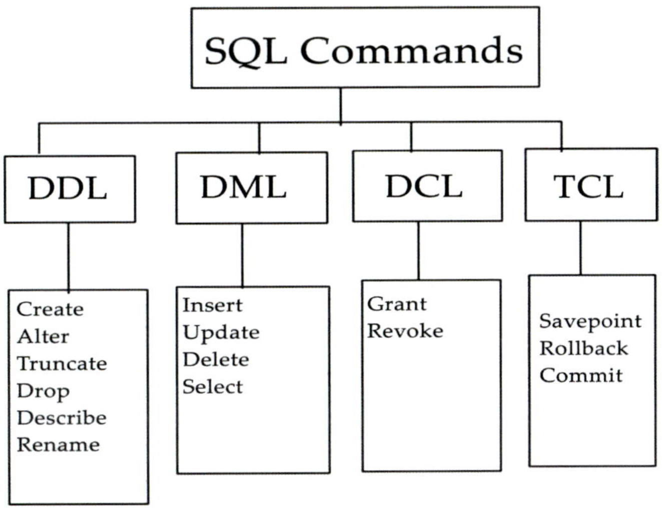

Figure 5.1. *Types of SQL database.*

The design of an information system is crucial for the efficient administration of data. The design process is directed by standardization that is grounded in the relational framework. This strategy aids in the eradication of data abnormalities and the reduction of redundancy. This chapter explores the notion of normalization forms, namely 1NF, 2NF, and 3NF, and their essential role in achieving a database design that is efficient and optimized. In addition, the content covers the notion of entity-relationship (ER) simulation, which is a methodology employed in the conceptual design of databases to represent entities, connections, and characteristics.

Efficient databases rely heavily on optimizing queries and system tuning for optimal functionality. The optimization of queries involves the conversion of requests from users by considering various factors, including selectivity, searching, and join operations. The performance tuning process encompasses the refinement of database arrangement, the optimization of index utilization, and the implementation of caching processes. The chapter provides an in-depth analysis of the optimization of queries along with performance tuning techniques, presenting valuable perspectives and optimal methodologies for enhancing query speed of execution and overall system efficiency.

The development of NoSQL database systems as a replacement for conventional relational ones can be attributed to the development of big information and the necessity to manage extensive volumes of semi-structured and unstructured information. Non-relational databases, commonly known as NoSQL databases, provide advantages such as enhanced scalability, adaptability, and superior performance. This chapter delves into the underlying incentives over NoSQL databases, delineates their distinctive attributes, and surveys the various classifications of NoSQL in the form of databases, including document-oriented, key-value, vertical, and diagram (Sallans & Lake, 2014). The concepts above hold significant importance in guaranteeing data credibility, uniformity, and effectiveness across interpersonal non-SQL database circumstances. Experts within data management might efficiently layout, optimize, and supervise databases by thoroughly understanding the fundamental principles. This enables them to fully exploit the immense value of their information assets within the present data-centric world (Provost & Fawcett, 2013) (Figure 5.2).

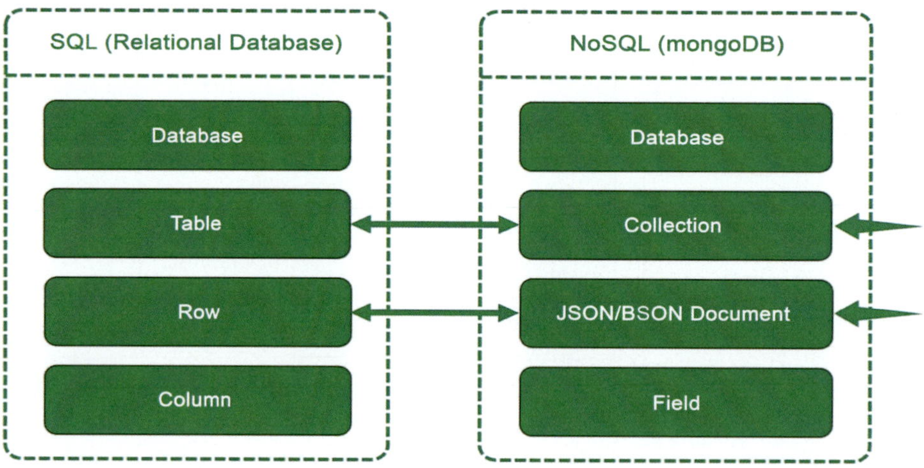

Figure 5.2. *Difference between SQL and non-SQL.*

5.1. RELATIONAL DATABASES

Learning Objectives

At the end of this section, readers will be able to:

- Explain the fundamental principles of a relational database, including the concepts of tables, rows, columns, and keys.
- Discuss the importance of data normalization in relational databases and its impact on data integrity and efficiency.
- Compare and contrast different types of database management systems (DBMS) used for relational databases, such as MySQL, PostgreSQL, and Microsoft SQL Server.

Relations databases play a fundamental role in data management within modern computer systems. Structured approaches are utilized for arranging and handling data, providing a dependable and effective means of storing, retrieving, and manipulating substantial amounts of data.

5.1.1. Definition of Relational Databases

A database with a relational structure is a structured assembly of interrelated data arranged in a tabular format, wherein data entities are stored in rows, and connections among those tables are created through common attributes. The term "relational" originates from depicting connections among entities by linking shared data attributes throughout tables. The aforementioned relational structure facilitates streamlined and adaptable querying, the influence of data, and the implementation of security measures.

5.1.2. Characteristics of Relational Databases

Databases with relationships are widely utilized and popular due to several basic features that they possess:

1. Tabular Structure: Relational databases utilize a tabular structure consisting of columns and rows for storing data. Every table corresponds to a distinct entity or idea in the tangible world, while the columns symbolize the characteristics or qualities of that particular entity. The columns, documents, or tuples comprise the factual data situations or values.

2. Data Independence: Databases with relationships between the physical preservation of data and its logical depiction. The partitioning of data enables independence from data, wherein the mathematical framework of the relational database may be utilized for writing applications or queries without being impacted by modifications in its physical location or arrangement.
3. Data Integrity: Integrity rules are enforced by SQL databases to preserve the coherence and precision of the data. Integrity constraints, including main key and foreign key limitations, verify constraints, guarantee data validity, preserve connections, and fulfill specific conditions.
4. Query Capability: Structured Query Language, also called SQL, is a robust query language supported by relational database systems. SQL enables users to extract, modify, and merge data from single or multiple tables through declarative statements. The interpersonal databases' ability to query facilitates the effective recovery of data according to diverse criteria and lets intricate data analysis.
5. ACID Properties: Relational databases conform to the ACID (Durability, Atomicity, Uniformity isolate) principles to guarantee dependable and resilient transaction processing. The concept of atomicity ensures that a transaction is regarded as an unbreakable and single section of work. The maintenance of a valid state of the database both before and after every transaction is ensured by consistency. The implementation of isolation prevents interference between concurrent actions; strength assures that any changes dedicated will remain enduring and survive any potential system errors.

5.1.3. Relational Model: Tables, Rows, and Columns

The interpersonal model offers a structured look at arranging data inside an interpersonal database. It is centered on tables, rows, and posts, which create the basic developing hinders for the interpersonal database framework.

1. Tables: These have a central organization within an interpersonal database. A set of interrelated data instances denotes the entities above or concepts. Every table possesses a distinctive name along with comprises rows along with columns. A corporate database could comprise distinct staff, divisions, and project tables.
2. Rows: Additionally referred to as documents or tuples, represent particular information instances within a piece of furniture. Every row in the table comprises data values related to the cells' characteristics or columns. For instance, in an employee surface, each row might indicate a staff, including data like staff ID, name, location, and earnings.
3. Columns: Referred to as characteristics and fields, specify the information's features or qualities in a given table. Every column possesses a distinct appellation and a particular data classification that ascertains what data it can accommodate. As an illustration, within a table

of employees, the columns may comprise characteristics such as the employee's identification number, full name, and corresponding salary.

The relational framework facilitates connections between tables by utilizing common characteristics or keys. The relational file can aptly depict intricate interactions and facilitate streamlined data retrieval via joins and additional relational activities by establishing links between interrelated tables based on shared attributes.

To conclude, relational database systems offer a methodical and effective approach to data management. The relational framework, which utilizes tables of information, rows, and columns, is the fundamental basis of relational databases. This model facilitates the systematic and coherent organization, retrieval, and modification of data.

5.2. STRUCTURED QUERY LANGUAGE (SQL)

Learning Objectives

At the end of this section, readers will be able to:

- Explain the fundamental principles of SQL.
- Discuss SQL query basics.
- Explore database design and normalization.
- Understand advanced SQL concepts.
- Practice SQL in real-world scenarios.

SQL represents a standardized and potent language facilitating interaction with relationship-based database management software (RDBMS). The tool offers extensive commands and constructs that enable data management and manipulation within databases. This section will comprehensively explore the diverse facets of SQL, encompassing its overview, significance in relational database management systems, data types, managers, expressions, and pivotal data definition language and data manipulation language statements. Furthermore, we shall delve into rudimentary SQL queries. The four fundamental operations in relational databases are SELECT, DELETE, UPDATE, or INSERT.

5.2.1. Importance of SQL in RDBMS

SQL is an explicit programming syntax developed to interact with relational database management systems (RDBMS). It provides syntax and semantics, permitting users to interact with records. Structured Query Language (SQL) is essential in managing information as it offers a uniform method for executing database operations throughout different systems vendors. The extensive utilization of this language has established it as the default choice for interacting with relational databases (Imieliński & Lipski, 1984).

SQL provides users diverse functionalities for manipulating databases, such as the ability to generate and alter database structures, retrieve, and query data, insert novel records, update pre-existing data, and remove records. The crucial skill set possessed by database managers, programmers, experts, and data researchers is attributed to the versatility and user-friendliness of the tool (Sahoo et al., 2009).

5.2.2. SQL Data Types, Operators, and Expressions

SQL provides support for a range of data types that specify the nature of the data, which can be accommodated within database columns of data. Practical SQL types of information involve integers, floats, fractions, strings, time frames, and Booleans (CJ Date, 1988). Comprehending the various data types at one's disposal and making informed decisions regarding their selection is paramount for optimizing data preservation and retrieval processes. This is because such decisions have a direct impact on the storage capacity, accuracy, and scope of values that can be effectively represented. Workers in SQL enable users to carry out operations upon data. Structured Query Language (SQL) offers a range of operators, including arithmetic operators such as addition (+), subtraction (–), multiplication (*), and division (/), comparison operators such as equals (=), not equals (<>), greater than (>), less than (<), greater than or equal to (>=), and less than or equal to (<=), logical operators such as AND, OR, and NOT, as well as a string encoding operator (||), among others (Figures 5.3–5.5).

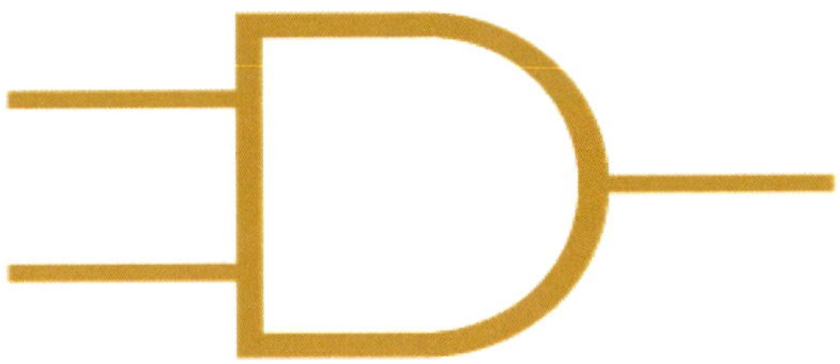

Figure 5.3. *AND operator.*

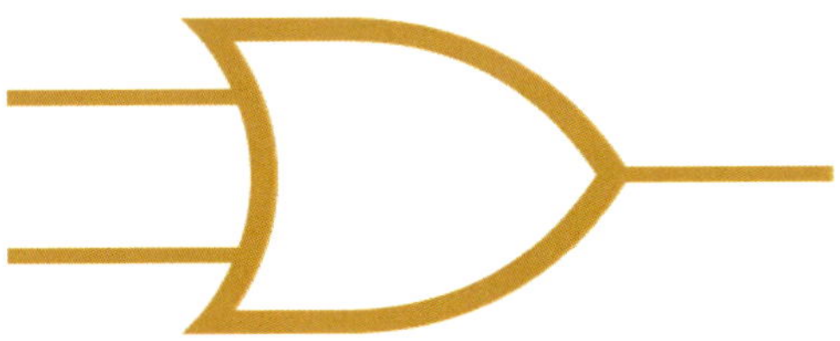

Figure 5.4. *OR operator.*

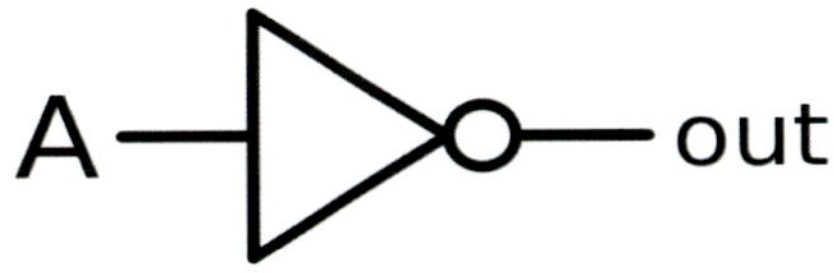

Figure 5.5. *NOT operator.*

Using employees within SQL queries allows for the execution of calculations, contrasts, and mathematical operations by users (Armbrust et al., 2015).

SQL phrases operators, operations, and literals, along with column values, to generate a singular value. SQL phrases are commonly utilized in various sections of SQL queries, such as WHERE provisions and choose financial statements. The platform enables users to perform computations, manipulate data, and apply filters to outcomes based on predetermined criteria. SQL offers a diverse range of pre-defined functions that can be utilized in expressions, encompassing numerical, string, date, and assembling functions.

5.2.3. DDL (Data Definition Language) and DML (Data Manipulation Language) Statements

SQL is split into two main groups about statements: Data Definition, The use of language (DDL), and Data Manipulation Language (DML). Statements in DDL are utilized for defining and handling the structure of records and objects in them. The fundamental Data Definition Language (DDL) assertions comprise CREATE, DROP, or ALTER. The CREATE statement generates novel objects such as databases, indexes, views, tables, and other related entities. The ALTER declaration enables users to alter the structure of previously created objects. The DROP declaration is a command to remove databases, tables of information, and additional objects. In contrast, Data Manipulation Language (DML) statements are employed to modify data stored within a database. The statements encompassed within this discussion's scope are SELECT, INSERT, UPDATE, and DELETE. The SELECT operator is the fundamental SQL statement utilized to retrieve data from any number of tables. The system enables users to extract particular columns, apply row-based filtering according to specified conditions, and execute diverse operations, including sorting and arrangement.

The INSERT declaration is a SQL command for adding new data records into a table. This functionality allows users to efficiently input one or more rows containing information into designated columns within a given table. The UPDATE declaration is a SQL command to alter or modify pre-existing data within a table. The feature enables users to modify particular rows or columns by applying specific criteria. The DELETE declaration is a database operation that facilitates the removal of information from the table according to predetermined conditions.

5.2.4. Basic SQL Queries: SELECT, INSERT, UPDATE, DELETE

The SELECT operator constitutes the fundamental element of SQL inquiries. The system enables users to extract information from singular or multiple tables by applying predetermined criteria. The SELECT statement provides diverse clauses, such as WHERE, GROUP BY, HAVING, ORDER BY, and JOINs. Utilizing such clauses facilitates data filtering, aggregation, sorting, and combination from various tables, producing significant result sets (Agrawal et al., 2005).

The INSERT declaration is a SQL command that adds fresh records to a database table. The feature enables users to designate specific values for insertion or retrieval from alternative tables. Including information databases, whether a solitary record or a large quantity of data, relies upon the pivotal INSERT statement. The UPDATE declaration is a SQL command utilized to alter or adjust the values of the current information in a specified table. The feature lets users modify columns or rows contingent on predetermined conditions. This assertion is crucial in upholding data precision and effecting modifications to the extant records. The DELETE declaration is a SQL command utilized to eliminate information within a table that has been modified. The feature enables users to selectively remove rows by applying predetermined criteria. The DELETE operation holds significant importance in maintaining the confidentiality of data and eliminating redundant or outdated records about databases.

In summary, Structured Query Language (SQL) seems a potent language that facilitates the management and manipulation of data within relational database systems. This section examines SQL's general outline and importance within relational database management systems (RDBMS). During the session, the operators, syntax of SQL types of data, managers, and expressions were deliberated upon, as they serve as the fundamental building blocks for modifying data and evaluations. Furthermore, we discussed the fundamental Data Definition Language (DDL) and Data Manipulation Language (DML) statements that establish the database framework and enable data manipulation. The study encompassed an analysis of the primary SQL queries, namely SELECT, INSERT, UPDATE, and DELETE, that constitute the fundamental procedures involved in the data.

5.3. NORMALIZATION AND DATABASE DESIGN

Learning Objectives

At the end of this section, readers will be able to:

- Explain the concept of normalization in database design and discuss its significance in reducing data redundancy and improving data integrity.
- Discuss the various normal forms (1NF, 2NF, 3NF, BCNF, and 4NF) and their requirements, highlighting the benefits and trade-offs associated with each.
- Analyze real-world database scenarios to identify when denormalization might be appropriate, and discuss the trade-offs involved in denormalizing a database.

5.3.1. Importance of Normalization in Database Design

The concept of normalization holds significant importance in the realm of database design because it strives to eradicate duplication and enhance the integrity of data. Normalization is a process that enhances the efficiency, flexibility, and maintainability of a database by arranging data into properly organized tables and minimizing data redundancy. Minimizing data anomalies, including revision, inserting, and deletion deviations, ensures data is kept consistently and without redundancy.

The principal objective of normalizing is to attain data integrity, which guarantees the accuracy and consistency of data across the database. Normalization is a process that involves the removal of redundant data and the establishment of associations among entities. This process is aimed at minimizing the occurrence of contradictions along with contradictions. This aspect holds significant importance in environments that involve several individuals or applications that may concurrently access and alter the database (Edwards, 2015).

5.3.2. Functional Dependencies and Normalization Forms (1NF, 2NF, 3NF)

Dependencies on function are of utmost importance in the process of normalization. A table establishes a functional connection when a particular attribute's contents can ascertain another characteristic's appreciation. Comprehending functional dependencies facilitates the identification of primary keys, ascertaining the connections between organizations, and implementing normalizing rules.

The normalization process encompasses multiple normalization forms, with each subsequent form developing upon the preceding one.

- According to the principle of the first usual form (1NF), it is necessary for every attribute present in a table to be atomic, which implies that it should consist solely of indivisible values. The process of eliminating duplicate groups and guaranteeing the uniqueness of every row within a table is achieved (Dongare et al., 2011).
- The additional normal shape (2NF) concept centers on removing limited dependencies. In database design, a partial dependence happens when an attribute is dependent solely on a portion of a primary key that is a composite. The second normal form (2NF) is achieved by breaking down a table through smaller ones and appropriately assigning characteristics to the following table. This process ensures that every attribute depends on the entire main key.
- The third standard form (3NF) concept pertains to eliminating temporary dependencies. In database design, a transitive dependency is said to arise when a property is functionally dependent on another property that does not constitute a constituent of the primary key. The third normal form (3NF) can attain a greater degree of normalizing and minimize data redundancy by breaking down tables and removing dependencies.

5.3.3. Denormalization and Trade-Offs

Although normalization is essential for preserving the confidentiality of information and minimizing redundant operations, there are still instances in which normalization might be suitable. Denormalization is a deliberate technique employed in database design to enhance performance by minimizing the number of joins necessary to retrieve data by introducing redundancy. This process is commonly employed in scenarios with a high emphasis on read operations or when intricate queries must be carried out. Denormalization is a technique that involves storing redundant data in a database. This approach may assist in lowering the amount of table connects necessary to retrieve information, which in turn can enhance the speed of queries. Nevertheless, denormalization entails certain trade-offs. The utilization of this approach may result in an escalation of data storage demands, the introduction of data inconsistencies in the event of inadequate update management, and the possible complication of data adaptations.

The decision of whether to renormalize necessitates meticulous contemplation of the demands of the program, the anticipated workload, and its performance ramifications. It is crucial to evaluate the potential advantages compared with the disadvantages and analyze the effect on the integrity of information and the complexity of upkeep (Helland, 2019).

5.3.4. Entity-Relationship (ER) Modeling and Database Design

The Entity-Relationship (ER) modeling process is widely utilized for conceptualizing and designing databases. The system is depicted visually by illustrating its constituent entities, deemed significant, and their interconnections. ER diagrams utilize diverse terminologies and symbols to show entities, attributes, connections, and cardinality.

Within ER modeling, a person or thing is used to signify a tangible or intangible object or notion within the real world. Examples of such entities may include a client as well as an order. Attributes refer to the inherent features or qualities of entities, including the nomenclature or chronological age of a patron. The concept of relationships pertains to how entities are interconnected, exemplified by the correlation between a patron and a purchase order (Dhabe et al., 2010) (Figure 5.6).

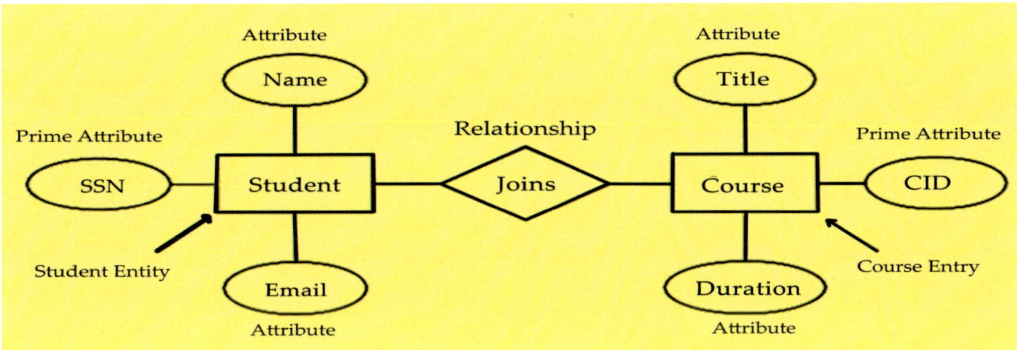

Figure 5.6. *Illustration of entity-relationship (ER) modeling.*

ER modeling facilitates comprehension of the database's structure, recognition of organizations' characteristics, and visualization of the interconnections among entities. The ER model provides a fundamental basis for the subsequent logical design phase, wherein it is transformed into a database's structure. The resultant schema encompasses various components such as rows, posts, primary and secondary keys, and additional constraints that are imperative to the system's database design.

A comprehensive comprehension of the business demands, and the inter-entity relationships is imperative for proficient ER simulation. The process aids in verifying that the database architecture effectively reflects actual situations in the physical world and facilitates the intended tasks of the entire system (Hussain et al., 2003).

Incorporating normalizing or database layouts is essential in constructing effective, resilient, and sustainable databases. Normalization is imperative in maintaining data integrity and minimizing redundancy through systematically arranging data into structured tables. Comprehending functional dependencies and implementing normalization forms such as the first normal form (1NF), second normal form (2NF), and third normal form (3NF) can facilitate the attainment of elevated levels of the normalization process. Denormalization might be employed as a strategic measure to enhance performance, albeit at the expense of introducing trade-offs. Moreover, Entity-Relationship (ER) modeling offers a graphical depiction of relationships, attributes, and entities and simplifies the creation of databases. Through the implementation of those concepts and methods, database designers can construct database architectures that are improved and scalable, thereby satisfying the demands of the software or system.

5.4. QUERY OPTIMIZATION AND PERFORMANCE TUNING

Learning Objectives

At the end of this section, readers will be able to:

- Explain the concept of query optimization and its significance in database management.
- Discuss the factors that can impact the performance of database queries and how to identify performance bottlenecks.
- Explore various query optimization techniques, such as indexing, query rewriting, and query plan analysis.

Optimization of queries and performance adjusting are essential components of handling information in any relational database management system (RDBMS). The procedures above are designed to enhance the efficacy and velocity of data retrieval procedures, guaranteeing peak performance even when dealing with extensive datasets. The forthcoming section will undertake an in-depth examination of various query optimization, methodologies, optimization algorithms, executing query strategies, indexed techniques (which include B-trees, encode indexes, along with a bitmap index), as well as performance enhancement factors, including searching, table partitioning, along with caching.

Improving queries in relational database management systems (RDBMS) entails examining and restructuring queries to reduce the computing power needed for their implementation. The aim is to produce an optimal plan for executing a query that minimizes the time required or maximizes the use of resources. Relational database management systems (RDBMS) utilize advanced query optimization techniques that use statistical data, cost-based analysis, and heuristics to ascertain the optimal method for executing a given query. The creation of question execution strategies is a crucial element in optimizing queries. As mentioned earlier, the plans delineate the sequential procedures that the Relational Database Management System (RDBMS) will undertake to procure the data that has been solicited. The optimization process considers multiple variables, including but not limited to the dimensions of the data table, the number of indexes available, and the resources the system has at its disposal to determine the optimal plan of execution. The execution plans may be depicted through various formats, such as textual depictions, visualizations, or a series of operations. The execution plans of queries offer valuable insights into the strategies that the relational database management system (RDBMS) will use in accessing and joining tables, implementing filters along with aggregations, and utilizing optimization methods such as indexes.

The relational database management system (RDBMS) utilizes algorithms for optimization to produce the most efficient execution plan. The methods under consideration assess various tactics and merging techniques while considering factors like selectivity, cardinality approximations, and expenses. The optimization process involves an analysis of various plans, accompanied by selecting the strategy via the lowest calculated cost, as determined by the chosen optimization algorithm. Exhaustive look, dynamic code, and heuristics-based methods are frequently employed in algorithms for optimization. The algorithms evaluate the compromises among various approaches for executing queries to ascertain the optimal plan with the highest efficiency. The process of indexing is crucial in enhancing the efficiency of query execution. Data recovery can be greatly sped up by building the right indexes. B-trees, hashing indexes, and image indexes are among the most prevalent indexing techniques in RDBMS. B-trees are frequently used for equality checks and range queries. By reducing the amount of disk, I/O needed, they preserve a healthy tree structure, enabling effective search operations. B-trees are highly useful in cases when the data is constantly updated.

Hash indexes are appropriate for precise match searches. They quickly perform lookup tasks using hashing algorithms to assign keys to particular locations in storage. Hash indexes are particularly effective for read-intensive applications that have low update frequency. Bitmap indexes are a valuable tool for columns with low cardinality. In such cases, the index stores a bitmap for every unique value. The utilization of indexes facilitates expedited recovery of records through bit manipulations, rendering them especially effective for decision-making systems and information warehouse management.

Performance optimization entails more than just the optimization of queries and indexing. Implementing supplementary methodologies, like table splitting and caching, may augment the system's overall efficiency. The process of table splitting entails the fragmentation of extensive tables through smaller, more controllable partitions, which are categorized based on a predetermined criterion, including a particular column or an assortment of values. The partitioning technique facilitates the execution of queries in parallel and enhances the speed of data retrieval by diminishing the volume of data that necessitates scanning. The implementation of data pruning enables efficient data management and has the potential to notably enhance query speed, particularly when dealing with extensive datasets.

Caching is a highly effective method for optimizing efficiency. Storing frequently within memory, known as caching, enables subsequent queries to be served immediately from the cache, removing the requirement for costly disk input/output operations. The use of caching processes may be deployed at diverse tiers, such as query outcome caching, caching at the database level, or caching at the application level. The practice of storing the outcomes of frequently carried out queries, which enables subsequent deaths to be served via the cache, is known as query outcome caching. Database-level caching entails caching complete tables from databases or frequently obtained data structures within the memory. Implementing an application-level cache involves integrating it into the application logic, where it selectively caches particular data or computation outcomes to minimize the frequency of database access. To achieve optimal performance, it is imperative to consider various factors, including cache dimensions and uniformity, when devising appropriate caching tactics.

5.5. NOSQL DATABASES

Learning Objectives

At the end of this section, readers will be able to:

- Explain the concept of NoSQL databases.
- Discuss the various types of NoSQL databases.
- Compare and contrast NoSQL databases with SQL databases.
- Describe common use cases for NoSQL databases.
- Explore popular NoSQL database management systems.

5.5.1. Evolution and Motivations Behind NoSQL Databases

Non-relational databases, commonly called NoSQL databases, have become a viable substitute for conventional Relational Database Management Systems (RDBMS) like Oracle, MySQL, and SQL Server. The acronym "NoSQL" denotes "Not Only SQL," implying that these databases offer a departure from the inflexible organization and querying functionalities of SQL-based systems. The emergence of NoSQL databases may be attributed to the beginning of the 2000s, during which web-scale enterprises such as Facebook, Amazon, and Google encountered difficulties effectively handling their swiftly expanding data (Scherzinger et al., 2006).

The principal impetus for the emergence of NoSQL databases proved the necessity to manage copious quantities of unstructured or partially structured data produced by web-based applications. Relational database management systems (RDBMS) encountered difficulties in horizontal scaling and delivering the required efficiency for these workloads due to their inflexible schemas and queries being processed on joins. In contrast, NoSQL databases provided a data structure that was more adaptable and structures that were distributed, enabling seamless expansion to accommodate extensive amounts of data.

The pursuit of high levels of availability and tolerance for faults was another influential factor in the emergence of NoSQL databases. Despite potential hardware malfunctions or network partitions, web-based applications frequently require an uninterrupted operation. NoSQL databases have adopted eventual consistency examples and distributed reproduction strategies to guarantee the persistence and accessibility of data, even in unfavorable circumstances.

5.5.2. Characteristics and Advantages of NoSQL Databases

NoSQL databases possess distinct features that differentiate them from conventional relational database management systems (RDBMS). Comprehending these attributes is imperative to comprehend the advantages they provide:

1. Flexible Data Model: NoSQL databases facilitate schema-less architecture, enabling data to be maintained in a more dynamic and adaptable format in contrast to the inflexible tabular arrangement of a relational database Document-oriented files, such as those that utilize JSON along with BSON format, possess the capability to conform to evolving needs for data readily (Han et al., 2011).
2. Horizontal Scalability: The architecture of database systems using NoSQL is intended to facilitate horizontal scaling, which involves data distribution across numerous servers or clusters. The ability to scale enables organizations to manage substantial information and meet traffic by incorporating additional ordinary servers (Moniruzzaman et al., 2013).
3. High Performance: NoSQL databases may improve writing and reading, emphasizing versatility and scalability. Frequently, denormalization, which caching processes and optimized preservation formats are utilized to augment the velocity of retrieving information and processing.
4. Distributed Architecture: NoSQL database systems are designed to function in distributed settings using distributed tables of identifiers and shared-nothing designs. The strategy mentioned above guarantees fault tolerance and elevated availability using data replication across numerous nodes, enabling local execution of operations (Nayak et al., 2013).
5. Support for Unstructured Data: NoSQL databases are proficient in managing various data types, including feeds from social media, information from sensors, or log records. The pliability of their data models facilitates effortless preservation and retrieval of heterogeneous data categories, obviating the necessity for substantial schema alterations.
6. Agile Development: Utilizing NoSQL databases provides developers with increased flexibility and adaptability by facilitating swift prototyping and continual improvement. These tools facilitate rapid iterations and diminish the time to market for novel features or uses by eliminating the necessity for advanced schema design.

5.5.3. Choose NoSQL Over RDBMS

Although databases built with NoSQL along with RDBMS each have respective merits and demerits, there exist particular circumstances were opting for NoSQL could prove to be more beneficial:

1. Large-Scale Data: NoSQL databases demonstrate their superiority when confronted with extensive data amounts surpassing a solitary server's abilities. Horizontal scaling enables data distribution across numerous nodes, thereby facilitating

the processing thousands of gigabytes of information.

2. Flexible Data Requirements: Databases using NoSQL provides greater flexibility for data that undergoes frequent modifications or has an intricate structure that is not easily accommodated within a fixed tabular schema. Document-oriented records are particularly suitable for situations where the structure may undergo changes or vary throughout various entities.
3. High Performance and Low Latency: NoSQL databases are specifically engineered to facilitate rapid data retrieval with minimal delay and handle large volumes of data processing efficiently. NoSQL database systems can offer notable performance improvements over conventional RDBMS for applications requiring swift information retrieval or immediate analysis.
4. Agile Development and Scalability: NoSQL databases facilitate agile creation methods and can scale effortlessly to cope with expanding user populations or evolving demands. The absence of a fixed schema and the utilization of decentralized architectures facilitate uninterrupted scalability.
5. Unstructured or Semi-Structured Data: In cases where the data comprises partially or completely structured formats, including content created by users, social networking posts, or data from sensors, NoSQL databases may provide a more suitable solution. The system facilitates storing and retrieving heterogeneous data categories without necessitating intricate schema alterations.

It is imperative to acknowledge that the selection of NoSQL across RDBMS necessitates a meticulous assessment of the particular prerequisites and limitations of the project. It is advisable to consider various factors, such as the necessity for data consistency, transactional prerequisites, and the existence of specific characteristics or tools of every kind for the database. Polyglot tenacity, which utilizes SQL and non-SQL databases, can be optimal in certain scenarios. This strategy capitalizes on each system's unique capabilities to cater to a program's distinct aspects.

To conclude, NoSQL databases have helped significantly transform information management by offering adaptable, expandable, and efficient options instead of conventional RDBMS. The rise and growth of NoSQL databases were primarily motivated by the necessity to manage vast amounts of data, ensure robust availability, and facilitate flexible development methodologies. NoSQL databases possess distinctive attributes and benefits, such as their adaptable data models, capacity for horizontal expansion, and ability to accommodate unstructured information, making them highly appealing for particular utilization scenarios. It is imperative to evaluate the prerequisites and limitations of the project before selecting NoSQL along with RDBMS, given that each database category possesses unique advantages and drawbacks. One can arrive at informed judgments under their data administration requirements by comprehending the incentives, attributes, and suitable application scenarios for NoSQL databases (Figure 5.7).

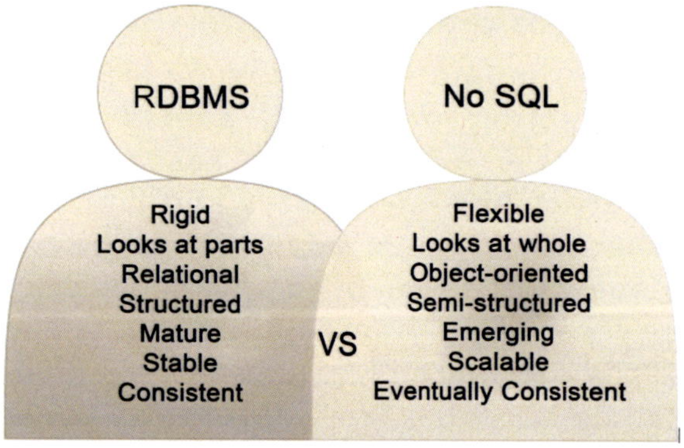

Figure 5.7. *Difference NoSQL and RDBMS.*

5.5.4. Types of NoSQL Databases

5.5.4.1. Document-Oriented Databases

In contemporary times, documents-oriented databases have emerged as a prominent category of NoSQL databases, garnering substantial attention. These databases are engineered to efficiently store and handle data in a versatile and non-structured approach, rendering them appropriate for use in applications that experience dynamic data demands. Document-oriented records differ from relational databases in that they store information in self-describing papers, commonly represented in formats such as JSON or BSON, instead of organizing information with predetermined schemas (Lourenço et al., 2015; Mason, 2015; Kumar & Mohanavalli, 2017; Vera et al., 2015).

5.5.4.2. JSON and BSON Data Formats

JSON, which stands for JavaScript Object Notation, is an information exchange format that is both lightweight and easily readable by humans. The representation of structured information, such as keys and values, arrays, along with nested objects, is facilitated by a straightforward and user-friendly approach. JSON documents are frequently utilized in document-oriented databases, their ease of comprehension and broad support across various programming languages or systems. JSON's versatility and ease of use make it a highly suitable option for web-based applications requiring common data exchange among the user's device and the server (Nayak et al., 2013).

BSON, also known as Binary JSON, represents a variant of the JSON format that incorporates supplementary data types and binary encoding. BSON preserves the fundamental characteristics and organization of JSON while concurrently augmenting its operational speed and storage effectiveness. The technology provides a condensed binary format for data, thereby minimizing the memory bandwidth on the network needed. BSON offers expanded support for diverse data types, including but not limited to dates. These data are binary and numeric types, enhancing the scope of expressive capabilities for representation and manipulation. BSON is the fundamental data structure in certain document-centric databases, such as MongoDB (Zhang et al., 2014; Raut, 2017; Kaur & Rani, 2013).

5.5.4.3. MongoDB: Features and Data Modeling

MongoDB's free document-oriented file has gained significant popularity and widespread adoption. The software provides many functionalities, rendering it a flexible option for diverse applications. This study aims to examine MongoDB's fundamental characteristics and principles in conjunction with its methodology for data modeling.

1. Flexible Schema: The schema-less architecture of MongoDB enables adaptable and versatile data modeling. In contrast to relational

databases that impose a strict schema framework, MongoDB permits documents to exhibit diverse structures within a single collection. The malleability of the data model allows developers to modify it by the evolution of the application, needing to necessitate intricate and protracted schema migrations.

2. High Scalability: The MongoDB database management system is specifically engineered to manage and accommodate extensive scalability demands effectively. Sharding splitting horizontal scaling by providing data across numerous computers or clusters. Through the process of sharding information, MongoDB is capable of effectively managing substantial datasets and accommodating intensive reading and writing workloads. Splitting can be set up using diverse criteria, including range-based splitting or hashed division, which enables effective data shipping and enhanced performance.
3. Indexing and Querying: The MongoDB platform offers comprehensive indexing functionalities designed to enhance query processing efficiency. The system supports various index types, encompassing single-field, substance, geospatial, and writing indexes designed to facilitate full-text search functionality. Indexes may affect the effectiveness of the database's search for pertinent documents, diminishing the necessity of scanning extensive collections. The optimization of indexes can have a substantial impact on the efficiency of data recovery processes.
4. Replication and High Availability: MongoDB provides inherent replication functionalities that guarantee elevated availability and data persistence. The replication process entails preserving numerous data duplicates across distinct servers, thereby establishing a set of replicas. In case of a malfunctioning elementary server, the backup set can autonomously select another main server to sustain reading and writing requests. The replication process facilitates the creation of duplicate copies of data, thereby ensuring redundancy and enabling the possibility of data recuperation in the event of hardware breakdowns or other catastrophic events (Tang & Fan, 2016).
5. Data Modeling: The process of data demonstration in MongoDB entails the creation of a well-designed framework for organizing and interconnecting documents to facilitate optimized query processing. Although document-driven databases such as MongoDB provide versatility in expressing data, it is crucial to devise the schema to enhance efficiency meticulously. A crucial factor is the denormalization of data pertains to the incorporation of interconnected data inside a solitary document or the replication of data across numerous documents. The implementation of denormalization has the potential to enhance the efficiency of queries by mitigating the necessity for intricate join operations. However, it also presents difficulties in preserving data integrity throughout denormalized information.

The data modeling process within MongoDB is generally influenced by the particular methods of access along with query prerequisites of the application. The process entails the identification of crucial entities and their relationships, the determination of the structure of the document, and the optimization of indexes to enhance the efficiency of query execution. The malleability of MongoDB's structure affords the capacity for incremental and nimble data modeling, empowering programmers to hone and modify the data structure in tandem with the application's progression.

MongoDB's extensive range of features, such as its adaptable schema layout, capacity for high scaling, indexing functionalities, replication, and effective data modeling, render it a highly attractive option for uses that necessitate flexibility, scalability, and optimal performance. Comprehending the characteristics and optimal methodologies for modeling data within MongoDB is imperative to effectively exploit its potential in practical situations.

5.6. DATA MODELING IN NOSQL DATABASES

Learning Objectives

At the end of this section, readers will be able to:

- Explain the fundamentals of NoSQL databases and their importance in modern data management.
- Discuss the differences between NoSQL data models (e.g., document, key-value, column-family, and graph) and their use cases.
- Analyze the challenges and advantages of schema-less data modeling in NoSQL databases.

Data demonstration is of utmost importance in the design of files, as it establishes the structure and arrangement of data storage and retrieval within a given system. Although the basic concepts of modeling data to traditional relational database management systems (RDBMS) and NoSQL databases exist, notable distinctions exist in their methodologies. This part will provide an in-depth analysis of data demonstrated in NoSQL databases, highlighting the subtle distinctions between them and RDBMS.

5.6.1. Data Modeling Differences Between NoSQL and RDBMS

The process of data demonstrating in RDBMS is centered on the relational framework, which entails organizing information into tables with predetermined schemas. The objective is to attain a database with a standard schema, mitigating duplication and guaranteeing data consistency. The establishment of relationships between tables is facilitated through the utilization of primary and foreign keys, which in turn allows for the efficient execution of joins when querying data. Conversely, NoSQL databases adopt an alternative framework to increase adaptability and scaling. In contrast to relational database management systems (RDBMS), NoSQL database systems are free from inflexible schemas, thereby facilitating the creation of schema-less or adaptable schema structures. The attribute of flexibility holds particular benefits in cases where the information structure is exposed to dynamic alterations or when managing partially or completely structured information.

5.6.2. Aggregation and Denormalization in NoSQL Databases

Databases using NoSQL exhibit a paradigm shift in emphasis from normalizing to denormalization accumulation. Normalization is a fundamental principle in relational database management systems (RDBMS) aimed at reducing redundancy. However, NoSQL databases tend to promote data denormalization to enhance the speed of queries.

The aggregation process entails consolidating interconnected data into a unified document or entity, expediting retrieval, and mitigating the necessity for intricate joins. In document-oriented databases such as MongoDB, the denormalization of related data inside a document obviates the need for expensive joins across numerous tables. Incorporating associated information immediately into a given document enables retrieval procedures to be executed in a solitary read, thereby augmenting efficiency, and streamlining data accessibility.

Denormalization is a technique that facilitates the duplication of associated data across numerous documents and collections, thereby allowing for redundant data. Using redundant facilitates expedited queries and circumvents expensive joins, albeit at the cost of augmented storage necessities. The determination of whether or not to denormalize information stored in databases using NoSQL is contingent upon the particular query patterns and the given application's performance criteria.

5.6.3. Schema-Less Design and Flexible Schemas

Non-relational databases, commonly called NoSQL databases, are characterized by their schema-less architecture, which sets them apart from traditional relational database management systems (RDBMS). Relational database management systems (RDBMS) have rigid schema enforcement, whereas non-relational databases (NoSQL) offer greater adaptability to data schema.

NoSQL databases, including document-oriented files, exhibit heterogeneity in data structures inside a given collection or document. The adaptability of NoSQL databases to changing information needs is attributed to their adaptability, which obviates the necessity of modifying the database structure when fresh fields or characteristics are added. The flexibility of not being bound by predetermined schemas enables developers to incorporate or alter fields, thereby enhancing the agility of the creation process. In addition, the schema-less architecture of NoSQL databases provides a more efficient means of accommodating semi-structured and unstructured information. No-SQL database systems are capable of accommodating a wide range of data kinds and dynamic data models, rendering them highly suitable for functions that involve intricate or rapidly shifting data, owing to the absence of a predetermined structure that must be followed.

5.6.4. Consistency Models in NoSQL Databases

In the context of NoSQL databases, uniformity models specify how data is disseminated and harmonized across disparate systems. In contrast to relational database management systems (RDBMS), which generally operate using robust uniformity as the failure mode, NoSQL database systems provide a variety of uniformity models to tackle the difficulties posed by distributed systems (Diogo et al., 2019).

Certain NoSQL databases, including those utilizing key-value storage, adopt a consistent paradigm. In the present model, modifications performed on the database's contents can be promptly observed on the current replica. However, there may be a delay in disseminating these changes across other replicas. In due course, all duplicates attain a uniform state. The concept of eventual consistency confers the advantage of ensuring high reliability and tolerance for partitions, albeit at the cost of potential, albeit transient, data inconsistencies. Certain NoSQL databases offer robust consistency assurances that are comparable to those of relational database management systems (RDBMS). The model guarantees strict data consistency by enabling immediate visibility of updates across all replicas. Attaining robust reliability in distributed computing environments frequently results in increased latency and decreased availability due to the requirement for coordination along with synchronization.

In addition to providing ultimately strong and weak consistency, several NoSQL databases present uniformity models on a spectrum among these two polarities. Causal uniformity and session alignment are instances of models that exemplify this notion. Causal consistency is a fundamental property that guarantees the preservation of causal dependencies by enforcing a strict ordering of causally related operations. Meeting consistency pertains to maintaining data consistency within a particular session or a client's perspective toward the data. This approach enables the provision of more robust assurances while simultaneously loosening the consistency across different sessions. The selection of a suitable reliability model is contingent upon the particular demands of an application. Determining the most appropriate model is significantly influenced by various factors, including but not limited to information access trends, scalability requirements, and the degree of tolerance for future consistency.

5.7. SCALABILITY AND PERFORMANCE CONSIDERATIONS

Learning Objectives

At the end of this section, readers will be able to:

- Explain the concept of scalability in computing and its challenges in NoSQL Database.
- Discuss the key factors that influence the performance of software applications and systems, including hardware, software design, and network considerations.
- Analyze the trade-offs between scalability and performance, highlighting scenarios where optimizing one may lead to compromises in the other.

5.7.1. Scalability Challenges in NoSQL Databases

The scalability issue holds significant importance in contemporary information management systems, particularly when considering applications of extensive magnitude and data of substantial size. NoSQL databases are engineered to manage extensive volumes of data and offer horizontal scalability, enabling further servers or nodes to spread the data along with the workload. Notwithstanding, attaining scalability within NoSQL databases presents distinct challenges.

Data distribution poses a significant scalability problem for NoSQL databases. In contrast to conventional relational database systems that depend on vertical expansion to enhance the computing power of one server, NoSQL databases can employ horizontal expansion to disseminate data across numerous servers. The present distribution of data presents challenges in maintaining consistent information and optimizing data access efficiency.

When data is dispersed among many servers, it's imperative to consider the partitioning of information and queries through the relevant nodes. Maintaining uniform distribution of data across fragments or divisions is imperative to avoid the occurrence of hotspots, wherein specific nodes are burdened with an inequitable share of data along with queries. Attaining equitable data distribution necessitates meticulous deliberation of the fragment key, which ascertains how information is partitioned (Mapanga & Kadebu, 2013).

Consistency in data poses an additional difficulty. NoSQL databases frequently prioritize the attributes of high reliability and tolerance for partitions, as per the capacity availability theorem, over strict consistency. The compromise above facilitates enhanced operational efficiency and resilience within distributed systems, albeit at the expense of eventual consistency, which may result in momentary discrepancies among data replicas. Achieving optimal performance over an application while maintaining consistency requirements necessitates finding an appropriate equilibrium.

5.7.2. Horizontal Scaling and Sharding

Implementing horizontal growth is a fundamental strategy for scaling databases using NoSQL. The process entails the dispersion of data among numerous servers or just nodes to manage augmented workloads and quantities. Sharding is a commonly employed method in which a given dataset is partitioned into fewer subsets, called shards or divisions, and subsequently stored on distinct servers.

The partitioning process entails the selection of a shard key that governs the partitioning of data. The selection of the shard key necessitates meticulous consideration to ensure the equitable dispersion of data among shards and circumvent the occurrence of hotspots or disproportionate workloads. Typical strategies employed for fragmented key selection encompass utilizing a unique identification or a field that denotes the locality of the data, such as geographical location. Implementing splitting yields various advantages, such as the heightened capacity for storage, enhanced reading and writing performance, and faults. Through data distribution, individual shards can manage a specific subset of the overall workload, facilitating concurrent processing and mitigating contention. Furthermore, in the event of a shard along with server failure, the remaining fragments can persistently provide data, guaranteeing high availability.

Nevertheless, the implementation of sharding also presents certain difficulties. Co-located data, which refers to data that must be accessed in conjunction, may be distributed across multiple shards, necessitating further synchronization and potentially compromising system efficiency. The effective scaling of a system necessitates meticulous observation and realignment of shards to sustain a uniform dispersion of information and workload (Abdelhafiz & Elhadef, 2021).

5.7.3. CAP Theorem and Trade-Offs in Distributed Systems

Brewer's theorem, commonly called the theory of CAP, posits that a networked data system cannot feasibly offer reliability, accessibility, and partition tolerance concurrently. Consistency refers to the property of all nodes perceiving identical information, while availability denotes the capacity of the infrastructure to respond to all requests, even in the face of errors. Partition tolerance, upon the other hand, pertains to the system's capacity to continue functioning despite partitions within the network.

NoSQL databases are primarily intended for scaling and high availability and therefore tend to put tolerance for partitions and availability across strict consistency. In the event of network divisions or mistakes, continued accessibility, and tolerance for partitions over consistency. The trade-off above gives rise to distinct consistency models, including eventual or related consistency, wherein data replicas may undergo temporary divergence but ultimately converge (Gilbert & Lynch, 2012).

Comprehending the trade-offs linked with the concept of CAP is crucial in designing and utilizing NoSQL databases. The selection of consistency models may differ based on the particular demands of an application. Certain programs require eventual uniformity, whereas others necessitate strong consistency assurances. Selecting a suitable consistency framework for a given use case requires architects and developers to evaluate the associated compromises thoroughly.

5.7.4. Performance Tuning in NoSQL Databases: Caching, Indexing, and Partitioning

A range of methodologies can be implemented to enhance the efficiency of databases that use NoSQL, such as caching, searching, and partitioning.

1. Caching: The caching process entails retaining frequently used data near the program in memory, aiming to mitigate latency and enhance response times. Incorporating cached information in memory systems, like Redis or Memcached, alongside NoSQL relational databases can facilitate expedited retrieval of frequently utilized data. Caching techniques like the most recently executed (LRU) or time-dependent removal can be utilized to administer the cache proficiently (Hsieh et al., 2011).
2. Indexing: It constitutes a pivotal facet of optimizing performance. Similar to relational databases, databases built with NoSQL employ indexes to facilitate effective information retrieval by constructing data structures that enable rapid lookup based on particular fields. Various indexing methods can be employed based on the type of database, including B-trees and LSM-trees. It is advisable to exercise caution while choosing suitable fields for indexed strike a balance between query execution efficiency and the upkeep overhead of the index (Pandey et al., 2018).
3. Partitioning: As previously mentioned, partitioning refers to fragmenting the dataset into smaller parts or partitions. Effective partitioning techniques can enhance system efficiency by providing information and workload among numerous servers. Selecting a suitable shard key and preventing hotspots or uneven partitions are critical factors in achieving effective data sharing and reducing bottlenecks.

Apart from caches, indexing, and splitting, additional techniques for enhancing performance encompass optimization of queries, data denormalization; however, and appropriate hardware provisioning. The query optimization process entails examining and enhancing question execution schedules from responses. The deliberate introduction of redundant data, known as data denormalization, can enhance read performance while incurring higher storage demands. The general efficiency of NoSQL tables can be significantly influenced by appropriate hardware provisioning, which may involve the utilization of solid-state disks (SSDs) or optimizing network arrangements (Chawla et al., 2020).

By implementing performance optimization strategies, entities can guarantee that their MySQL databases can effectively manage extensive workloads and deliver the necessary level of responsiveness to satisfy the requirements of contemporary applications.

5.8. ADVANCED SQL TECHNIQUES

Learning Objectives

At the end of this section, readers will be able to:

- Discuss the optimization techniques for improving SQL query performance, including indexing, query rewriting, and query execution plans.
- Explore advanced SQL joins such as self-joins, outer joins, and cross joins, and illustrate their usage in solving real-world data problems.
- Describe the principles of data normalization and denormalization in SQL databases and discuss when to apply each technique for efficient data storage and retrieval.

5.8.1. Advanced Querying

The utilization of advanced searching methods in SQL empowers users to extract and handle data more intricately than conventional SELECT declarations. This section delves into three crucial facets of sophisticated querying: subqueries, correlated queries, prevalent table phrases (CTEs), and recurrent queries, which are instrumental in managing hierarchical data. Subqueries are used, and associated queries are potent instruments that enable the nesting of queries inside additional queries. A subquery refers to a query incorporated within the primary query and may be utilized in different sections of the SQL query, including the SELECT clause and the WHERE section. Subqueries offer a means to execute computations, filtering, or collection on a certain amount of data before the execution of the primary query. An illustrative scenario involves retrieving employees whose salaries exceed the mean salary of their respective departments. One possible approach to accomplish this task is to employ a subquery that computes the average wage for each division and subsequently contrasts this with the median wage of every worker in the primary query (Woods et al., 2014).

Correlated queries extend the functionality of subqueries by incorporating references to columns derived from the exterior query inside the subquery. The correlation above facilitates the subquery's dependence on the outcomes of the exterior query. Correlated searches are valuable for conducting row-by-row contrasts or filtering according to principles from the outside query. Subsequently, we shall examine the ubiquitous table expressions known as common table expressions (CTEs). Common table expressions (CTEs) are a type of short-term lead set that may be utilized within a query. They are particularly advantageous in situations where intricate and repeatable subqueries are necessary. Common table expressions (CTEs) enhance the comprehensibility and sustainability of code by enabling the definition of a designated temporary following table expression which can be invoked repeatedly in a query.

The initial step in utilizing a common table expression (CTE) involves its definition through the WITH clause, wherein the CTE's name and column definitions are specified. The common table expression (CTE) is subsequently alluded to within the primary query in a manner that resembles a conventional table or view. Common table expressions (CTEs) have the potential to enhance the efficiency of intricate queries by decomposing them into more comprehensible segments, thereby facilitating the reuse of code. An instance of utilizing a common table expression (CTE) is when there is necessary to identify the highest-selling commodities within every category. One may generate a common table expression (CTE) that employs sales volume to rank products within respective categories and subsequently merge the CTE alongside the primary query to obtain the intended outcomes (Olsen, 2000).

Recursive queries represent an advanced SQL methodology employed to query hierarchical data. Hierarchical information depicts connections among entities according to a hierarchical arrangement, such as those found in genealogy databases or organizational diagrams. Recursive queries facilitate the traversal of a hierarchy by enabling the navigation of parent-child connections data. To execute a recursive inquiry, it is customary to employ a common table conveying (CTE) that refers to its structure. The recursive component of the inquiry encompasses the primary inquiry seed, also referred to as the anchor member, and the recursive expression that specifies how the inquiry should advance by merging with the common table expression (CTE) itself. As mentioned, the procedure persists until a specified termination criterion is satisfied.

As an illustration, consider a tabular representation of a corporate structure featuring attributes such as employee identification number, name, and manager identification number. Formulating a recursive query to retrieve comprehensive information on employees and their interpersonal connections is possible. This query would commence at the highest level of the organizational hierarchy, namely the CEO, and proceed downwards through the lowest-level staff members.

To conclude, utilizing advanced SQL searching techniques offers potent means for modifying and finding data more intricately. Subqueries and associated queries facilitate the nesting of queries, thereby enabling intricate computations and filtration. Using common table expressions (CTEs) can improve the comprehensibility and adaptability of queries by generating provisional outcome sets. Recursive queries are highly useful in the context of searching structures of data that exhibit a hierarchical organization. Proficiency in advanced SQL techniques can enhance one's query abilities while allowing the efficient handling of intricate retrieval of information tasks.

5.8.1.1. Advanced Indexing

The indexing process is paramount in enhancing the efficiency and effectiveness of database management systems. Creating an organized data version facilitates efficient data extraction, enabling expedited access according to particular search criteria. The upcoming chapter will delve into diverse advanced indexed methodologies that have the potential to augment the efficiency of databases substantially. The present study will explore various indexing methods that can be employed to enhance system performance. Specifically, the study will examine the benefits of bitmap indices, full-text indexed along with search, and geographic indexed as applied to data related to geography (Li et al., 2005).

5.8.1.2. Indexing Strategies for Improved Performance

Indexing is a fundamental methodology employed in databases to enhance the expediency of data retrieval. B-trees and other conventional indexing methods are extensively employed and offer effective data retrieval in various contexts. Nevertheless, supplementary indexing techniques can enhance performance even further in the case of extensive databases that entail complex queries and information types (Habimana, 2015).

A strategy that can be employed is the utilization of combined indexes, which entail the establishment of an index on several columns as opposed to a solitary column. The relational database can effectively leverage the combined index to fulfill queries with multiple search criteria through this approach. Implementing this technique can significantly reduce the number of data accesses needed, yielding expedited execution of query durations.

An additional approach to indexing is the implementation of function-based indexes. The methodology generates an index by executing an operator or conveying on the dataset. Using function-based indexes can prove advantageous, especially in scenarios involving intricate data manipulations or computations. Through precomputation and indexing, the relational database efficiently retrieves the needed information without incurring the expenses associated with on-the-fly calculation.

5.8.1.3. Bitmap Indexes and Their Advantages

Bitmap indexing is a distinct methodology that can offer considerable performance advantages in specific situations. In contrast to conventional indices that retain value suggestions to the associated data, bitmap indices maintain a bitmap for every unique value in a given column. The bitmap utilizes individual bits to indicate the presence or absence of a particular value within a given row.

Bitmap indexes offer a notable benefit in effectively managing queries encompassing various criteria. The bitwise operations applied to the bitmaps are the relational database expeditiously ascertains the rows that meet the specified search parameters. The implementation of this technique has the potential to significantly enhance the speed of query execution, particularly in cases where intricate queries encompassing numerous predicates are involved.

Bitmap indices are highly appropriate for datasets that exhibit low cardinality, wherein the total amount of unique values in a given column is relatively diminutive compared with the overall number of rows. In instances of this nature, bitmap indexes possess the potential for significant compression, thereby reducing storage demands. Furthermore, bitmap indexes exhibit high efficiency in managing set operations, including union, connection, and distinction, rendering them appropriate for analytical inquiries and data warehousing contexts (Wu et al., 2008).

5.8.1.4. Full-Text Indexing and Search

Conventional indexing methods are predominantly centered on precise matches, rendering them less efficacious for textual data that necessitates keyword searches and using natural languages in query formulation. The limitation of inefficient searching inside text fields can be overcome by utilizing full-text indexed search methods, which enable the efficient retrieval of information using phrases or words.

Full-text indexing entails generating a database of textual information, such as items or documents, by examining the content and identifying pertinent terms. This index facilitates expedient searches based on keywords, thereby enabling prompt retrieval of relevant documents in response to user queries. To accomplish this task, full-text indexing employs stemming, tokenization, and stop-word elimination techniques to produce a condensed index framework.

Similar text analysis methods are employed to process the query when conducting a full-text search. The process involves matching the query terms with the indexed terms, following which the search engine generates a list of the most pertinent documents. The order of importance of these documents is determined by various factors such as frequency range, proximity, and significance ranking computation.

The utilization of full-text indexed and search methodologies is prevalent in diverse applications, such as archives of documents, content management systems, and search engines. Implementing these methods results in improved user experience and enhanced performance of applications that handle textual information, facilitating efficient written investigating.

5.8.1.5. Spatial Indexing and Geographic Data

Spatial searching is a distinct indexing methodology employed to preserve and access geographical information effectively. Using spatial data management systems facilitates the efficient processing of inquiries about spatial entities such as points, lines, and polygons. This capability empowers software applications to execute functions such as location-based searching, closeness analysis, and graphical representation of geographic information (Jones et al., 2004).

This frequently employed spatial indexing method utilizes a tree-based data structure to facilitate data indexing in multiple dimensions. The R-tree is a hierarchical data structure that arranges spatial entities in a tree-like form. Each node within the tree denotes a leaping geographical area, a group of entities. Utilizing a hierarchical structure facilitates expedient spatial search procedures, diminishing the number of entities necessitating scrutiny throughout processing queries.

Spatial indexing facilitates spatial inquiries such as range queries, closest neighbor inquiries, and spatial unions. The software offers efficient functionality for managing intricate spatial operations such as intersection, confinement, and separation computations. The operations above hold significant importance in applications of geographic information systems (GIS), navigational systems, and services that use location.

The significance of geographic information has risen across multiple fields, such as travel, urban planning, and ecological sciences. Consequently, spatial indexed has become an essential component of contemporary database systems. The tool's capacity to enhance the analysis of geographic queries renders it an invaluable tool for proficiently handling and evaluating geographic information.

To summarize, utilizing advanced indexed techniques is crucial in augmenting the efficiency of databases. Utilizing techniques that include composite indexes and function-based indices can enhance the efficiency of executing queries and facilitate intricate data transformations. Bitmap indexes offer benefits in efficiently managing various circumstances and set activities. Full-text indexing facilitates expedited searches based on keywords within textual data, whereas spatial indexing streamlines the handling of geographical data queries. Using sophisticated indexing methodologies, databases can enhance the speed and efficacy of data retrieval, ultimately improving the system's effectiveness.

5.8.2. Transactions and Concurrency Control

The proper management of transactions, along with control over concurrency, is of utmost importance in upholding data integrity and preserving an information system's coherence. This section will delve into the multifaceted components of deals and cooperation control. Specifically, it will examine the ACID characteristics of transactions, cooperation control techniques, including securing and MVCC, separation levels, and approaches for averting and handling deadlocks.

5.8.2.1. ACID Properties of Transactions

ACID is a condensed form of Atomicity, Consistency, and Isolation. The properties above establish the fundamental attributes of an agreement and guarantee its dependability and accuracy. The principle of atomicity ensures that an activity is regarded as an indivisible entity of operation. The statement implies that the transaction's modifications are either entirely stored in the database's structure or not. In the event of a transactional failure, the entirety of the transaction is reverted, resulting in the database retaining its original state.

Maintaining consistency guarantees that a given transaction results in the transition of the relational database from an initial in-line state to a final in-keeping state. The database is ensured to maintain its validity throughout the transaction by enforcing integrity limitations, such as uniqueness constraints or foreign key relationships. The concept of isolation pertains to the ability of concurrent transactions to execute simultaneously without interference. The implementation of isolation guarantees the absence of interference among transactions. It ensures that every transaction perceives a coherent database perspective, notwithstanding other transactions' concurrent modification of identical data. The attribute of durability ensures that the outcomes of a transaction remain intact and enduring even in the event of any subsequent system failures, thereby providing a guarantee of permanence. The alterations are retained in a persistent storage medium-sized, such as a hard drive, and can be retrieved during a system malfunction or power outage.

5.8.2.2. Concurrency Control Mechanisms: Locking and MVCC

Concurrency controls are utilized to manage scenarios where multiple transactions simultaneously have access to and alter identical data. Securing along with Multi-Version Concurrency Control are two frequently employed mechanisms. The locking mechanism is extensively employed to ensure data consistency by providing sole access to a particular resource. Lock acquisition can occur at varying levels, including a database, table, and row level. For an operation to gain access to a particular resource, it is necessary to obtain the corresponding lock. If a different transaction already holds a lock, the requester transactions may be required to wait or stop until the security key is released. By keeping several copies of a piece of information, MVCC, on the opposite hand, enables simultaneous viewing and modification of data by numerous transactions. A picture of the database's structure as it was at the time of the operation is shown for each transaction. Before they are committed, additional transactions aren't impacted by changes made by one. With this method, concurrency is increased, and explicit barring is unnecessary (Neumann et al., 2015).

5.8.2.3. Isolation Levels and Their Impact on Performance

The concept of isolation levels pertains to the extent of isolation among tandem transactions and the scope of visibility that modifications performed by a single transaction have for other transactions. Various isolation levels are available, such as Read Uncommitted, Serializable, Repeatable Read, Read Committed, or presenting a distinct proportion of multitasking.

The Read Uncommitted separation level is the least restrictive isolation level, allowing a transaction to access and read indifferent modifications made by other concurrent transactions. Although it offers superior concurrency, this approach compromises data uniformity. The Read Committed isolation level ensures that a transaction can solely access committed modifications carried out by other operations, thereby preventing the occurrence of dirty reads. Repeatable The Read operation guarantees that the identical query executed repetitively yields coherent outcomes in the context of a transaction, notwithstanding any alterations made to the data by subsequent transactions. The Serializable feature guarantees the utmost level of information uniformity by ensuring that operations happen in a manner that mimics serial execution. However, this feature may lead to reduced concurrency due to heightened locking (Larson et al., 2011).

The selection of the separation level is contingent upon the particular demands of the application in question. Elevated levels of isolation guarantee the uniformity of data. However, they may hurt cooperation and efficiency. The judicious selection of the suitable isolation level is crucial in achieving an optimal trade-off between maintaining consistent data and enhancing system performance.

5.8.2.4. Deadlocks and Deadlock Prevention Strategies

A state of deadlock arises in a system of concurrent transactions if multiple transactions are mutually blocked and indefinitely awaiting one another to relinquish resources. Deadlocks can cause a system to cease functioning and necessitate intervention for resolution. To avert deadlocks, diverse tactics can be implemented. A viable strategy involves the implementation of a resource-requesting protocol, wherein transactions are designed to solicit and relinquish resources in a pre-established sequence. As mentioned earlier, the action effectively eradicates the potential for circular waits, a prevalent instigator of deadlock occurrences. An additional approach involves implementing timeouts, whereby a transaction that fails to obtain an object within a designated period relinquishes its presently held materials and attempts to acquire them again later. Deadlock detection programs might be utilized to periodically examine the existence of deadlocks and implement suitable measures for resolving them.

Concurrency controls, such as locking along with MVCC, prevent impasses by regulating the acquisition of resources by deals. Deadlocks may be prevented or reduced by providing exclusive utilization of resources.

Incorporating transactions and cooperation control mechanisms is imperative for establishing a resilient and dependable database infrastructure. Comprehending the ACID characteristics of transactions, cooperation management techniques such as locking along with MVCC, separation levels, and techniques for preventing deadlocks is imperative for devising and administering database systems that exhibit superior performance. Transactions and cooperation control mechanisms are crucial for efficiently operating databases in a multi-user and concurrent environment. These mechanisms ensure the accuracy of data and uniformity and avoid deadlocks.

SUMMARY

This chapter delves into various aspects of managing data, starting with relational databases (RDBMS). It begins by defining relational databases and discussing their characteristics, such as organizing data into tables, rows, and columns. Structured Query Language (SQL) is then introduced as a crucial tool for interacting with RDBMS, covering its data types, operators, and expressions, as well as DDL and DML statements for database definition and manipulation.

Normalization and database design are highlighted as essential practices for ensuring data integrity and efficiency. This section explores functional dependencies, normalization forms (1NF, 2NF, 3NF), denormalization, and entity-relationship modeling.

Query optimization and performance tuning are vital for improving database efficiency, ensuring that queries run quickly and effectively. The chapter also introduces NoSQL databases, discussing their evolution, characteristics, advantages, and when to choose them over RDBMS. Different types of NoSQL databases are explored, along with data modeling differences, aggregation, denormalization, schema-less design, and consistency models.

Scalability and performance considerations are crucial in both RDBMS and NoSQL databases, with challenges such as horizontal scaling, sharding, and trade-offs discussed. The CAP theorem is introduced to explain the trade-offs in distributed systems. Performance tuning techniques, including caching, indexing, and partitioning, are also covered.

Finally, advanced SQL techniques are presented, offering insights into more sophisticated ways of querying, and manipulating data within RDBMS.

Overall, this chapter provides a comprehensive overview of fundamental concepts in data management, from relational databases and SQL to NoSQL databases, normalization, database design, query optimization, and performance tuning. It equips readers with the knowledge necessary to effectively manage data in various environments and make informed decisions about database technologies and practices.

REVIEW QUESTIONS

1. What is the purpose of SQL in relational databases?
2. Name two types of SQL statements.
3. Explain the importance of normalization in database design.
4. What are the different normalization forms?

MULTIPLE CHOICE QUESTIONS

1. **Which of the following best describes the term "data management"?**
   a. Storing data in physical files and folders.
   b. Organizing data in a structured manner for efficient use and retrieval.
   c. Creating complex data visualizations.
   d. Deleting obsolete data from the system.
2. **What is the primary objective of data normalization in database management?**
   a. Maximizing data redundancy.
   c. Minimizing data consistency.
   d. Reducing data duplication and anomalies.
   e. Increasing data complexity.
3. **Which of the following statements best describes the concept of a "database schema"?**
   a. A graphical representation of data relationships.
   b. A set of rules defining data types and constraints in a database.
   c. A programming language used for database management.
   d. A physical storage location for database files.
4. **What role does a Data Dictionary serve in data management?**
   a. It is used to encrypt sensitive data in the database.
   b. It provides a detailed description of data elements and their meanings.
   c. It is a tool for generating random data for testing purposes.
   d. It stores backup copies of the database.
5. **Which of the following is NOT a common data manipulation operation in database management?**
   a. Inserting new records into a database table.
   b. Deleting existing records from a database table.
   c. Modifying data values within a database table.
   d. Backing up the entire database to an external drive.

Answers to Multiple Choice Questions

1. (b); 2. (c); 3. (b); 4. (b); 5. (d);

REFERENCES

1. Abbas, Q., Shafiq, H., Ahmad, I., & Tharanidharan, S., (2016). Concurrency control in distributed database system. In: *2016 International Conference on Computer Communication and Informatics (ICCCI)* (pp. 1–4). IEEE.

2. Abdelhafiz, B. M., & Elhadef, M., (2021). Sharding database for fault tolerance and scalability of data. In: *2021 2nd International Conference on Computation, Automation and Knowledge Management (ICCAKM)* (pp. 17–24). IEEE.
3. Aboutorabi[a], S. H., Rezapour, M., Moradi, M., & Ghadiri, N., (2015). Performance evaluation of SQL and MongoDB databases for big e-commerce data. In: *2015 International Symposium on Computer Science and Software Engineering (CSSE)* (pp. 1–7). IEEE.
4. Armbrust, M., Xin, R. S., Lian, C., Huai, Y., Liu, D., Bradley, J. K., & Zaharia, M., (2015). Spark SQL: Relational data processing in spark. In: *Proceedings of the 2015 ACM SIGMOD International Conference on Management of Data* (pp. 1383–1394).
5. Atzeni, P., Bugiotti, F., Cabibbo, L., & Torlone, R., (2020). Data modeling in the NoSQL world. *Computer Standards & Interfaces, 67*, 103149.
6. Bahmani, A. H., Naghibzadeh, M., & Bahmani, B., (2008). Automatic database normalization and primary key generation. In: *2008 Canadian Conference on Electrical and Computer Engineering* (pp. 000011–000016). IEEE.
7. Banerjee, S., & Sarkar, A., (2016). Modeling NoSQL databases: From conceptual to logical level design. In: *3rd International Conference Applications and Innovations in Mobile Computing (AIMoC 2016)* (pp. 10–12). Kolkata, India.
8. Barghouti, N. S., & Kaiser, G. E., (1991). Concurrency control in advanced database applications. *ACM Computing Surveys (CSUR), 23*(3), 269–317.
9. Berry, M. A., & Linoff, G. S., (2000). Mastering data mining: The art and science of customer relationship management. *Industrial Management & Data Systems, 100*(5), 245–246.
10. Dhabe, P. S., Patwardhan, M. S., Deshpande, A. A., Dhore, M. L., Barbadekar, B. V., & Abhyankar, H. K., (2010). Articulated entity relationship (AER) diagram for complete automation of relational database normalization. *International Journal of Database Management Systems, 2*(2), 84–100.
11. Dhulavvagol, P. M., & Totad, S. G., (2023). Performance enhancement of distributed system using HDFS federation and sharding. *Procedia Computer Science, 218*, 2830–2841.
12. Di Sanzo, P., Ciciani, B., Quaglia, F., & Romano, P., (2008). A performance model of multi-version concurrency control. In: *2008 IEEE International Symposium on Modeling, Analysis and Simulation of Computers and Telecommunication Systems* (pp. 1–10). IEEE.
13. Diack, B. W., Ndiaye, S., & Slimani, Y., (2013). CAP theorem between claims and misunderstandings: What is to be sacrificed. *International Journal of Advanced Science and Technology, 56*, 1–12.
14. Diogo, M., Cabral, B., & Bernardino, J., (2019). Consistency models of NoSQL databases. *Future Internet, 11*(2), 43.
15. Dongare, Y. V., Dhabe, P. S., & Deshmukh, S. V., (2011). *RDBNorma: A Semi-Automated Tool for Relational Database Schema Normalization up to Third Normal Form*. arXiv preprint arXiv:1103.0633.

16. Eisenberg, A., & Melton, J., (2002). SQL/XML is making good progress. *ACM Sigmod Record, 31*(2), 101–108.

17. Hashim, F., Shuaib, K., & Zaki, N., (2022). Sharding for scalable blockchain networks. *SN Computer Science, 4*(1), 2.

18. Helland, P., (2019). The trade-offs between write and read. *Communications of the ACM, 62*(11), 111–113.

19. Hillenbrand, A., Störl, U., Levchenko, M., Nabiyev, S., & Klettke, M., (2020). Towards self-adapting data migration in the context of schema evolution in NoSQL databases. In: *2020 IEEE 36th International Conference on Data Engineering Workshops (ICDEW)* (pp. 133–138). IEEE.

20. Hsieh, M. J., Chang, C. R., Ho, L. Y., Wu, J. J., & Liu, P., (2011). SQLMR: A scalable database management system for cloud computing. In: *2011 International Conference on Parallel Processing* (pp. 315–324). IEEE.

21. Hussain, T., Shamail, S., & Awais, M. M., (2003). Eliminating process of normalization in relational database design. In: *7th International Multi Topic Conference, 2003; INMIC 2003* (pp. 408–413). IEEE.

22. Imieli⊠ski, T., & Lipski, Jr. W., (1984). Incomplete information in relational databases. *Journal of the ACM (JACM), 31*(4), 761–791.

23. Jahan, A., & Edwards, K. L., (2015). A state-of-the-art survey on the influence of normalization techniques in ranking: Improving the materials selection process in engineering design. *Materials & Design (1980–2015), 65*, 335–342.

24. Jones, C. B., Abdelmoty, A. I., Finch, D., Fu, G., & Vaid, S., (2004). The SPIRIT spatial search engine: Architecture, ontologies, and spatial indexing. In: *Geographic Information Science: Third International Conference, GIScience 2004, Adelphi, MD, USA, Proceedings 3* (pp. 125–139). Springer Berlin Heidelberg.

25. Kamatkar, S. J., Kamble, A., Viloria, A., Hernández-Fernandez, L., & Cali, E. G., (2018). Database performance tuning and query optimization. In: *Data Mining and Big Data: Third International Conference, DMBD 2018, Shanghai, China, Proceedings 3* (pp. 3–11). Springer International Publishing.

26. Khan, W., Kumar, T., Zhang, C., Raj, K., Roy, A. M., & Luo, B., (2023). SQL and NoSQL database software architecture performance analysis and assessments—A systematic literature review. *Big Data and Cognitive Computing, 7*(2), 97.

27. Köhler, H., & Link, S., (2016). SQL schema design: Foundations, normal forms, and normalization. In: *Proceedings of the 2016 International Conference on Management of Data* (pp. 267–279).

28. Koltsidas, I., & Viglas, S. D., (2011). Data management over flash memory. In: *Proceedings of the 2011 ACM SIGMOD International Conference on Management of Data* (pp. 1209–1212).

29. Koonce, D., Huang, L., & Judd, R., (1998). EQL an express query language. *Computers & Industrial Engineering, 35*(1, 2), 271–274.

30. Kulkarni, K., & Michels, J. E., (2012). Temporal features in SQL: 2011. *ACM Sigmod Record, 41*(3), 34–43.

31. Kumar, K. S., & Mohanavalli, S., (2017). A performance comparison of document oriented NoSQL databases. In: *2017 International Conference on Computer, Communication and Signal Processing (ICCCSP)* (pp. 1–6). IEEE.

32. Kunda, D., & Phiri, H., (2017). A comparative study of NoSQL and relational database. *Zambia ICT Journal, 1*(1), 1–4.

33. Kung, H. J., & Tung, H. L., (2006). *A Web-Based Tool to Enhance Teaching/Learning Database* Normalization (Vol. 1, No. 1, pp. 1–20).

34. Li, X., Bian, F., Zhang, H., Diot, C., Govindan, R., Hong, W. H., & Lannaccone, G., (2005). Advanced indexing techniques for wide-area network monitoring. In: *21st International Conference on Data Engineering Workshops (ICDEW'05)* (pp. 1184–1184). IEEE.

35. Liu, Z. H., Hammerschmidt, B., & McMahon, D., (2014). JSON data management: Supporting schema-less development in RDBMS. In: *Proceedings of the 2014 ACM SIGMOD International Conference on Management of Data* (pp. 1247–1258).

36. Lourenço, J. R., Cabral, B., Carreiro, P., Vieira, M., & Bernardino, J., (2015). Choosing the right NoSQL database for the job: A quality attribute evaluation. *Journal of Big Data, 2*(1), 1–26.

37. Mapanga, I., & Kadebu, P., (2013). Database management systems: A NoSQL analysis. *International Journal of Modern Communication Technologies & Research (IJMCTR), 1*, 12–18.

38. Mason, R. T., (2015). NoSQL databases and data modeling techniques for a document-oriented NoSQL database. In: *Proceedings of Informing Science & IT Education Conference (In SITE)* (Vol. 3, No. 4, pp. 259–268).

39. McClure, R. A., & Krüger, I. H., (2005). SQL DOM: Compile time checking of dynamic SQL statements. In: *Proceedings of the 27th International Conference on Software Engineering* (pp. 88–96).

40. Melnik, S., Raghavan, S., Yang, B., & Garcia-Molina, H., (2001). Building a distributed full-text index for the web. In: *Proceedings of the 10th International Conference on World Wide Web* (pp. 396–406).

41. Melton, J., Michels, J. E., Josifovski, V., Kulkarni, K., & Schwarz, P., (2002). SQL/MED: A status report. *ACM SIGMOD Record, 31*(3), 81–89.

42. Mishra, P., & Eich, M. H., (1992). Join processing in relational databases. *ACM Computing Surveys (CSUR), 24*(1), 63–113.

43. Mohamed, M. A., Altrafi, O. G., & Ismail, M. O., (2014). Relational vs. NoSQL databases: A survey. *International Journal of Computer and Information Technology, 3*(3), 598–601.

44. Moniruzzaman, A. B. M., & Hossain, S. A., (2013). *NoSQL Database: New Era of Databases for Big Data Analytics-Classification, Characteristics, and Comparison.* arXiv preprint arXiv:1307.0191.

45. Nayak, A., Poriya, A., & Poojary, D., (2013). Type of NOSQL databases and its comparison with relational databases. *International Journal of Applied Information Systems, 5*(4), 16–19.

46. Neumann, T., Mühlbauer, T., & Kemper, A., (2015). Fast serializable multi-version concurrency control for main-memory database systems. In: *Proceedings of the 2015 ACM SIGMOD International Conference on Management of Data* (pp. 677–689).

47. Olsen, D. H., (2000). Accounting database design and SQL implementation revisited. *Review of Business Information Systems (RBIS), 4*(2), 53–68.

48. Oussous, A., Benjelloun, F. Z., Lahcen, A. A., & Belfkih, S., (2013). Comparison and classification of NoSQL databases for big data. *International Journal of Database Theory and Application, 6*(4.2013).

49. Pandey, V., Kipf, A., Neumann, T., & Kemper, A., (2018). How good are modern spatial analytics systems? *Proceedings of the VLDB Endowment, 11*(11), 1661–1673.

50. Parsons, R. G., Dale, A. G., & Yurkanan, C. V., (1974). Data manipulation language requirements for database management systems. *The Computer Journal, 17*(2), 99–103.

51. Rivero, C., & Ruiz, D., (2002). An advanced query capability description framework implementation. In: *International Conference on Enterprise Information System* (pp. 1–8). IEEE.

52. Rys, M., (2005). XML and relational database management systems: Inside Microsoft® SQL Server™ 2005. In: *Proceedings of the 2005 ACM SIGMOD International Conference on Management of Data* (pp. 958–962).

53. Sahatqija, K., Ajdari, J., Zenuni, X., Raufi, B., & Ismaili, F., (2018). Comparison between relational and NOSQL databases. In: *2018 41st International Convention on Information and Communication Technology, Electronics, and Microelectronics (MIPRO)* (pp. 0216–0221). IEEE.

54. Sahoo, S. S., Halb, W., Hellmann, S., Idehen, K., Thibodeau, Jr. T., Auer, S., & Ezzat, A., (2009). A survey of current approaches for mapping of relational databases to RDF. *W3C RDB2RDF Incubator Group Report, 1*, 113–130.

55. Sallans, A., & Lake, S., (2014). Data management assessment and planning tools. *Research Data Management: Practical Strategies for Information Professionals*, 87–107.

56. Sanders, G. L., & Shin, S., (2001). Denormalization effects on performance of RDBMS. In: *Proceedings of the 34th Annual Hawaii International Conference on System Sciences* (pp. 9-pp). IEEE.

57. Santos, M. Y., & Costa, C., (2016). Data models in NoSQL databases for big data contexts. In: *Data Mining and Big Data: First International Conference, DMBD 2016, Bali, Indonesia; Proceedings 1* (pp. 475–485). Springer International Publishing.

58. Sareen, P., & Kumar, P., (2015). NoSQL database and its comparison with SQL database. *International Journal of Computer Science & Communication Networks, 5*(5), 293–298.

59. Scherzinger, S., & Sidortschuck, S., (2020). An empirical study on the design and evolution of NoSQL database schemas. In: *Conceptual Modeling: 39th International Conference, ER 2020, Vienna, Austria, Proceedings 39* (pp. 441–455). Springer International Publishing.

60. Schiefer, K. B., & Valentin, G., (1999). DB2 universal database performance tuning. *IEEE Data Eng. Bull., 22*(2), 12–19.

61. Schnaitter, K., Abiteboul, S., Milo, T., & Polyzotis, N., (2006). Colt: Continuous on-line tuning. In: *Proceedings of the 2006 ACM SIGMOD International Conference on Management of Data* (pp. 793–795).

62. Seshadri, P., & Paskin, M., (1997). PREDATOR: An OR-DBMS with enhanced data types. *ACM SIGMOD Record, 26*(2), 568–571.

63. Setiyadi, D., (2021). Database system development life cycle (DSDLC) on system libraries for data manipulation language (DML) using SQL Server 2008. *Jurnal Mantik, 5*(2), 1065–1071.

64. Sharma, V., & Dave, M., (2012). SQL and NoSQL databases. *International Journal of Advanced Research in Computer Science and Software Engineering, 2*(8).

65. Shin, S. K., & Sanders, G. L., (2006). Denormalization strategies for data retrieval from data warehouses. *Decision Support Systems, 42*(1), 267–282.

66. Shoval, P., & Even-Chaime, M., (1987). Database schema design: An experimental comparison between normalization and information analysis. *ACM SIGMIS Database: The Database* for *Advances in Information Systems, 18*(3), 30–39.

67. Sidi, E., El, M., & Amin, E., (2016). Star schema advantages on data warehouse: Using bitmap index and partitioned fact tables. *International Journal of Computer Applications, 134*(13), 11–13.

68. Swaminathan, S. N., & Elmasri, R., (2016). Quantitative analysis of scalable NoSQL databases. In: *2016 IEEE International Congress on Big Data (BigData Congress)* (pp. 323–326). IEEE.

69. Tang, E., & Fan, Y., (2016). Performance comparison between five NoSQL databases. In: *2016 7th International Conference on Cloud Computing and Big Data (CCBD)* (pp. 105–109). IEEE.

70. Tang, F., You, I., Yu, S., Wang, C. L., Guo, M., & Liu, W., (2012). An efficient deadlock prevention approach for service oriented transaction processing. *Computers & Mathematics with Applications, 63*(2), 458–468.

71. Teorey, T. J., Yang, D., & Fry, J. P., (1986). A logical design methodology for relational databases using the extended entity-relationship model. *ACM Computing Surveys (CSUR), 18*(2), 197–222.

72. Amornchewin, R. (2018). The development of sql language skills in data definition and data manipulation languages using exercises with Quizizz for students' learning engagement. Indonesian Journal of Informatics Education, 2(2), 85-90.

73. Tiffany, R., (2003). Data manipulation language. In: *SQL Server CE Database Development with the. NET Compact Framework* (pp. 139–179). Berkeley, CA: A Press.

74. Truica, C. O., Boicea, A., & Trifan, I., (2013). CRUD operations in MongoDB. In: *2013 International Conference on Advanced Computer Science and Electronics Information (ICACSEI 2013)* (pp. 347–350). Atlantis Press.

75. Van, D. B. H., Van, D. L. R., & Visser, J., (2007). Quality assessment for embedded SQL. In: *Seventh IEEE International Working Conference on Source Code Analysis and Manipulation (SCAM 2007)* (pp. 163–170). IEEE.

76. Vera, H., Boaventura, W., Holanda, M., Guimaraes, V., & Hondo, F., (2015). Data modeling for NoSQL document-oriented databases. In: *CEUR Workshop Proceedings* (Vol. 1478, pp. 129–135).

77. Vera-Olivera, H., Guo, R., Huacarpuma, R. C., Da Silva, A. P. B., Mariano, A. M., & Holanda, M., (2021). Data modeling and NoSQL databases-a systematic mapping review. *ACM Computing Surveys (CSUR), 54*(6), 1–26.

78. Vyverman, M., De Baets, B., Fack, V., & Dawyndt, P., (2012). Prospects and limitations of full-text index structures in genome analysis. *Nucleic Acids Research, 40*(15), 6993–7015.

79. Wells, G., & Wells, G., (2001). DML: Inserting, updating, and deleting data. *Code Centric: T-SQL Programming with Stored Procedures and Triggers,* 133–148.

80. Woods, L., István, Z., & Alonso, G., (2014). Ibex: An intelligent storage engine with support for advanced SQL offloading. *Proceedings of the VLDB Endowment, 7*(11), 963–974.

81. Wu, K., Otoo, E. J., & Shoshani, A., (2001). A performance comparison of bitmap indexes. In: *Proceedings of the Tenth International Conference on Information and Knowledge Management* (pp. 559–561).

82. Wu, K., Stockinger, K., & Shoshani, A., (2008). Breaking the curse of cardinality on bitmap indexes. In: *Scientific and Statistical Database Management: 20th International Conference, SSDBM 2008, Hong Kong, China, 2008 Proceedings 20* (pp. 348–365). Springer Berlin Heidelberg.

83. Wu, M. C., & Buchmann, A. P., (1998). Encoded bitmap indexing for data warehouses. In: *Proceedings 14th International Conference on Data Engineering* (pp. 220–230). IEEE.

84. Xie, C., Su, C., Littley, C., Alvisi, L., Kapritsos, M., & Wang, Y., (2015). High-performance ACID via modular concurrency control. In: *Proceedings of the 25th Symposium on Operating Systems Principles* (pp. 279–294).

85. Yalamanchi, A., Srinivasan, J., & Gawlick, D., (2003). *Managing Expressions as Data in Relational Database Systems*. In CIDR.

86. Yang, X., Procopiuc, C. M., & Srivastava, D., (2009). Summarizing relational databases. *Proceedings of the VLDB Endowment, 2*(1), 634–645.

87. Zaki, A. K., (2014). NoSQL databases: New millennium database for big data, big users, cloud computing and its security challenges. *International Journal of Research in Engineering and Technology (IJRET), 3*(15), 403–409.

88. Zhang, X., Song, W., & Liu, L., (2014). An implementation approach to store GIS spatial data on NoSQL database. In: *2014 22nd International Conference on Geoinformatics* (pp. 1–5). IEEE.

89. Zhou, J., Bruno, N., & Lin, W., (2012). Advanced partitioning techniques for massively distributed computation. In: *Proceedings of the 2012 ACM SIGMOD International Conference on Management of Data* (pp. 13–24).

90. Zhu, Q., Gong, J., & Zhang, Y., (2007). An efficient 3D R-tree spatial index method for virtual geographic environments. *ISPRS Journal of Photogrammetry and Remote Sensing, 62*(3), 217–224.

CHAPTER

6

Relational Database Constraints and Relational Data Model

LEARNING OBJECTIVES

After studying this chapter, you will be able to:

- The importance of relational model concepts
- The different between relational model constraints and relational database schemes
- Benefits of Relational Database Constraints
- Update Operations, Transactions, and Deal with Constraint Violations

"Relational database constraints and the relational data model are the cornerstones of data integrity and precision, ensuring that every piece of information finds its rightful place in the digital world."

INTRODUCTORY EXAMPLE

Imagine you are tasked with designing a database system for a library. In this library, you need to keep track of various aspects of the books, such as their titles, authors, publication dates, and availability. To ensure that the data in your database is accurate, consistent, and meaningful, you decide to apply the principles of the relational data model and employ various relational database constraints.

One of the constraints you implement is the "Unique Constraint." This constraint ensures that each book title is unique in the database, preventing the accidental insertion of duplicate book titles. For instance, if you try to add a new book with the title "The Catcher in the Rye" when there's already a record for this book, the database system will reject the insertion, maintaining data integrity.

Another important constraint you utilize is the "Foreign Key Constraint." To keep track of the relationship between books and their authors, you create two separate tables: one for books and another for authors. By using foreign keys, you establish a link between these tables, ensuring that each book is associated with a valid author from the author table. If someone tries to delete an author who has books associated with them, the foreign key constraint prevents it, preventing orphaned records and maintaining referential integrity.

Lastly, you implement a "Check Constraint" to ensure that the publication date of a book is within a reasonable range, preventing the insertion of books with unrealistic publication dates, such as those in the future or too far in the past.

These relational database constraints, along with the relational data model, allow you to create a structured and reliable database for the library, ensuring that the data remains consistent, accurate, and well-organized as the library continues to manage its collection of books. In this example, you can see how the principles of the relational data model and constraints play a crucial role in database design and management.

UNIT INTRODUCTION

A relational data model constitutes a fundamental database management system (DBMS) concept. Utilizing a relational database offers a systematic and methodical approach to storing and administrating data. Edgar F. Codd introduced the relational model during the 1970s, subsequently gaining widespread adoption as the predominant data model in the industry (Demuth & Hussmann, 1999) (Figure 6.1).

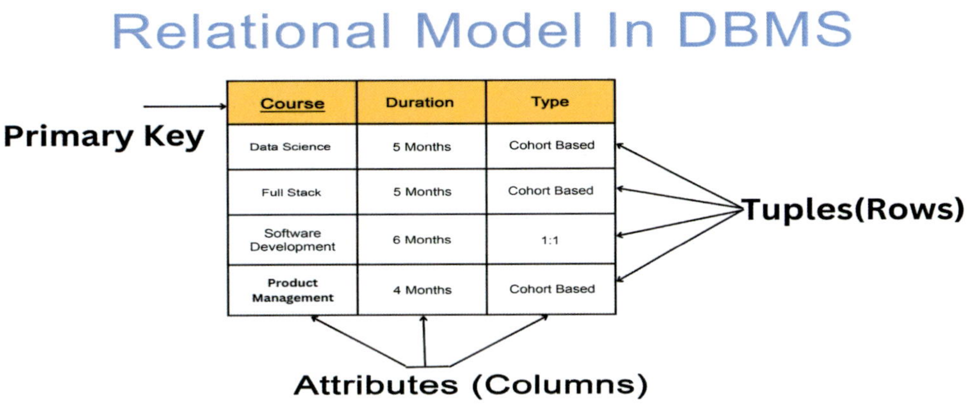

Figure 6.1. *Relational model in DBMS.*

Tables comprising rows and columns form the fundamental structure of relational data model. In context of tabular data, it can be observed that every row corresponds to a distinct entity or record. In contrast, each column pertains to an attribute or characteristic associated with that entity. As an illustration, within a database containing customer information, a table could contain various columns, including but not limited to "customer_id," "name," "email," and "phone_number" (Giese, 2022).

The relational data model is advantageous because it can establish connections between tables. Establishing relationships within a table is facilitated using keys, which serve as distinctive identifiers. The relational model typically employs two distinct categories of keys: primary and foreign.

A fundamental concept in database design is the primary key, which refers to a singular column or a composite of columns that distinguishes each record within a given table. Implementing a unique identifier for each record in a table guarantees its distinctiveness and facilitates the effective retrieval and manipulation of data. As an illustration, the column denoted as "employee_id" may be assigned as the primary key within a tabular representation of staff members. Foreign keys establish inter-table relationships by referencing the primary key of another table. Referential integrity is enforced through their utilization, guaranteeing data consistency and accuracy in interrelated tables. In the context of relational databases, it is possible to establish a relationship between two tables, such as orders and customers, by utilizing a foreign key. Specifically, "employee_id" column in orders table can be designated as foreign key, which references primary key "employee_id" in customers' table.

A relational data model encompasses a collection of limitations and regulations, known as constraints, which govern the data housed within a database and the notion of keys. The implementation of constraints serves the purpose of upholding the integrity and consistency of data by obstructing the insertion of data that is deemed invalid or inconsistent. Various constraints are frequently employed in relational databases:

1. Entity Integrity Constraint: This restriction guarantees that the primary key attribute of a given table possesses a distinct and non-null value. The primary key attribute ensures the unique identification of each entity within a table and prohibits the absence or ambiguity of its corresponding value.
2. Referential Integrity Constraint: The enforcement of the relationship between tables is achieved using foreign keys as a constraint. The foreign key constraint guarantees that the values contained within the column designated as a foreign key in a given table correspond to values of a primary key in referenced table. The limitation mentioned above impedes the formation of isolated records and upholds the integrity of the data (Lin, 1988).
3. Domain Constraint: It is a specification that establishes the permissible scope of values for a given column. The column's data type, length, format, and other attributes are specified by it. For instance, a column categorized as an "integer" might feature a domain constraint that restricts the permissible values to a particular range.
4. Key Constraint: A crucial limitation guarantees that the values in particular group or column maintain uniqueness within given table. Implementing a mechanism that prohibits the insertion of redundant values and guarantees the fulfillment of the primary key constraint (He & Naughton, 2008).
5. Check Constraint: It is a logical expression that specifies a condition that must be satisfied by the data stored in a particular column or a group of columns. This feature facilitates the implementation of intricate data validation mechanisms that surpass the basic requirements of ensuring uniqueness or non-nullability. A check constraint can be employed to guarantee that a specific column representing an individual's age comprises values greater than zero and less than 150.
6. Nullability Constraint: This restriction dictates whether a given column can accommodate null values. In database management, a "not null" column is restricted from containing any missing or undefined values. In contrast, a column designated as "null" permits the non-existence of a value.
7. Integrity Constraint: These refer to regulations that impose particular business rules or demands on the data. The database architect establishes the limitations in accordance with the particular requirements of the entity. An instance of an integrity constraint could entail that the remuneration allocated to an employee must not possess a negative value.

The imposition of these limitations by the relational model serves to safeguard the precision, coherence, and dependability of the information housed within a given database. In the event of a constraint violation, the database management system (DBMS) will impede the operation that resulted in the violation, be it an insertion, update, or deletion of a record (Sumathi & Esakkirajan, 2007) (Figure 6.2).

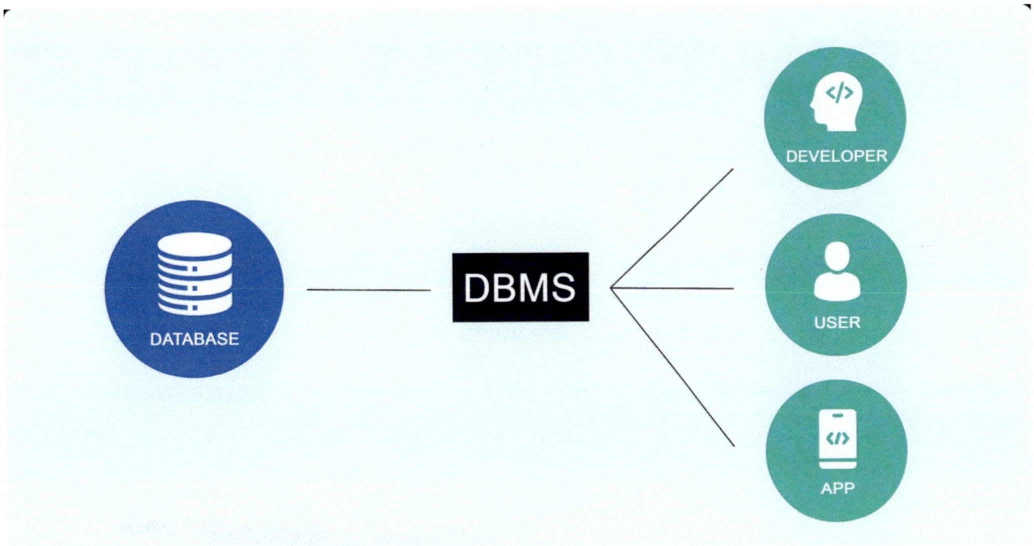

Figure 6.2. *Database management system (DBMS).*

Relational database management systems offer means to establish and implement these limitations. Developers can define table constraints by utilizing SQL (Structured Query Language) statements. The database management system (DBMS) automatically verifies and implements the constraints while performing data manipulation operations (Halpin & Morgan, 2010).

6.1. RELATIONAL MODEL CONCEPTS

Learning Objectives

At the end of this section, readers will be able to:

- Explain the fundamental principles of the relational model in database management.
- Discuss the importance of data integrity and constraints in the context of the relational model.
- Describe the key components of a relational database, including tables, rows, and columns.

The database is represented by a collection of relations in the relational model. In casual setting, it's noticeable that each relationship exhibits similarities to a value table or, to some extent, a record flat file. The term "flat file" is derived from the characteristic feature of its constituent records, which exhibit a simple and sequential format. The collection of records exhibits similarities to the depiction of the fundamental relational model.

When relation is conceptualized as tabular arrangement of values, each row within table denotes set of interrelated data values. The factual representation known as a row in a database often correlates to an object or connection in the real world. Terminology of table and its constituent columns facilitates the comprehension of the signification of the data contained in each row. The nomenclature of the columns, namely Name, Class, Student_number, & Major, delineate how data values in each row are to be comprehended, contingent upon the specific column in which the value is situated. Each element within a given column possesses an identical data type. In formal relational model context, tuple is term used to refer to a row, while an attribute is a term used to describe a column header.

Additionally, a relation is the term used to denote a table. The domain of possible values represents data type that characterizes types of values which may be present in each column. The following terms, namely domain, tuple, attribute, and relation, shall be defined formally.

6.1.1. Domains, Relations, Tuples, and Attributes

In computer science, domain D refers to collection of fundamental and indivisible values. The term "atomic" refers to the indivisibility of each value within the domain in the context of the formal relational model. A prevalent approach to defining a domain involves specifying a particular data type from where constituent domain's data values are derived. Assigning name to domain can be advantageous as it aids in comprehending its values. The following are domains examples:

1 Usa_phone_numbers: A collection of 10-digit telephone numbers deemed legitimate within jurisdiction of United States.

2 Local_phone_numbers: This refers to collection of telephone numbers comprising seven digits that are deemed valid within a specific geographic region code in USA. The employment of local area phone numbers is swiftly becoming obsolete and being supplanted by traditional 10-digit phone numbers.

3 Social_security_numbers: A collection of legitimate Social Security numbers consisting of 9 digits. Social Security Number (SSN) is distinctive alphanumeric identifier allocated to individuals in United States for employment, taxation, and benefits (Figure 6.3).

4 Names: A collection of character sequences that denote the appellations of individuals.

5 Grade_point_averages: Feasible numerical outcomes for calculated grade point averages are restricted to real numbers within the range of 0 to 4.

Figure 6.3. *Image of social security number (SSN).*

6 Employee_ages: The permissible range for the age of employees in a company is limited to integer values falling within the interval of 15 to 80.

7 Academic_department_names: A assemblage of nomenclatures for academic departments within a university, encompassing disciplines including Economics, Computer Science, and Physics.

8 Academic_department_codes: This is a compilation of academic department codes, encompassing designations such as 'CS,' 'ECON,' and 'PHYS.'

Those mentioned above are referred to as logical definitions of domains. Each domain is associated with a specified data type or format. One possible declaration for data type of domain "Usa_phone_numbers" is a character string which conforms to format of (ddd)ddd-dddd, where each character in the string represents a decimal digit and initial three digits correspond to legitimate telephone area code. Employee_ ages variable is classified as an integer data type with values between 15 and 80. The data type assigned to Academic_ department_names comprise a collection of character strings which accurately represent legitimate department names. Domain is assigned nomenclature, a specific data category, and a structure. Supplementary details about the interpretation of domain values may be provided. For instance, a numerical domain such as Person_weights ought to include corresponding units of measurement, such as kgs or lbs. The structure of a relation schema, denoted as $R(A_1, A_2, \ldots, A_n)$, comprises a name for the relation, R, and set of attributes, $A_1, A_2, \ldots, A_n$. In the relation schema R, each attribute Ai denotes a role fulfilled by a domain D. The domain of Ai is referred to as D and is symbolized by dom(Ai). A relation schema is a formal representation used to describe the structure of relation. The relation itself is identified by the name R. Numerical value denoting the number of attributes, represented by the symbol 'n,' within a relation schema is commonly referred to as the degree or arity of a relation. A septenary relation about the domain of university students would encompass seven distinct attributes that delineate the characteristics of each student. The following text is presented below (Codd, 1979):

STUDENT(Name: string, Ssn: string, Home_phone: string, Address: string, Office_phone: string, Age: integer, Gpa: real)

The STUDENT entity represents a subject in the relational model and consists of seven attributes. Each attribute can be assigned a specific data type:

- Name: string
- Ssn: string
- Home_phone: string
- Address: string
- Office_phone: string
- Age: integer
- Gpa: real

To define the domains for each attribute, we can map them to predefined types:

- dom(Name) = Names
- dom(Ssn) = Social_security_numbers
- dom(Home_phone) = USA_phone_numbers3
- dom(Address) = Addresses
- dom(Office_phone) = USA_phone_numbers
- dom(Age) = Integers
- dom(Gpa) = Grade_point_averages (with greater precision)

Based on the description, the attributes within the STUDENT relation can be identified by their position:

- Name is the 1st attribute of the STUDENT relation.
- Ssn is the 2nd attribute of STUDENT relation.
- Home_phone is 3rd attribute of the STUDENT relation.
- Address is 4th attribute of the STUDENT relation.
- Office_phone is fifth attribute of STUDENT relation.
- Age is the sixth attribute of the STUDENT relation.
- Gpa is the seventh attribute of STUDENT relation.

This provides a clearer understanding of the characteristics and placement of the attributes within the STUDENT relation schema (Tansel, 1986).

A set of n-tuples defined by the symbol r(R), where $R(A_1, A_2, \ldots, A_n)$ is relation schema, is referred to as a "relation" (or "relation state"). This set is represented as $r = \{t_1, t_2, \ldots, t_m\}$. Every n-tuple, denoted as t, represents a sequentially arranged list of n values $t = <v_1, v_2, \ldots, v_n>$. Each value vi, where vi, $1 \leq i \leq n$, is a member of dom(Ai) or is a unique NULL value. i^{th} element within the tuple t, denoting attribute Ai, is commonly denoted as t[Ai] or t.Ai (alternatively, t[i] if positional notation is employed). A concepts of relation intention and relation extension are frequently employed in schema R and relation state r(R), respectively (Codd, 1971).

Every tuple within relation denotes distinct student entity or object. Relation is represented in tabular form, wherein every tuple is represented as row, and every attribute is denoted by column header that signifies the function or meaning of values contained in particular column. The presence of NULL values in a STUDENT tuple indicates that certain attributes either have an unknown value or don't exist for that specific person.

Relation definition can be expressed more rigorously by utilizing concepts from set theory, as follows.

The concept of a relation, denoted as r(R), is a mathematical construct that represents a relation state. It corresponds to a relation with a degree of n, defined on domains A_1, A_2, ..., A_n. This relation is essentially a subset of the Cartesian product (represented by the symbol '×') of the domains that define R:

$$r(R) \subseteq (\text{dom}(A_1) \times \text{dom}(A_2) \times \ldots \times \text{dom}(A_n))$$

Cartesian product comprehensively delineates the complete set of feasible permutations of values derived from the respective underlying domains. The total number of tuples in the Cartesian product can be calculated by multiplying the cardinalities, denoted as |D|, of each individual domain D within a particular relation. It is important to note that this calculation assumes that all domains are finite.

By taking the Cartesian product of domains A_1, A_2, ..., A_n, the resulting set will consist of tuples where each element of the tuple is selected from one of the domains. The number of tuples in the Cartesian product can be determined by multiplying the cardinalities of each domain (Li et al., 2005):

$$\text{Total number of tuples} = |A_1| \times |A_2| \times \ldots \times |A_n|$$

This calculation provides an estimation of the total number of possible tuples within the Cartesian product, representing the entire set of combinations of values from the defined domains.

$$|\text{dom}(A_1)| \times |\text{dom}(A_2)| \times \ldots \times |\text{dom}(A_n)|$$

The cardinality product of all domains denotes maximum number of potential tuples or instances which could conceivably exist within any given state of a relation r(R). The current relation state, among various feasible combinations, exclusively represents the valid tuples corresponding to a specific state of actual world. Generally speaking, state of real world undergoes changes that result in a transformation of the relational state. The schema R is characterized by high stability and infrequent modifications, such as including an attribute to represent novel information that was not initially stored in the relation.

Multiple attributes can share a common domain. The nomenclature assigned to attributes denotes distinct functions or connotations within the domain. In STUDENT entity, domain USA_phone_numbers serve as both Home_phone and Office_phone roles, denoting the respective phone numbers for a student's home and office. An additional attribute, which has not been illustrated, but shares the same domain, is the Mobile_phone attribute (Codd, 1972).

6.1.2. Characteristics of Relations

An antecedent relations definition encompasses distinct attributes which differentiate a relation from a table or a file. The following section will address several of characteristics mentioned above (Table 6.1):

1. Ordering of Tuples in a Relation: A relation is defined by a set of tuples. From a mathematical standpoint, it is important to note that the elements within a set do not possess any inherent order. As a result, it follows that tuples contained within a relation lack any specific order. Stated differently, the ordering of tuples does not affect the sensitivity of a relation. In file storage, records are arranged in a specific order as they are physically stored on a disk or in memory. The sequence above denotes the file's initial, subsequent, i^{th}, and final entries. Likewise, the arrangement of rows is predetermined in presenting a relation as a table (Ng & Levene, 1997).

The absence of tuple ordering in a relation definition can be attributed to relations aiming to represent abstract facts. A single relation can have many tuples ordering specified. As an illustration, the tuples present in STUDENT relation have the potential to be arranged based on the values of attributes such as Name, Ssn, Age, or any other attribute. Relation definition is agnostic towards order, as it does not exhibit a bias towards any particular ordering. Thus, it can be inferred that the correlation is equivalent. In the context of data management, it is possible to specify a specific order for records of a file or rows of a table when representing a relation in the form of file or table (Tatarinov et al., 2002).

2. Value Ordering in a Tuple and Different Definition of Relation: As per definition of relation provided earlier, it can be inferred that an n-tuple denotes a sequence of n values arranged in a specific order. Therefore, it can be concluded that the order of values in tuple, and consequently the arrangement of attributes in a relation schema, holds significant importance. At higher level of abstraction, significance of attributes order and their respective values are relatively inconsequential, provided that the association between attributes and values remains intact.

An alternative definition of a relation can be given, making the ordering of values in a tuple unnecessary. In this definition, a relation schema $R = \{A_1, A_2, ..., A_n\}$ is a set of attributes (instead of a list), and a relation state r(R) is a finite set of mappings $r = \{t_1, t_2, ..., t_m\}$, where each tuple ti is a mapping from R to D, and D is the union (denoted by ∪) of the attribute domains; that is, $D = dom(A_1) \cup dom(A_2) \cup ... \cup dom(A_n)$. In this definition, t[Ai] must be in dom(Ai) for $1 \leq i \leq n$ for each mapping t in r. Each mapping ti is called tuple. (Wu et al., 2016).

According to tuple definition as mapping, it can be considered grouping of pairs consisting of an attribute and its corresponding value. Each pair denotes the correspondence between a specific attribute Ai and its corresponding value vi from domain of Ai, denoted as dom(Ai). An impact of attribute ordering is inconsequential since the attribute identifier is consistently accompanied by its corresponding value. Tabular representation of connection

STUDENT with a different tuple order

Table 6.1. *Tabular Representation of Connection STUDENT with a Different Tuple Order*

Name	Ssn	Home_phone	Address	Office_ phone	Age	Gpa
Dick Davidson	422-11-2320	NULL	3452 Elgin Road	(817)749-1253	25	3.53
Barbara Benson	533-69-1238	(817)839-8461	7384 Fontana Lane	NULL	19	3.25
Rohan Panchal	489-22-1100	(817)376-9821	265 Lark Lane	(817)749-6492	28	3.93
Chung-Cha Kim	381-62-1245	(817)375-4409	125 Kirby Road	NULL	18	2.89
Benjamin Bayer	305-61-2435	(817)373-1616	2918 Bluebonnet Lane	NULL	19	3.21

3. STUDENT: According to this particular definition, it can be inferred that the two tuples exhibit complete similarity. This proposition is logical in a theoretical context, as there exists no rationale to prioritize the occurrence of one attribute value over another within tuple. The characteristics are organized as fields within a record in a predefined physical sequence when relation is implemented as file. Typically, primary definition of relation that we employ involves the imposition of order on attributes and values within tuples. This approach is favored due to its ability to streamline notation. Nevertheless, the alternate definition provided in this context is more comprehensive.
4. Values and NULLs in Tuples: In the basic relational model, each element within tuple is considered an inseparable atomic value and cannot be further decomposed into smaller components. Therefore, using composite and multivalued attributes is prohibited in this context. The flat relational model is a nomenclature sometimes utilized to refer to this particular model. The foundational principles of the relational model were largely formulated with the underlying premise of 1st normal form assumption. Therefore, in fundamental relational model, it's necessary to depict multivalued attributes through distinct relations, while composite attributes are exclusively represented by component attributes (Zaniolo, 1982).

NULL values are crucial in database management systems as they denote attribute values that may be indeterminate or inapplicable to a given tuple. In such instances, a distinct value known as NULL is employed. Certain STUDENT tuples exhibit NULL values for their office phone attribute, which can be attributed to the absence of office space for these students, rendering the office phone attribute inapplicable. The student in question may have a missing value for their home phone, which could indicate either the absence of a home phone or a lack of knowledge regarding its existence. Typically, multiple interpretations exist for NULL values, including but not limited to an unknown value, an existing value that is inaccessible, or an attribute which is inapplicable to the given tuple (alternatively referred to as undefined value). An instance of the final category of NULL arises when introducing a Visa status attribute to the STUDENT entity, which exclusively pertains to tuples denoting international students. Formulating distinct codes to represent various interpretations of NULL values is feasible. Including various forms of NULL values in relational model operations has presented challenges and is beyond purview of our discourse (Biskup, 1984).

When a NULL value is subjected to arithmetic aggregations or comparisons with other values, its behavior is determined by a precise interpretation of the value. An instance of comparing two NULL values can result in ambiguities. In the scenario where both Customer A and B possess NULL addresses, it cannot be inferred that they share the same address. In designing a database, minimizing the usage of NULL values is advisable (Scannapieco & Batini, 2004).

5. Interpretation (Meaning) of a Relation: A schema of a relation can be construed as declaration or form of assertion. The schema of STUDENT relation posits typical student entity possesses attributes such as Name, Ssn, Home_phone, Address, Office_phone, Age, and Gpa. Each tuple within relation can be construed as factual statement or specific occurrence of assertion. The initial tuple affirms the existence of a STUDENT entity, denoted by the Name attribute "Benjamin Bayer," the Ssn attribute "305-61-2435," the Age attribute "19," and so forth (Wand et al., 1999).

It should be noted that certain relations may pertain to information regarding entities, while others may pertain to information regarding relationships. An illustration of a relation schema is MAJORS (Student_ssn, Department_code), affirming that students pursue academic disciplines as their majors (Dey & Sarkar, 1996). The relation contains a tuple that establishes a correlation between students and their corresponding major discipline. Thus, relational model uniformly presents information about entities and relationships by utilizing relations. At times, the comprehensibility of a given relation may be affected when there is uncertainty about whether it represents an entity or a relationship type. This ambiguity can make it challenging to understand the nature and purpose of the relation (Zvieli & Chen, 1986).

A possible alternative perspective on a relation schema is to view it as a predicate. Under this framework, the values contained within each tuple are construed as values that fulfill the predicate. Predicate denoted as STUDENT (Name, Ssn,) holds for the set of five tuples in the STUDENT relation. The tuples above denote five distinct propositions or factual statements about the physical world. The interpretation mentioned above holds significant utility in the domain of logical programming languages, particularly in Prolog, as it facilitates the integration of the relational model into these languages. The closed world assumption is a postulate that posits the veracity of solely those facts contained within the extension or state of the relation(s) in the universe. Any alternative combination of values renders the predicate invalid (Shenoi & Melton, 1989).

6.1.3. Relational Model Notation

The following notation will be used in our presentation:

1. The notation $R(A_1, A_2, \ldots, A_n)$ represents a relation schema R of degree n.
2. An uppercase letters Q, R, and S denote the relation names.
3. A lowercase letters q, r, and s represent states of relation.
4. Symbols t, u, and v are used to represent tuples.

5. Typically, nomenclature of relation schema, including STUDENT, denotes present collection of tuples within that relation, known as the current relation state. Conversely, STUDENT(Name, Ssn,...) pertains solely to relation schema (Marcos et al., 2003).
6. The dot notation R.A can qualify an attribute A with its corresponding relation name R, such as in the STUDENT case. Please provide your name and age as a student. This phenomenon occurs due to the potential for identical nomenclature to be assigned to two distinct attributes across disparate relations. Each attribute name within a given relation must be unique.
7. In relation r(R), an n-tuple t can be represented as $t = <v_1, v_2, ..., v_n>$, where each vi corresponds to the value of attribute Ai. The notation presented pertains to values of components within tuples:
8. Notations t[Ai], t.Ai, and occasionally t[i] are used interchangeably to denote value vi in t corresponding to the attribute (Getoor & Sahami, 1999).
9. The subtype of values <vu, vw, ..., vz> from t, corresponding to attributes listed in R as Au, Aw, ..., Az, can be denoted as either t[Au, Aw, ..., Az] or t.(Au, Aw, ..., Az) (Liu et al., 2003).

An illustrative instance to contemplate is the tuple denoted by t, which comprises the following attributes: 'Barbara Benson' denoting the name, '533-69-1238' and '(817)839-8461' representing the phone numbers, '7384 Fontana Lane' indicating the address, NULL signifying the absence of a value for a particular attribute, 19 indicating the age, and 3.25 representing a numerical attribute. Based on the STUDENT entity, it can be inferred that t[Name] corresponds to the value of <'Barbara Benson'>, while t[Ssn, Gpa, Age] corresponds to the values of <'533-69-1238,' 3.25, 19> (Pieris, 2013).

6.2. RELATIONAL MODEL CONSTRAINTS AND RELATIONAL DATABASE SCHEMAS

Learning Objectives

At the end of this section, readers will be able to:

- Explain the concept of relational model constraints and their significance in ensuring data integrity within a relational database system.
- Discuss the various types of constraints, including primary key, foreign key, unique key, and check constraints, and their role in defining and maintaining the relational database schema.
- Describe how primary key constraints uniquely identify records within a relational database table and the implications of using them for data retrieval and modification.

Up to this point, an analysis has been conducted on the characteristics of personal relationships. Within the realm of relational databases, it is a frequent occurrence to come across numerous relations that contain tuples showcasing a variety of forms of interdependence. At particular point in time, the comprehensive condition of database will correspond to conditions of each its relations. Database states are commonly constrained by various limitations or restrictions governing their values. The limitations mentioned are inferred from the regulations inherent in the microcosm that the database represents.

The section pertains to delineating limitations imposed on data within a relational database, which can be expressed as constraints. The limitations imposed on databases can typically be classified into three primary groupings:

1 The limitations that are intrinsic to the data model. The constraints based on model itself or not explicitly stated are commonly referred to as inherent model-based or implicit constraints.

2 Limitations which are explicitly stated in schemas of data model, often by defining them in Data Definition Language (DDL). The constraints based on a

schema or explicitly defined are called schema-based constraints.

3 Certain constraints are not directly expressible in schemas of a data model. Consequently, these constraints must be articulated and enforced by application programs. The constraints or rules based on applications, semantics, or business are called application-based, semantic, or business constraints (Markowitz & Makowsky, 1990).

The attributes of relationships pertain to the fundamental limitations of the relational paradigm and are classified under the primary category. An instance of an inherent constraint is the restriction which a relation cannot contain duplicate tuples. The constraints under consideration in this section belong to second category, which refers to constraints which can be articulated within schema of relational model through Data Definition Language (DDL). Limitations falling under the third category are broader, about both the semantics and conduct of attributes, and are arduous to articulate and implement within data model. As a result, they're typically verified by application programs responsible for executing database updates (Yan & Ling, 1993) (Figure 6.4).

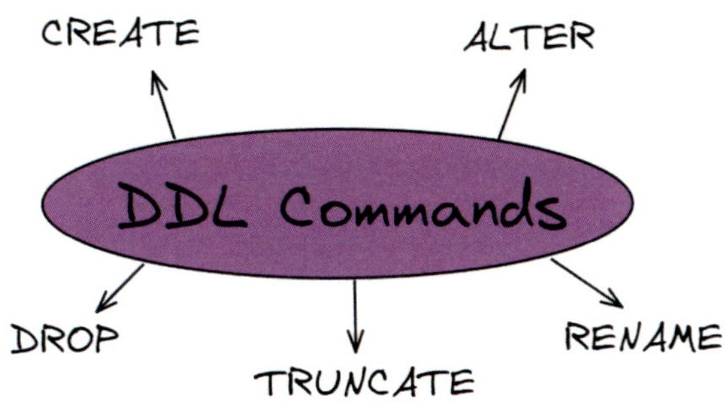

Figure 6.4. *DDL commands.*

Data dependencies constitute a significant category of constraints, encompassing functional and multivalued dependencies. Relational database testing primarily involves assessing the efficacy of the design and is commonly executed through the normalization process. The constraints based on schema include but are not limited to domain constraints, constraints on NULLs, key constraints, referential integrity constraints, entity integrity constraints.

6.2.1. Domain Constraints

According to domain constraints, each attribute A in a tuple must have an atomic value that comes from domain dom(A). Domains are commonly associated with data types that encompass numeric values. These data types may include standard integer data types, including integer, short and long integer, as well as real number data types, such as float and double-precision float. In addition to standard data types, such as integers and floats, various other data types are also available in programming. These include characters, Booleans, fixed-length strings, and variable-length strings. Furthermore, specialized data types, such as time, timestamp, date, and money, are also available in programming. It is plausible to depict additional domains as values subset from a given data type or as an enumerated data type that explicitly enlists each feasible value.

6.2.2. Key Constraints and Constraints on NULL Values

Formal relational model defines relation as tuples collection. As per the definition, it can be inferred that each element within a set is unique. Therefore, all tuples present in relation must also be unique. It implies that no 2 tuples will have an identical value amalgamation across all their attributes. Typically, relation schema R comprises additional attribute subsets that possess the characteristic whereby no 2 tuples within any given relation state r of R may share an identical combination of values for said attributes. Let SK be a subset of attributes in relation state R. There is a constraint like this for any two different tuples in R (Candan et al., 1997):

$t_1[SK] \neq t_2[SK]$

Relation schema R can be associated with a set of attributes SK, referred to as a super key. A superkey, denoted as SK, establishes a uniqueness constraint whereby it is impossible for two separate tuples within any given state r of R to possess identical values for SK. It is a commonly accepted fact in database management that every relation possesses a default superkey, essentially complete attributes set associated with it. A superkey may contain redundant attributes, whereas a key is a more valuable concept as it lacks redundancy. In the context of relation schema R, key K is considered superkey with added characteristic that removal of any attribute A from K results in a set of attributes K,' which no longer qualifies as a superkey of R. Therefore, key exhibits 2 distinct properties (Halpin & Ritson, 1992):

1. A fundamental principle in relational databases is that no two tuples within a given state of a relation can possess identical values for the attributes that comprise key. The characteristic as mentioned above is also applicable to superkey.
2. The aforementioned is minimal superkey, meaning it's superkey that satisfies the uniqueness constraint in condition 1 and cannot have any attributes removed from it. The presence of this attribute does not constitute a necessity for a superkey.

While the initial characteristic pertains to keys and superkeys, the subsequent characteristic is solely necessary for keys. Therefore, it can be stated that a key possesses the characteristic of being a superkey, but the reverse is not necessarily true. STUDENT relation. Set of attributes {Ssn} is considered primary key of the entity STUDENT, as it ensures that there cannot exist two tuples within the STUDENT entity with identical values for the attribute Ssn.8 A superkey is any collection of attributes that encompasses Ssn, such as {Ssn, Name, Age}. Superkey {Ssn, Name, Age} does not qualify as key for the entity STUDENT since removing either Name or Age or both from the set as mentioned above would still result in a superkey. Any superkey that is constituted by a solitary attribute is concurrently key. For key to possess the uniqueness property, it is imperative that all of its attributes collectively satisfy this requirement in a multi-attribute scenario (Morfuni, 1986).

The identification of each tuple within a relationship can be achieved by utilizing a key attribute that possesses a unique value. The SSN value of 305-61-2435 serves as a unique identifier for the tuple that pertains to Benjamin Bayer within the STUDENT relation. It should be noted that a collection of characteristics that make up a key is an inherent feature of the relation schema. This represents a limitation that must be satisfied by all legitimate relation states within the schema. The determination of a key is based on the semantic interpretation of the attributes, and the property of being time-invariant is inherent. The integrity constraint must remain valid even upon the insertion of additional tuples into the relation. The designation of the Name attribute of the STUDENT relation as a key is not feasible nor advisable due to the potential existence of two students with identical names in a valid state.

It is common for a relational schema to possess multiple keys. In this instance, every individual key is called candidate key. The CAR relationship possesses two potential keys, namely License_number and Engine_serial_number. It's customary to assign one of candidate keys as primary key for given relation. The candidate key is a set of values that serves the purpose of identifying tuples within the relation. The customary practice is to underline attributes which constitute primary key of a relation schema. It's crucial to remember that choosing a primary key can be arbitrary when a relational schema has several candidate keys. Nonetheless, it is generally advisable to opt for primary key that comprises a single attribute or a limited number of attributes. The candidate keys that remain are distinguished as being unique and not denoted by an underline.

One additional limitation on attributes pertains to the allowance or disallowance of NULL values. As an illustration, if each tuple about STUDENT must possess a legitimate and non-NULL value for Name, then the attribute of Name for STUDENT is restricted to NOT NULL.

6.2.3. Integrity, Referential Integrity, and Foreign Keys

Principle of entity integrity constraint posits which it is impermissible for any primary key value to assume a NULL state. The rationale behind this is primary key's value serves as a unique identifier for distinct tuples within a given relation. NULL values in the primary key indicate the inability to identify certain tuples. If multiple tuples possess NULL values for their primary keys, it may not be feasible to differentiate between them when attempting to reference them from other relations (Calero et al., 2001).

Individual relations are subject to the specification of key and entity integrity constraints. Referential integrity constraint pertains to the specification between two relations upholding the coherence of tuples within said relations. Referential integrity constraint is an informal principle stipulating that a tuple within one relation that references another must reference a pre-existing tuple within that relation. Attribute Dno of the EMPLOYEE entity provides department number corresponding to the department where each employee is employed. Therefore, the value of Dno in each tuple of EMPLOYEE must correspond to Dnumber value of a tuple in DEPARTMENT relation (Levene & Loizou, 2001).

To provide a formal definition of referential integrity, it is necessary first to establish concept of a foreign key. Following conditions pertain to foreign key and establish referential integrity constraint between two relational schemas, R_1 and R_2. In a relational schema, a collection of attributes is denoted as FK. Relation R_1 is said to have a foreign key which references relation R_2 if it adheres to prescribed rules (Meurice et al., 2014):

i. Attributes contained within foreign key (FK) possess identical domains as primary key (PK) attributes of R_2. As a result, attributes within FK are commonly referred to as referencing or referring to R_2 relation.
ii. In current state of $r_1(R_1)$, tuple t_1 contains an FK value that is either a PK value for a tuple t_2 in current state of $r_2(R_2)$ or it is NULL. When $t_1[FK]$ is equal to $t_2[PK]$, it can be stated that tuple t_1 is referencing or referring to the tuple t_2 (Reinert, 1995).

The nomenclature employed in this definition designates R_1 as referencing relation, while R_2 is identified as referenced relation. Provided that these two criteria are met, it can be stated that referential integrity constraint exists between R_1 and R_2. In a database comprising numerous relations, it is common to encounter many referential integrity constraints.

To delineate these limitations, it is imperative to possess a lucid comprehension of significance or function that every attribute or group of attributes fulfills in diverse relation schemas of the database. Referential integrity constraints commonly emerge from the interconnections among the entities depicted by the relation schemas. An instance that can be considered is the database. The attribute Dno in the EMPLOYEE relation denotes the department where an employee is employed. Therefore, Dno is identified as a foreign key of EMPLOYEE that references DEPARTMENT relation. The aforementioned statement states that the value of Dno for any tuple t_1 in the EMPLOYEE relation must coincide with a value of the Dnumber attribute in any tuple t_2 of the DEPARTMENT relation, which is the main key for DEPARTMENT. Alternatively, the value of Dno may be NULL if the employee does not already belong to a department or will be assigned to one in the future. The tuple about the employee named 'John Smith' refers to the tuple associated with the 'Research' department, thereby signifying that 'John Smith' is employed by this particular department (Vidaković et al., 2016).

It should be noted that a foreign key can reference its relation. The attribute "Super_ssn" in the "EMPLOYEE" relation denotes the superior of an employee, who is also an employee and is represented by a tuple in the same "EMPLOYEE" relation. Therefore, Super_ssn attribute is a foreign key that establishes a reference to the EMPLOYEE relation within itself. The tuple about employee 'John Smith' refers to the tuple of employee 'Franklin Wong,' thereby implying that 'Franklin Wong' holds the supervisor position for 'John Smith.' Referential integrity constraints can be visually represented through diagrams, wherein a directed arc is drawn from each foreign key to the relation it references. To enhance clarity, the arrowhead can indicate the primary key of the relation being referenced. The referential integrity constraints of the schema are presented in the format. To enforce integrity constraints on the database states, said constraints must be explicitly specified on the relational database schema as an integral part of its definition (Aleksić et al., 2011).

Therefore, Data Definition Language (DDL) incorporates clauses for defining diverse categories of constraints, enabling the Database Management System (DBMS) to enforce them automatically. Most relational database management systems support constraints related to entity integrity, key, and referential integrity. The abovementioned limitations are explicitly outlined as component of the data definition language (DDL) (Yue, 2022).

6.2.4. Other Types of Constraints

An antecedent integrity constraint has been incorporated into the data definition language due to their ubiquitous presence in most database applications. Notwithstanding, relational databases do not encompass a broad category of overall limitations, denoted as semantic integrity constraints, which may necessitate explicit specification and implementation. Illustrations of such limitations include the provision that an employee's remuneration ought not to surpass that of their immediate superior and the ceiling on the total number of hours that an employee may devote to all projects in a given week being 56. Constraints may be defined and implemented in the database-updating application programs or by utilizing a constraint specification language that is not specific to any particular purpose. Triggers and assertions represent viable mechanisms that can be employed. Using CREATE ASSERTION and CREATE TRIGGER statements in SQL can serve this objective. In practice, application programs are frequently employed to verify constraints of this nature instead of utilizing constraint specification languages, which can prove challenging and intricate to navigate (Luković et al., 2007).

The functional dependency constraint is type of constraint that creates functional relationship between two sets of attributes, namely X and Y.

Functional dependency X not equal to Y is constraint which mandates the determination of a singular value of Y in every relation state based on value of X.

Constraints that have been previously discussed may be classified as state constraints, as they establish limitations which legitimate state of database must adhere to. Transition constraints can be established to address alterations in the database's state, constituting an additional category of constraints. One instance of a transition constraint is, "The remuneration of a staff member can solely experience an upward trend." The enforcement of such limitations is commonly carried out by application programs or designated through active rules and triggers (Maatuk et al., 2008).

6.3. UPDATE OPERATIONS, TRANSACTIONS, AND DEAL WITH CONSTRAINT VIOLATIONS

Learning Objectives

At the end of this section, readers will be able to:

- Explain the concept of update operations in a database management system.
- Discuss the importance of using transactions in database management and their role in ensuring data consistency.
- Describe different types of constraint violations that can occur in a database.

Relational model encompasses two main operations categories: retrievals and updates. A new relation is created when algebraic operators are applied to a set of preexisting relations using a relational algebra expression. Primary purpose of this operation is to retrieve information from a database through querying. The user constructs a query that defines the target data and utilizes relational operators to extract said data, resulting in the formation of a novel relation. A resultant relation represents the outcome of the user's inquiry (Di Nitto & Tanca, 1996).

This section is focused on the operations related to modifying or updating a database. The fundamental actions that can alter the states of relations within a database are Insertion, Deletion, and Modification (or Update). The users can perform various operations on data records, such as inserting new data, deleting old data, or modifying existing data. The insertion operation, called "Insert," adds one or more new tuples to given relation. The deletion operation, "Delete," removes tuples from the relation. Lastly, the modification operation "Update" or "Modify" is utilized to alter values of certain attributes within existing tuples (Gehani & Jagadish, 1991). The application of these operations mustn't result in any violation of the integrity constraints that have been specified in the schema of the relational database. This section entails a discussion of the various constraint types which could potentially be breached by each operation and corresponding actions which may be implemented in response to such violations. The database is utilized for illustrative purposes, focusing exclusively on a key, entity, and referential integrity constraints. Examples are provided for every operation type, and any potential constraints each operation may violate are discussed (Boydens et al., 1998).

6.3.1. The Insert Operation

Inserting a new tuple t into a relation R involves providing a list of attribute values through the Insert operation. The act of inserting can potentially contravene any of the four categories of constraints that were previously expounded upon. The violation of domain constraints may occur when an attribute value is provided which either doesn't belong to corresponding domain or isn't of suitable data type. The violation of key constraints may occur when key value present in a new tuple t is already present in another tuple within relation r(R). Entity integrity violation may occur if any constituent of primary key of a newly introduced tuple, denoted as t, is rendered NULL. The violation of referential integrity may occur if a tuple referenced in a relationship does not exist, as indicated by value of a foreign key in t. The following examples are presented to elucidate the discourse mentioned above (Jajodia & Sandhu, 1991).

1. Please execute the command to insert the tuple <'Cecilia,' 'F,' 'Kolonsky,' NULL, '1960-04-05,' '6357 Windy Lane, Katy, TX,' F, 28000, NULL, 4> into the EMPLOYEE relation. The insertion mentioned above is deemed invalid as it breaches entity integrity constraint, specifically primary key Ssn being assigned a NULL value, thus leading to its rejection.
2. The following SQL command is proposed for the insertion of a new record into the EMPLOYEE table: INSERT INTO EMPLOYEE (FIRST_NAME, MIDDLE_INITIAL, LAST_NAME, SSN, BIRTH_DATE, ADDRESS, GENDER, SALARY, SUPER_SSN, DEPT_NUM) VALUES ('Alicia,' 'J,' 'Zelaya,' '999887777,' '1960-04-05,' '6357 Windy Lane, Katy, TX,' 'F,' 28000, '987654321,' 4); The attempted insertion is deemed invalid due to a key constraint violation. This is because another tuple already exists with identical Ssn value in the EMPLOYEE relation. As a result, the insertion is rejected.
3. The following command is to be executed to insert the tuple <'Cecilia,' 'F,' 'Kolonsky,' '677678989,' '1960-04-05,' '6357 Windswept, Katy, TX,' F, 28000, '987654321,' 7> into the EMPLOYEE relation. The insertion mentioned above is in contravention of the referential integrity constraint that has been stipulated on Dno in the EMPLOYEE table. This is due to the absence of a corresponding tuple in DEPARTMENT table with a Dnumber value of 7, the referenced value.
4. The following SQL statement is proposed for new record insertion into EMPLOYEE table: INSERT INTO EMPLOYEE (First_name, last_name, gender, ssn, birth_date, address, marital_status, salary, supervisor_ssn, department_number) VALUES ('Cecilia,' 'F,' 'Kolonsky,' '677678989,' '1960-04-05,' '6357 Windy Lane, Katy, TX,' 'F,' 28000, NULL, 4). The insertion mentioned above meets

each specified criterion and thus can be deemed permissible (Elmasri et al., 1985).

If an insertion contravenes one or multiple constraints, the standard course of action is to decline the insertion. It would be advantageous if the database management system (DBMS) could furnish a rationale to the user regarding the cause of the insertion's rejection in this scenario. An alternative approach involves rectifying the cause of the rejection. However, this method is not commonly employed for violations arising from the Insert operation. Instead, it is frequently utilized to address Delete and Update operations violations. During the initial operation, DBMS may prompt user to input a value for Ssn and subsequently authorize insertion if legitimate Ssn value is supplied. During operation 3, the DBMS can prompt the user to modify the value of Dno to a valid value or set it to NULL. Alternatively, DBMS may request the user to insert a DEPARTMENT tuple with Dnumber equal to 7 before accepting the original insertion. If a user inserts a department 7 tuple with a Mgr_ssn that isn't in EMPLOYEE relation, it could cascade (Ben-Zvi, 1982).

6.3.2. Delete Operation

Deleting data can solely result in a breach of referential integrity. This phenomenon arises when the tuple that is being deleted is referred to by foreign keys from other tuples within database. To perform a deletion operation, criterion based on attributes of relation is utilized to identify tuple or tuples that are to be removed. The following are instances (Arqués & Michel, 1993).

1. Remove tuple with combination of Essn = '999887777' and Pno = 10 from the WORKS_ON relation. The deletion operation is deemed acceptable as it precisely removes a single tuple.
2. Remove the tuple with the attribute Ssn equal to '999887777' from the EMPLOYEE relation. The deletion cannot be deemed acceptable as tuples in the WORKS_ON relation which refer to the tuple mentioned above exist. Therefore, deleting the tuple in the EMPLOYEE table would lead to referential integrity violations.
3. Remove the tuple with the attribute Ssn equal to '333445555' from the EMPLOYEE relation. Removing this tuple is anticipated to exacerbate referential integrity violations, as tuples from various relations including EMPLOYEE, DEPARTMENT, WORKS_ON, and DEPENDENT, are currently referencing it (Adya et al., 2002).

There exist multiple alternatives in case a deletion operation results in a breach. The initial alternative, "restrict," involves declining the removal. The alternative approach, cascade, involves attempting to propagate deletion process by eliminating tuples which refer to deleted tuple. In the second operation, the database management system can automatically remove the problematic tuples from the WORKS_ON table where social security number of employee is '999887777.' The third alternative, "set null" or "set default," involves altering values of referencing attributes responsible for violation. Every value is either replaced with NULL or substituted with a different valid tuple that serves as the new reference. It should be noted that it is not possible to give a reference property in a primary key that results in a violation a NULL value. Doing so would result in a breach of entity integrity.

It is also feasible to have various combinations of these three alternatives. To circumvent the occurrence of a violation resulting from operation 3, database management system (DBMS) may execute an automatic deletion of all tuples from the tables WORKS_ON and DEPENDENT, wherein the attribute Essn is equal to '333445555.' The tuples present in the EMPLOYEE table that have the attribute Super_ssn equal to '333445555' and tuple in DEPARTMENT table with the attribute Mgr_ssn equal to '333445555' are subject to modification of their Mgr_ssn and Super_ssn values, which can be replaced by other valid values or set to NULL.

Automatically eliminating WORKS_ON and DEPENDENT tuples that are associated with an EMPLOYEE tuple may be a reasonable approach. However, it may not be reasonable to remove other EMPLOYEE tuples or a DEPARTMENT tuple.

When a referential integrity restriction is stated in Data Definition Language (DDL), it is often, Database Management System (DBMS) enables database designer to designate appropriate option in the event of a constraint violation (Ai & Zhang, 2019).

6.3.3. The Update Operation

A given relation's tuples' attribute values can be changed through Update operation. To select tuple or tuples that require modification, and it's imperative to specify condition of relation attributes. Following are instances.

1. Modify the EMPLOYEE tuple with the Ssn value of '999887777' to reflect a salary 28000. The outcome of the situation is deemed satisfactory and meets the required standards.
2. Modify Dno attribute of EMPLOYEE tuple where the Ssn attribute is equal to '999887777' to have a value of 1. The outcome of the situation is deemed satisfactory and meets the required standards.
3. Modify Dno attribute of EMPLOYEE tuple where Ssn equals '999887777' to a value of 7. The outcome is deemed unsatisfactory as it breaches the principle of referential integrity (Dayal & Bernstein, 1982).
4. Modify SSN attribute of EMPLOYEE tuple, specifically the one with an SSN value of '999887777,' to '987654321.' The outcome is deemed unacceptable due to violating the primary key constraint, wherein a value already existing as primary key in another tuple has been repeated. Furthermore, it violates referential integrity constraints since there are other relations which reference pre-existing values of Ssn attribute (Baumann et al., 2005).

Modifying a non-primary key and non-foreign key attribute typically does not result in any complications. The database management system (DBMS) must verify that the updated value matches the appropriate data type and domain. The process of altering primary key value resembles deleting tuple and subsequently inserting a new one in its stead, as the primary key identifies tuples. Therefore, the abovementioned concerns regarding (Insert) and (Delete) are relevant. In the event of a modification to a foreign key attribute, the database management system (DBMS) must ensure that updated value pertains to an extant tuple within referenced relation or is alternatively assigned a NULL value. Analogous alternatives are available to address referential integrity breaches resulting from

Update, akin to the solutions deliberated for the Delete function. In the context of database management, the establishment of a referential integrity constraint through the use of data definition language (DDL) prompts database management system (DBMS) to offer discrete alternatives for addressing a violation that may arise from either a Delete or an Update operation (Pannirselvam et al., 1999).

6.3.4. The Transaction Concept

In the context of a relational database, it is common for a database application program to carry out one or multiple transactions Transaction refers to a program in execution that involves certain database operations, including reading from database or performing insertions, deletions, or updates to database. Upon transaction completion, it's imperative that database is left in valid and consistent state, which adheres to each of constraints outlined in database schema. Transaction can encompass multiple retrieval and update operations. The retrieval and update operations will collectively constitute a single, indivisible transactional unit performed on the database. In banking transactions, initiating a withdrawal from a user's account typically involves accessing the account record, verifying the availability of adequate funds, and subsequently modifying the record to reflect the withdrawal amount.

Online transaction processing (OLTP) systems used by many commercial applications that use relational databases are capable of processing transactions at rates surpassing several 100 per second (Chu & Ieong, 1993).

6.4. BENEFITS OF RELATIONAL DATABASE CONSTRAINTS

Learning Objectives

At the end of this section, readers will be able to:

- Discuss the primary benefits of using primary key constraints in relational databases, including their role in ensuring data uniqueness and facilitating data retrieval.
- Describe the advantages of foreign key constraints in relational databases, emphasizing their role in enforcing referential integrity and maintaining data relationships.
- Explain the benefits of using unique constraints in relational databases, including their role in preventing duplicate entries and improving data quality.

6.4.1. Ensuring Data Accuracy and Consistency

The principal advantage of incorporating relational database constraints lies in their capacity to guarantee precision and uniformity of data. Constraints aid in preserving the accuracy and consistency of the information contained within a database by imposing predetermined regulations and limitations. The imposition of constraints can play a significant role in enhancing the precision and uniformity of data:

1. Uniqueness: Limitations such as primary keys and unique keys guarantee the uniqueness of every entry within a given table. In the context of database management, a primary key refers to a specific column or a set of columns that serves the purpose of uniquely identifying each individual row within a given table. The primary key value is enforced as a rule to prevent the insertion of duplicate data, ensuring that no two rows possess the same value. Similarly, unique keys ensure that there are no duplicate values within a designated column or group of columns. Constraints prevent data redundancy and guarantee that each piece of information is accurately and uniquely represented within the database by preserving its uniqueness (Hill et al., 2013).

2. Referential Integrity: The constraint of referential integrity serves to institute and uphold connections among tables using foreign keys. A foreign key is a database constraint that establishes a relationship between two tables, whereby column or columns set in one table is linked to primary key in another table. Constraints guarantee the coherence of data by imposing referential integrity, which mandates that the values contained in foreign key column of a given table correspond to values of the primary key in the table being referenced. By implementing this measure, orphaned records are avoided, and the coherence of data is maintained throughout interconnected tables. The referential integrity constraint guarantees a valid association between the orders and customers' tables. Specifically, it verifies that the customer ID in the orders table corresponds to a valid customer ID in the customer's table (Barak et al., 2007).
3. Data Validation Constraints: Such as domain and check constraints, impose regulations on the permissible range and structure of data contained within columns. A domain constraint is a specification that defines a column's acceptable data types, lengths, formats, and other attributes. The function of data validation is to ensure that the information contained within a given column conforms to the predetermined criteria. An instance of a domain constraint can be observed where a particular column that denotes a date is restricted to only accept dates that conform to a predetermined range and format (Khalfi et al., 2017). Check constraints enable the implementation of intricate data validation measures that go beyond the scope of ensuring uniqueness and nullability. Organizations can define custom conditions to ensure data is inserted into the database only after meeting specific requirements. Exemplar employment of a check constraint is to guarantee that a specific column denoting an individual's age solely permits affirmative numerical values. Constraints validate data against predetermined criteria, thereby preventing the insertion of invalid or inconsistent data. This, in turn, helps to uphold the accuracy and dependability of the database (Mohanty et al., 2007).

6.4.2. Preventing Invalid and Inconsistent Data

Relational database constraints serve as protective measures to prevent the insertion of data that is invalid or inconsistent. Constraints are implemented to ensure that the database only accepts data that adheres to predetermined rules and limitations. This prevents the inclusion of data that fails to meet the specified criteria. Several methods exist by which constraints aid in the prevention of invalid and inconsistent data:

1. Nullability Constraints: These of a column dictate its ability to accept null values. The concept of null value pertains to the absence of data or an unknown value. Constraints guarantee the presence of crucial data by indicating whether a column permits null values or not. Implementing measures to prevent the inclusion of incomplete

or unidentified data is crucial in ensuring the accuracy of analyzes and the validity of outcomes. If a column denoting a customer's phone number disallows null values, the database shall implement the constraint and disapprove any endeavor to insert a record lacking a phone number (Kupzyk & Cohen, 2015).

2. Key Constraints: Primary and unique keys are essential constraints that restrict the insertion of repetitive values in particular columns or groups of columns. The primary key serves as a distinct identifier for every record in a table, whereas a unique key guarantees uniqueness within a designated column or group of columns. The database system guarantees the absence of duplicate primary key or unique key values across multiple rows by implementing key constraints. Eliminating data redundancy mitigates the possibility of duplicity and promotes the preservation of data consistency and precision. Suppose a table possesses a unique key constraint on the email column. In that case, the database will decline any endeavor to insert a record containing an email address that already exists within the table (Soares & Borba, 2002).
3. Check Constraints: These enable the implementation of intricate data validation measures that go beyond the scope of ensuring uniqueness and nullability. Organizations can establish custom conditions to authenticate data prior to its insertion into database. An example of the utilization of check constraint is to guarantee that a particular column, which denotes a discount percentage, solely accepts values ranging from 0 to 100. The database system effectively averts the inclusion of data that fails to meet the prescribed criteria by implementing check constraints. This, in turn, precludes the existence of erroneous or incongruous data (Kent, 1983).

6.4.3. Supporting Data Integrity and Reliability

Implementing relational database constraints plays a crucial role in ensuring integrity and dependability of the data stored within database. Process of ensuring that the data conforms to predetermined rules and requirements serves to mitigate the possibility of errors and inconsistencies. The implementation of constraints can provide significant support for maintaining data integrity and reliability:

1. Data Consistency: The implementation of constraints, such as primary keys, foreign keys, and referential integrity constraints, serves to guarantee the precise maintenance of data relationships. In order to avoid potential inconsistencies that may arise from incomplete or mismatched data references, measures are taken to prevent such occurrences. If foreign key is linked to primary key in separate table, the referential integrity constraint guarantees the presence of the referenced key within the referenced table. Data consistency is maintained throughout the database by preventing the creation of orphaned records or invalid references (Park et al., 2013).

2. Error Prevention: The database management system (DBMS) ensures data integrity by imposing constraints during data insertion, update, and deletion operations, thereby preventing errors. Constraints serve as a mechanism for regulating data input into a database, permitting solely accurate and coherent information to be stored. Suppose a record is attempted to be inserted which violates a uniqueness constraint. In that case, the database management system (DBMS) will decline the operation and generate an error, thereby obstructing the insertion of erroneous data (Almassabi et al., 2018).
3. Data Quality and Reliability: Implementing relational database constraints has been shown to enhance the overall quality and dependability of data. Constraints play a crucial role in maintaining accuracy, reliability, and suitability of the data stored in a database for critical business operations, reporting, and decision-making processes. This is achieved by preventing the insertion of invalid or inconsistent data. Organizations can rely on the data stored within the database, assuring that it conforms to predetermined regulations and limitations, thereby augmenting the credibility and practicality of the data (Azzini et al., 2019).

SUMMARY

The present chapter expounded upon modeling concepts, data structures, and constraints that relational data model furnishes. The initial step involved the introduction of fundamental notions such as domains, tuples, and attributes. Subsequently, relation schema was established as an inventory of attributes which delineate configuration of relation. A relation, also known as a relation state, can be defined as a collection of tuples that adhere to a specific schema.

Several distinguishing features set relations apart from conventional tables or files. One of the fundamental properties of a relation is its insensitivity to tuples ordering. Second aspect pertains to arrangement of attributes within relation schema and corresponding arrangement of values within tuple. An alternative conceptualization of the term "relation" was introduced, which doesn't require the existence of 2 distinct orderings. However, for the sake of convenience, we opted to employ the initial definition that mandates the ordering of attributes and tuple values. Subsequently, the topic of values within tuples was deliberated upon, wherein the concept of NULL values was introduced to signify the absence or uncertainty of information. It was emphasized that minimizing the usage of NULL values is advisable.

The categorization of database constraints includes three distinct types: inherent model-based constraints, explicit schema-based constraints, and application-based constraints, which're also referred to as semantic constraints or business rules. Subsequently, we engaged in a discourse regarding the limitations imposed by the schema.

In regard to the relational model, it is necessary to begin with domain constraints and subsequently address key constraints, which encompass the notions of superkey, candidate key, and primary key, as well as NOT NULL constraint applied to attributes. Relational databases and their corresponding schemas were established. One of the relational constraints that can be considered is entity integrity constraint. This constraint disallows primary key attributes from having a NULL value. Referential integrity constraint is a mechanism utilized to maintain references consistency among tuples that come from different relations, as explained in text.

REVIEW QUESTIONS

1. Define following terms as they apply to the relational model of data: domain, attribute, n-tuple, relation schema, relation state, degree of a relation, relational database schema, and relational database state.
2. Why are tuples in relation not ordered?
3. Why are duplicate tuples not allowed in a relation?
4. What is the difference between superkey and key?
5. What is the rationale behind selecting a specific candidate key as the primary key for a relation?

MULTIPLE CHOICE QUESTIONS

1. **Which of the following is a primary key constraint in a relational database?**
   a. Unique constraint
   b. Not null constraint
   c. Foreign key constraint
   d. Check constraint
2. **In a relational database, what does the foreign key constraint ensure?**
   a. That a column cannot contain NULL values
   b. That each row in a table has a unique identifier
   c. That values in a column must match values in another table's primary key column
   d. That values in a column satisfy a specified condition
3. **Which constraint ensures that a column cannot have NULL values?**
   a. Unique constraint
   b. Primary key constraint
   c. Not null constraint
   d. Check constraint
4. **What is the purpose of a check constraint in a relational database?**
   a. To ensure that each row in a table has a unique identifier
   b. To enforce a condition on the values allowed in a column
   c. To establish a relationship between two tables
   d. To prevent duplicate values in a column
5. **In the relational data model, what is a tuple?**
   a. A unique identifier for each record in a table
   b. A collection of related attributes representing a single entity
   c. A table within a database
   d. A constraint that ensures data integrity

Answers to Multiple Choice Questions

1. (a); 2. (c); 3. (c); 4. (b); 5. (b);

REFERENCES

1. Adya, A., Bolosky, W. J., Castro, M., Cermak, G., Chaiken, R., Douceur, J. R., & Wattenhofer, R. P., (2002). FARSITE: Federated, available, and reliable storage for an incompletely trusted environment. *ACM SIGOPS Operating Systems Review*, *36*(SI), 1–14.

2. Ai, T., & Zhang, Q., (2019). The application and research of cloud platform in practice teaching integrated service. In: *Journal of Physics: Conference Series* (Vol. 1213, pp. 042035). IOP Publishing.
3. Aleksić, S., Ristić, S., & Luković, I., (2011). *An Approach to Generating Server Implementation of the Inverse Referential Integrity Constraints; Proceedings* (Vol. 2, pp. 85–86). AL-Zaytoonah University of Jordan, Amman, Jordan.
4. Almassabi, A., Bawazeer, O., & Adam, S., (2018). Top NewSQL databases and features classification. *International Journal of Database Management Systems*, *10*(2), 11–31.
5. Arqués, D., & Michel, C. (1993). A model of gene evolution based on recognizable languages and on insertion and deletion operations. International Journal of Modelling and Simulation, 13(3), 110-113.
6. Cerbah, F., (2008). Learning highly structured semantic repositories from relational databases: The RDBToOnto tool. *Lecture Notes in Computer Science*, *5021*, 777–781.
7. Chen, P. P. S., (1976). The entity-relationship model—Toward a unified view of data. *ACM Transactions on Database Systems (TODS)*, *1*(1), 9–36.
8. Chiang, R. H., Barron, T. M., & Storey, V. C., (1994). Reverse engineering of relational databases: Extraction of an EER model from a relational database. *Data & Knowledge Engineering*, *12*(2), 107–142.
9. Chu, W. W., & Ieong, I. T., (1993). A transaction-based approach to vertical partitioning for relational database systems. *IEEE Transactions on Software Engineering*, *19*(8), 804–812.
10. Clifford, J., & Croker, A., (1987). The historical relational data model (HRDM) and algebra based on lifespans. In: *1987 IEEE Third International Conference on Data Engineering* (Vol. 2, pp. 528–537). IEEE.
11. Codd, E. F., (1971). A data base sublanguage founded on the relational calculus. In: *Proceedings of the 1971 ACM SIGFIDET (now SIGMOD) Workshop on Data Description, Access, and Control* (Vol. 1, pp. 35–68).
12. Fahrner, C., & Vossen, G., (1995). Transforming relational database schemas into object-oriented schemas according to ODMG-93. In: *Deductive and Object-Oriented Databases: Fourth International Conference, DOOD'95 Singapore, Proceedings 4* (Vol. 1, pp. 429–446). Springer Berlin Heidelberg.
13. Fonkam, M. M., & Gray, W. A., (1992). An approach to eliciting the semantics of relational databases. In: *Advanced Information Systems Engineering: 4th International Conference CAiSE'92 Manchester, UK, Proceedings 4* (Vol. 1, pp. 463–480). Springer Berlin Heidelberg.
14. Gadia, S. K., (1988). A homogeneous relational model and query languages for temporal databases. *ACM Transactions on Database Systems (TODS)*, *13*(4), 418–448.
15. Galan, J., (2020). Towards a relational model for emerging urban nature concepts: A practical application and an external assessment in landscape planning education. *Sustainability*, *12*(6), 2465.

16. Gehani, N. H., & Jagadish, H. V., (1991). Ode as an active database: Constraints and triggers. In: *VLDB* (Vol. 91, pp. 327–336).
17. Getoor, L., & Sahami, M., (1999). Using probabilistic relational models for collaborative filtering. In: *Workshop on Web Usage Analysis and User Profiling (WEBKDD'99)* (Vol. 2, pp. 1–6).
18. Goldstein, B. S., (1981). Constraints on null values in relational databases. In: *Proceedings of the Seventh International Conference on Very Large Data Bases-Volume 7* (Vol. 1, pp. 101–110).
19. Halpin, T. A., & Ritson, P. R., (1992). Fact-oriented modelling and null values. *Research and Practical Issues in Databases, 321*, 1122–1123.
20. Halpin, T., & Morgan, T., (2010). Information modeling and relational databases. *Morgan Kaufmann, 6*(6), 990–1000.
21. He, J. S. K. T. G., & Naughton, C. Z. D. D. J., (2008). Relational databases for querying XML documents: Limitations and opportunities. *Proceedings of VLDB*, 302–314.
22. Hill, C., Gordon, I. E., Rothman, L. S., & Tennyson, J., (2013). A new relational database structure and online interface for the HITRAN database. *Journal of Quantitative Spectroscopy and Radiative Transfer*, *130*, 51–61.
23. Hui, K. Y., & Gray, P. M., (2000). Developing finite domain constraints-a data model approach. *Lecture Notes in Computer Science*, *78*, 448–462.
24. Lerat, N., & Lipski, Jr. W., (1986). Nonapplicable nulls. *Theoretical Computer Science*, *46*, 67–82.
25. Levene, M., & Loizou, G., (2001). A generalization of entity and referential integrity in relational databases. *RAIRO-Theoretical Informatics and Applications*, *35*(2), 113–127.
26. Levene, M., & Loizou, G., (2012). *A Guided Tour of Relational Databases and Beyond* (Vol. 2, pp. 253–255). Springer Science & Business Media.
27. Li, M., Du, X. Y., & Wang, S., (2005). Learning ontology from relational database. In: *2005 International Conference on Machine Learning and Cybernetics* (Vol. 6, pp. 3410–3415). IEEE.
28. Lin, T. Y., (1988). Neighborhood systems and approximation in relational databases and knowledge bases. In: *Proceedings of the 4th International Symposium on Methodologies of Intelligent Systems* (Vol. 2, pp. 75–86). California State University Northridge CA.
29. Liu, Z., Jifeng, H., Li, X., & Chen, Y., (2003). A relational model for formal object-oriented requirement analysis in UML. In: *Formal Methods and Software Engineering: 5th International Conference on Formal Engineering Methods, ICFEM 2003, Singapore, Proceedings 5* (Vol. 3, pp. 641–664). Springer Berlin Heidelberg.
30. Luković, I., Mogin, P., Pavićević, J., & Ristić, S., (2007). An approach to developing complex database schemas using form types. *Software: Practice and Experience*, *37*(15), 1621–1656.

31. Maatuk, A., Ali, A., & Rossiter, N., (2008). Relational database migration: A perspective. In: *Database and Expert Systems Applications: 19th International Conference, DEXA 2008, Turin, Italy, Proceedings 19* (Vol. 2, pp. 676–683). Springer Berlin Heidelberg.

32. Malinowski, E., & Zimányi, E., (2008). A conceptual model for temporal data warehouses and its transformation to the ER and the object-relational models. *Data & Knowledge Engineering*, *64*(1), 101–133.

33. Marcos, E., Vela, B., & Cavero, J. M., (2003). A methodological approach for object-relational database design using UML. *Software and Systems Modeling, 2*, 59–72.

34. Markowitz, V. M., & Makowsky, J. A., (1990). Identifying extended entity-relationship object structures in relational schemas. *IEEE Transactions on Software Engineering*, *16*(8), 777–790.

35. McMinn, P., Wright, C. J., McCurdy, C. J., & Kapfhammer, G. M., (2017). Automatic detection and removal of ineffective mutants for the mutation analysis of relational database schemas. *IEEE Transactions on Software Engineering*, *45*(5), 427–463.

36. Meier, A., Schindler, G., & Werro, N., (2008). Fuzzy classification on relational databases. In: *Handbook of Research on Fuzzy Information Processing in Databases* (Vol. 1, pp. 586–614). IGI Global.

37. Meurice, L., Ruiz, F. J. B., Weber, J. H., & Cleve, A., (2014). Establishing referential integrity in legacy information systems-reality bites! In: *2014 IEEE International Conference on Software Maintenance and Evolution* (Vol. 1, pp. 461–465). IEEE.

38. Mohanty, S. K., Piccoli, A. L., Devine, L. J., Patel, A. A., William, G. C., Winters, S. B., & Parwani, A. V., (2007). Synoptic tool for reporting of hematological and lymphoid neoplasms based on World Health Organization classification and College of American Pathologists checklist. *BMC Cancer*, 7, 1–9.

39. Ng, W., & Levene, M., (1997). An extension of SQL to support ordered domains in relational databases. In: *Proceedings of the 1997 International Database Engineering and Applications Symposium (Cat. No. 97TB100166)* (Vol. 1, pp. 358–367). IEEE.

40. Nyulas, C., O'connor, M., & Tu, S., (2007). DataMaster–a plug-in for importing schemas and data from relational databases into Protege. In: *10th International Protégé Conference* (Vol. 2, pp. 15–18).

41. Pannirselvam, G. P., Ferguson, L. A., Ash, R. C., & Siferd, S. P., (1999). Operations management research: An update for the 1990s. *Journal of Operations Management*, *18*(1), 95–112.

42. Paredaens, J., De Bra, P., Gyssens, M., & Van, G. D., (2012). *The Structure of the Relational Database Model* (Vol. 17, pp. 981–982). Springer Science & Business Media.

43. Park, S., Kelly, T., & Shen, K., (2013). Failure-atomic msync() a simple and efficient mechanism for preserving the integrity of durable data. In: *Proceedings of the 8th ACM European Conference on Computer Systems* (Vol. 2, pp. 225–238).

44. Pieris, D., (2013). *Modifying the Entity Relationship Modeling Notation: Towards High Quality Relational Databases from Better Notated ER Models* (pp. 852–855). arXiv preprint arXiv: 445.

45. Raghunathan, T. E., Lepkowski, J. M., Van, H. J., & Solenberger, P., (2001). A multivariate technique for multiply imputing missing values using a sequence of regression models. *Survey Methodology*, *27*(1), 85–96.

46. Reinert, J., (1995). Ambiguity for referential integrity is undecidable. In: *ESPRIT WG CONTESSA Workshop on Constraint Databases and Applications* (Vol. 1, pp. 132–147). Berlin, Heidelberg: Springer Berlin Heidelberg.

47. Scannapieco, M., & Batini, C., (2004). Completeness in the relational model: A comprehensive framework. In: *ICIQ* (Vol. 1, pp. 333–345).

48. Schek, H. J., & Scholl, M. H., (1986). The relational model with relation-valued attributes. *Information Systems*, *11*(2), 137–147.

49. Selinger, P. G., Astrahan, M. M., Chamberlin, D. D., Lorie, R. A., & Price, T. G., (1979). Access path selection in a relational database management system. In: *Proceedings of the 1979 ACM SIGMOD International Conference on Management of Data* (Vol. 1, pp. 23–34).

50. Shenoi, S., & Melton, A., (1989). Proximity relations in the fuzzy relational database model. *Fuzzy Sets and Systems*, *31*(3), 285–296.

51. Soares, S., & Borba, P., (2002). Concurrency control with Java and relational databases. In: *Proceedings 26th Annual International Computer Software and Applications* (Vol. 2, pp. 843–849). IEEE.

52. Sumathi, S., & Esakkirajan, S., (2007). *Fundamentals of Relational Database Management Systems* (Vol. 47, pp. 789–790). Springer.

53. Tansel, A. U., (1986). Adding time dimension to relational model and extending relational algebra. *Information Systems*, *11*(4), 343–355.

54. Tatarinov, I., Viglas, S. D., Beyer, K., Shanmugasundaram, J., Shekita, E., & Zhang, C., (2002). Storing and querying ordered XML using a relational database system. In: *Proceedings of the 2002 ACM SIGMOD International Conference on Management of Data* (Vol. 1, pp. 204–215).

55. Telnarova, Z., (2010). Relational database as a source of ontology creation. In: *Proceedings of the International Multiconference on Computer Science and Information Technology* (Vol. 1, pp. 135–139). IEEE.

56. Thapa, R. B., & Giese, M., (2022). *Mapping Relational Database Constraints to SHACL (Extended Version)* (pp. 528–530). Research report http://urn. nb. no/URN: NBN: 35.

57. Vidaković, J., Luković, I., & Kordić, S., (2016). Specification and validation of the referential integrity constraint in XML databases. In: *Proceedings of the 6th International Conference on Information Society and Technology* (Vol. 3, pp. 197–202).

58. Wand, Y., Storey, V. C., & Weber, R., (1999). An ontological analysis of the relationship construct in conceptual modeling. *ACM Transactions on Database Systems (TODS)*, *24*(4), 494–528.

59. Wu, J., Xiong, R., & Chiclana, F., (2016). Uninorm trust propagation and aggregation methods for group decision making in social network with four tuple information. *Knowledge-Based Systems*, *96*, 29–39.

60. Yan, L. L., & Ling, T. W., (1993). Translating relational schema with constraints into OODB schema. In: *Interoperable Database Systems (Ds-5)* (Vol. 2, pp. 69–85). North-Holland.

61. Yue, K. B., (2022). Assuring referential integrity in blockchain applications. In: *2022 Fourth International Conference on Blockchain Computing and Applications (BCCA)* (Vol. 1, pp. 47–54). IEEE.

62. Zaniolo, C., (1982). Database relations with null values. In: *Proceedings of the 1st ACM SIGACT-SIGMOD Symposium on Principles of Database Systems* (Vol. 1, pp. 27–33).

63. Zvieli, A., & Chen, P. P., (1986). Entity—Relationship modeling and fuzzy databases. In: *1986 IEEE Second International Conference on Data Engineering* (Vol. 1, pp. 320–327). IEEE.

CHAPTER

7 NoSQL Database

LEARNING OBJECTIVES

After studying this chapter, you will be able to:

- Understand the concept of NoSQL databases and distinguish them from traditional relational databases.
- Explore NoSQL data modeling techniques and schema design principles.
- Understand scalability features and performance considerations in NoSQL databases.
- Learn querying and data manipulation techniques in NoSQL databases.
- Identify common use cases and best practices for deploying and managing NoSQL databases.

"NoSQL databases unlock the potential of unstructured and semi-structured data, offering a flexible and scalable foundation for the data-driven future."

INTRODUCTORY EXAMPLE

Imagine you're the owner of a rapidly growing e-commerce platform, and your website is experiencing an influx of customers and transactions. Traditional relational databases have served you well for managing customer data, order history, and product details, but as your business scales, you start encountering performance bottlenecks and data modeling challenges. This is where NoSQL databases come into play, offering a revolutionary approach to data management. In this introduction, we'll explore what NoSQL databases are and how they address the limitations of traditional relational databases in handling large and complex datasets while ensuring high availability and scalability.

UNIT INTRODUCTION

There has been a growing trend towards adopting dispersed web-based applications in recent years. Services such as YouTube, Google, and Amazon are required to maintain and analyze vast quantities of data due to their widespread usage. It is evident that managing such data using single-node platforms is not feasible. Hence dispersed storage methods are imperative. The potential for expanding a system for managing relational databases (RDBMS) by adding nodes is frequently restricted or nonexistent.

Numerous non-relational options for storage have appeared as a means of surpassing the constraints of scalability. Some instances of dispersed, non-relational records include Dynamo, which was created by Amazon, Google's The Big Table system, and Hadoop, which is utilized by Facebook. The expression "NoSQL" encompasses database platforms of this nature (Figure 7.1).

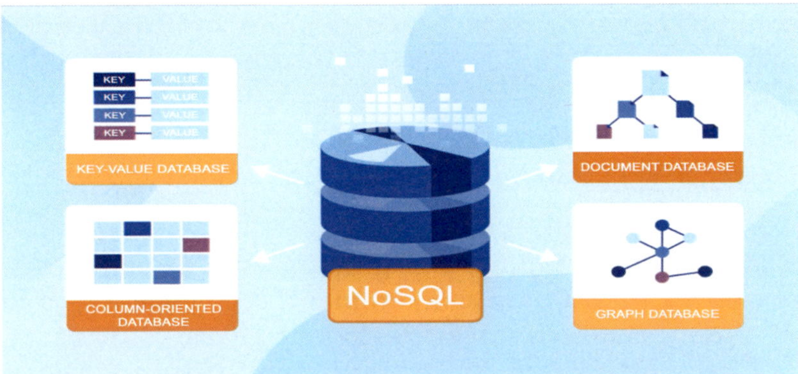

Figure 7.1. Components of NoSQL.

This discourse delves into the fundamental tenets of systems that do not use SQL and their primary distinctions from relational database management systems (RDBMS). To commence, a brief overview of the relational framework will be presented. Subsequently, the following section presents the fundamental principles of NoSQL databases and provides a comprehensive survey of the NoSQL domain (Moniruzzaman & Hossain, 2013).

7.1. BASICS CONCEPTS

This text examines the fundamental attributes of conventional, SQL-centric systems to comprehend the needs that various NoSQL methodologies endeavor to fulfill.

7.1.1. Relational Databases

Edgar F. Codd, credited with inventing the relational structure, outlines in the fundamental constituents that establish a data model:

i. Data Structure: The term "data structure" refers to the various data types used to construct a model.

ii. Operators: The operators refer to the set of available actions that can be performed to retrieve or control information contained in this particular structure.

iii. Integrity Rules: These refer to the fundamental regulations that establish coherent states for the data system.

Interactions, characteristics, tuples, and primary keys primarily define the relational information model's structure. In data management, it is common practice to represent relations in tables, where the attributes are organized as columns and the tuples are arranged as rows. The arrangement of attributes and tuples within the framework is not predetermined and, therefore, may be arbitrary (Strauch et al., 2011).

The utilization of LECT operations, which encompasses predictions and joins, is employed for data retrieval. Manipulative actions such as INSERT, UPDATE, and DELETE are also utilized for data manipulation.

The relational framework may be classified into two distinct categories of integrity rules. The enforcement of constraints, such as the requirement for primary keys to be unique, serves to maintain data integrity inside a given relation. Furthermore, independent referential integrity regulations exist among distinct relations (Okman et al., 2011).

7.1.2. ACID Properties

Transactions have been a crucial element in relational databases. Jim Gray established three fundamental attributes of a transaction in reference:atomic structure, consistency, and strength. Subsequently, Harder & Reuter condensed the characteristics and an additional isolation attribute into an abbreviation, ACID. While all four characteristics of ACID are widely recognized as crucial aspects of transactions within relational databases, uniformity is a particularly intriguing factor to consider when examining the capacity of a given system (Abramova et al., 2014) (Figure 7.2).

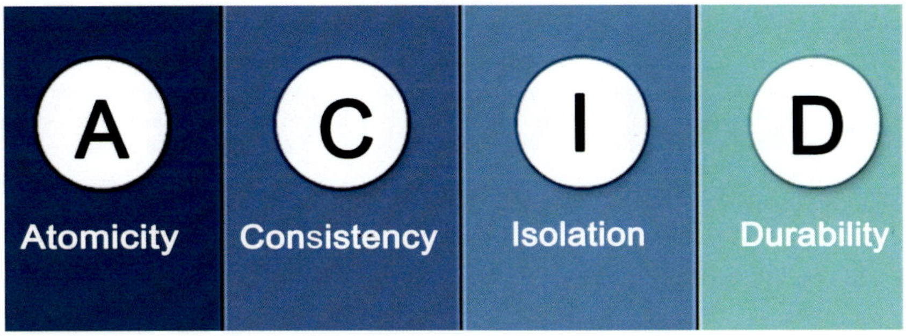

Figure 7.2. Schematic of the full form of ACID.

7.1.3. Scalability

The capacity for a system to handle an increasing workload is commonly referred to because of its ability to scale. In essence, a system has the potential to be scaled in two distinct manners: vertically along with horizontally. Vertical scaling, also known as "scale up," involves the augmentation of a system's nodes' ability. Enhanced performance can be attained through the utilization of more robust hardware. On the contrary, horizontal scaling, also known as "scaling out," involves the addition of more nodes to a system (Stonebraker, 2010).

The vertical expansion of systems is often constrained by the accessibility and cost-effectiveness of superior gadgets or tends to exhibit inefficiency. On the contrary, the horizontal expansion of systems has been found to enhance efficiency while utilizing cost-effective hardware. However, the process of horizontal scaling is frequently a complex undertaking. The primary reason is the difficulty in achieving consistency guarantees, given by ACID characteristics, within distributed systems (Leavitt, 2010).

7.2. NOSQL CONCEPTS

Learning Objectives

At the end of this section, readers will be able to:

- Describe the NoSQL databases and their significance in modern data management.
- Explain the fundamental differences between NoSQL and traditional relational databases.
- Discuss the various types of NoSQL databases, including document stores, key-value stores, column-family stores, and graph databases.

The nomenclature "NoSQL" was initially coined by Carlo Strozzi to christen a database management system (DBMS) that he created. Although founded on a relational framework, the system in question deliberately refrained from utilizing SQL as its querying language. Currently, "NoSQL" is frequently understood as "Not only SQL" and pertains to primarily decentralized non-relational databases (Sicari et al., 2022).

Initially, an outline of the classifications of NoSQL databases is presented. Subsequently, the paper delves into the discussion of the reliability guarantees that are inherent to NoSQL databases. The MapReduce paradigm is ultimately presented, serving as a robust structure for effectively handling vast quantities of data and as a crucial constituent of various NoSQL realizations (Tudorica & Bucur, 2011).

7.2.1. Types of NoSQL Systems

Edlich et al. (2016) have classified NoSQL systems into four categories, which they refer to as "Core-NoSQL" structures. These categories include Key-Value retail outlets, Wide column shops, Graph databases, and Document outlets. This classification was presented in reference, page 6. Storage options associated with NoSQL, such as Object or XML files, are called "soft-NoSQL" systems. A comprehensive compilation of recognized NoSQL implementations, classified based on this nomenclature, is available in reference. The following section will provide a detailed explanation of only the "Core" courses (Nayak et al., 2013).

7.2.1.1. Key-Value Stores

Key-Value storage networks are a type of data structure that utilizes associated arrays comprised of distinct keys and corresponding values.

To ensure unambiguous recognition of values, each key must be unique. Although keys are typically uncomplicated entities, values can encompass lists, sets, or even hashes, thereby facilitating the creation of more intricate structures for information.

The operations commonly available from Key-Value shops are analogous to those familiar to developers coming from Hash-Table executions (Reddy et al., 2022):

- Add new pairs of keys and values;
- Retrieve the value associated with a given key;
- The removal of a key and its corresponding value.

The Key-Value store's straightforward model enables it to operate quickly and effectively. The trade-off for achieving a simplified structure is a concomitant limitation in the range of query options available. Amazon's Dynamo is a well-known exemplar of Key-Value stores. Dynamo provides an archive system that is both efficient along with extremely scalable. However, it is important to note that its search interface is significantly limited, as evidenced within the context above (Gudivada et al., 2014).

7.2.1.2. Wide Column Stores

The category of systems for storage being referred to is commonly known as Extensible Write down Stores. A wide section store may be conceptualized as a Key-Value shop, wherein the key is two-dimensional. A column key and a row's key are utilized for referencing a saved value. A date and time stamp may expand the key further, as shown in Google's Big Table. The number of potential variations for the key may vary according to the specific execution, often referred to as "keyspaces" or "domains." The keys in broad column storage possess numerous dimensions, leading to a configuration akin to a multifaceted, associated array (Haseeb & Pattun, 2017).

7.2.1.3. Graph Databases

This system employs graphical representations to depict data, as its nomenclature suggests. According to scholarly literature, databases containing graphs are suitable for representing data that exhibits a substantial and adaptable variety of connections, particularly when the knowledge of those connections holds equivalent significance to the portrayed data. Examples of such data may include social relationships or geographic information. Graph databases facilitate queries on the graph topology, such as the relationships among nodes or determining the shortest paths. Effective support with these queries can be achieved using established algorithmic methods and graph databases (Burckhardt, 2014) (Figure 7.3).

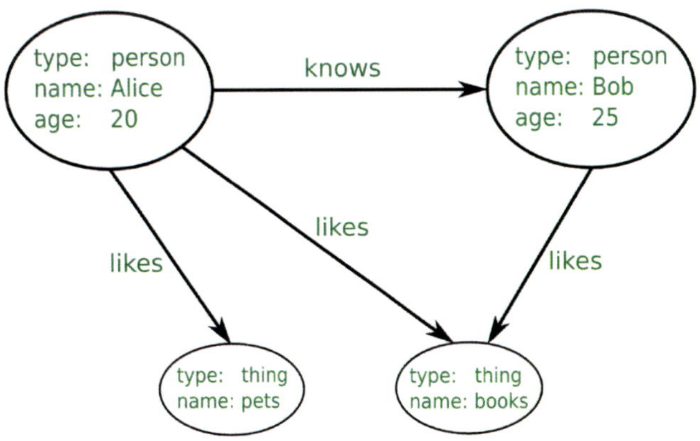

Figure 7.3. The graphical representation of data.

7.2.1.4. Document Stores

Information is retained in discrete pieces called documents within a paper-based database. The term "documents" within this context refers to any data structured in a certain manner. Examples of used formats are XML, BSON, and JSON. The specified data structure is often determined by the file that uses storage, although the data layout is flexible. As long as they adhere to the requirements of valid JSON files, it is conceivable to store disparate documents with different attribute sets in a JavaScript-based records store. The data representation within a document's file, with JSON serving as the underlying data format. The data archiving system can understand the chosen data format. Instead of using a Key-information architecture, the system can enable exact read-and-write writing procedures on a document's features because it often lacks a deeper grasp of the stored information (Bailis & Ghodsi, 2013).

MongoDB, an example of the type of document storage system. CouchDB is a popular storage solution in this group that heavily depends upon the MapReduce architecture for data searching (Figure 7.4).

people

```
{
  name:  "Alice",
  age:   20,
  likes: ["books", "pets"],
  knows: "Bob"
}
```

```
{
  name:  "Bob",
  age:   25,
  likes: ["books"]
}
```

Figure 7.4. The document preserve is utilized for displaying data through examples.

7.2.2. Eventual Consistency

A significant contrast between relational databases and NoSQL systems pertains to the uniformity of the offered models. NoSQL databases must relax the ACID assurances provided by interpersonal transactions to facilitate straight scalability. Initially, this discourse elucidates three desirable attributes across distributed structures and comprehends:

1. Consistency: The attainment of uniformity in a distributed system necessitates establishing a comprehensive order upon all operations executed across all nodes constituting the system, as posited by reference. For instance, this scenario would arise if all subsequent reading operations yielded the created value after a triumphant compose operation, irrespective of the node within which the actions are carried out (Bermbach & Tai, 2011).
2. Availability: The system is considered to fulfill the availability criterion when every operation carried out on a node within the system concludes with a response.
3. Partition Tolerance: A divided system comprises a minimum of two distinct sets of nodes, wherein nodes belonging to a single set can interact. In contrast, messages exchanged among nodes belonging to various sets cannot reach their intended destination. An instance of a partitioned system could be observed when a node becomes inaccessible due to a network malfunction. A system

can be deemed partition-accepting if it maintains both availability and consistency, despite the possibility of losing an arbitrary number of internal communications (Vogels, 2009).

Brewer proposed an idea in the year 2000, which posits that it is impossible for a web service to ensure reliability, accessibility, and tolerance for partitions simultaneously. After two years, the conjecture, commonly known as CAP Theorem and Brewer Theorem, was finally codified, and established by Gilbert and Lynch. In practical terms, this implies that distributed databases must sacrifice one of these properties. To prevent partitions, it is necessary to ensure continuous accessibility of each node within a system to the other nodes. However, this assurance cannot be ascertained in large-scale distributed systems, as stated in reference. Therefore, regarding scalable systems, the choice ultimately comes to deciding between being available alongside consistent (Condie et al., 2010).

Pritchett proposes BASE as a substitute for ACID. The acronym BASE denotes the principles of being essentially available, possessing a soft state, and ultimately consistent. The primary emphasis of this approach is on ensuring the accessibility of a system, even if it means relaxing its assurances of uniformity. The BASE system's integrity and eventual uniformity allow clients to access data that is inconsistent or outdated during certain periods. However, it ensures that those time intervals will ultimately conclude. A system possessing BASE (Basically Available, Soft state, eventually consistent) properties can overcome the constraints imposed by the CAP (Consistency, Availability, Partition tolerance) theorem, thereby providing significant potential for horizontal scaling. The chapter illustrates the irregular duration of instances for BASE structures using Amazon's S3 database as a case study. The authors have observed significant temporal fluctuations in inconsistency, ranging from a few milliseconds to moments (Dean & Ghemawat, 2008).

7.2.3. Map Reduce

The MapReduce structure, which originates in Google, is a programming language and framework specifically developed to handle vast quantities of data through the application of user-defined logic. The fundamental objective of the initial MapReduce architecture was to supply a conceptualization for handling data without encountering the complexities associated with scalabilities, such as parallelism load balancing, as stated in reference. The input for a MapReduce operation is a dictionary, a collection of data containing pairs of keys and values. The resulting data structure is once again a dictionary. The individual must implement two distinct functions, namely MAP and REDUCE and subsequently furnish these individuals with the structure (Hashem et al., 2016).

The MAP function is designed to accept a key and an amount as input parameters and generate an inventory of pairs of keys and values as an interim outcome. The MapReduce paradigm executes the designated MAP procedure on each element of the input map. Given the independence of function calls, the structure parallelizes the processing per its requirements. The initial data is partitioned into multiple segments, individually processed by distinct MAP procedures (Karloff et al., 2010).

In the middle outcomes, all key-value combinations are aggregated based on the keys, resulting in an inventory of values for each key. The reduced operation is called upon for each key. The system is designed to accept a key and a corresponding list of values as its input. The REDUCE operation performs the computation of values and aggregates them into a conclusive result value, subsequently linked with the corresponding key. All instances of the REDUCE function can be executed concurrently (Lee et al., 2012).

7.3. MONGODB

Learning Objectives

At the end of this section, readers will be able to:

- Explain the fundamental concepts and principles of MongoDB, including its document-oriented data model and NoSQL database architecture.
- Discuss the advantages and disadvantages of using MongoDB compared to traditional relational databases, highlighting its scalability, flexibility, and ease of development.
- Describe the key components of MongoDB, such as collections, documents, indexes, and queries, and demonstrate how they are used in real-world applications.

MongoDB has become an information database that is free to use and was created by 10gen, a software business that provides commercial support. The primary objective of MongoDB, as suggested by its nomenclature based on the term "humongous," is to manage vast quantities of data. Although MongoDB is coded in C^{++}, it employs JavaScript as its primary query language. The subsequent sections entail an analysis of the information model presented by MongoDB as the three fundamental constituents of data structures as previously defined. Most of the parts are derived from the present iteration of MongoDB's manual (Gyorodi et al., 2015).

7.3.1. Data Structure

MongoDB employs gathers as its fundamental units of data storage. A relationship (or table) is the interpersonal counterpart to a collection. Unlike relationships, an accumulation does not impose a rigid schema but can contain entirely disparate documents. Standardizing the structure for every record within a collection can facilitate streamlined and optimized data retrieval through querying (Boicea et al., 2012). Documents might be likened to interpersonal tuples and regarded as arrays of associations or hashes. MongoDB employs a data storage and transmission mechanism that uses BSON (Binary JSON) structure for documents. The BSON document primarily constitutes a binary manifestation of JSON paperwork, augmented with additional details to facilitate data parsing, such as duration prefixes. Like BSON documents, JSON items comprise attribute-value groups, wherein every value may be a basic type (such as string or integer), an intricate BSON object, or a set comprising either simple kinds or objects. Moreover, BSON expands upon the JSON requirements by incorporating a few basic data types, such as those over time and date values. The comprehensive BSON requirement is available for reference in the following location (Chauhan, 2019).

7.3.2. Operators

7.3.2.1. Reading Data

The FIND functioning holds significant importance in retrieving information from a MongoDB collection. Without supplementary parameters, the function yields all records contained within a given being collected. The FIND function receives an argument as a standards object organized within BSON. MongoDB employs a filtering mechanism that selects documents based on prescribed criteria, exclusively presenting query outcomes that satisfy all designated attributes and corresponding values. Furthermore, MongoDB has defined specific conditioned operators that can be incorporated into the criteria. The operators are available for use within the database encompass a spectrum of functionalities, ranging from basic contrasts such as "lt" denoting "lesser than" to traditional expressing and intricate JavaScript functions that can be customized by the user and subsequently examined by the database system (Wei-Ping et al., 2011).

An alternative method for retrieving data involves the utilization of the MAPREDUCE worker within MongoDB. The operator above requires a MAP and a REDUCE operation, provided in functions in JavaScript adhering to a stated format. As delineated in Section 1.3.3, the initial step involves the execution of the MAP function upon all the paperwork. Subsequently, the in-between outcomes are subjected to processing via the REDUCE function. The outcomes yielded by the REDUCE operation signify the outcome of the query. Listing 1.2 illustrates a specific instance (Lee et al., 2004).

```
db.people.find({name: 'Alice'})

// {_id: 1234, name: 'Alice,' age: 20, likes: ['books,' 'pets'], knows: ['Bob']}

db.people.find({age: 25})

// {_id: 5678, name: 'Bob,' age: 25, likes: ['books

']}

db.people.find({age: {$lt: 30}})

// [{_id: 1234, name: 'Alice,'...}, {_id: 5678, name: 'Bob,'...}]

db.people.find({knows: {$exists: true}})

// {_id: 1234, name: 'Alice,'...}

db.people.find({likes: {$size: 1}})

// {_id: 5678, name: 'Bob,'...}
```

7.3.2.2. Manipulating Data

Incorporating new documents into a collection is achieved through INSERT operations. The operational procedure receives the document for insertion in BSON format. Before storing the provided paperwork, MongoDB appends an extra attribute labeled "id" with a distinct value across the entire collection. Those above may be regarded as the main key, serving the purpose of distinguishing the document.

The UPDATE functioning can be employed to modify pre-existing objects within an assortment. The function requires a criteria object and an object representing the implemented modifications. If the latter object denotes a standard document, the initial document that satisfies the specified criteria undergoes a complete replacement. MongoDB offers supplementary alteration syntax to modify particular characteristics of matched paperwork exclusively. Listing 1.3 presents several examples (Gao & Qiu, 2010).

The act of removing documents can be achieved by utilizing the REMOVE operations. The requirements object may target the documents intended to be removed.

```
map = function() {
for (i in this.likes) {
emit(this.likes[i], {count: 1});
}
};
reduce = function(key, values) {
var total = 0;
for (i in values) {
total += values[i].count
}
return {count: total}
};
db.people.mapReduce(map, reduce)
// [{books: {count: 3}},
// {pets: {count: 4}}]
```

7.4. INTEGRITY RULES

Learning Objectives

At the end of this section, readers will be able to:

- Explain the concept of integrity rules in the context of data management and database systems.
- Discuss the importance of integrity rules in ensuring data accuracy, consistency, and reliability.
- Describe the types of integrity rules, including entity integrity, referential integrity, and domain integrity, and their specific purposes.

In contrast to relational databases, which provide diverse honesty regulations, MongoDB provides options for enforcing document distinctiveness. As previously stated, every document possesses an "id" attribute.

MongoDB lacks inherent assistance with record joining and provides no guidelines for maintaining the integrity of referential relationships.

7.5. INDEXING

Learning Objectives

At the end of this section, readers will be able to:

- Describe the purpose and importance of indexing in information retrieval systems.
- Explain the key principles and techniques involved in creating and maintaining an index.
- Discuss the advantages and disadvantages of various indexing methods, such as inverted indexes, B-trees, and hash tables.

Database searches are a crucial component in enhancing the efficiency of examining queries. By standard, the primary essential section in a relational database is usually indexed. The statement above holds valid for MongoDB paperwork's "id" link.

```
db.people.insert({name: 'Alice,' age: 20})
```

```
db.people.update({name: 'Alice'}, {name: 'Eve'})

db.people.find({name: 'Eve'})

// {_id: 123, name: 'Eve'}

db.people.insert({name: 'Alice,' age: 20})

db.people.update({name: 'Alice'}, {$set: {name: 'Eve

'}})

db.people.find({name: 'Eve'})

// {_id: 456, name: 'Eve,' age: 20}

db.people.insert({name: 'Alice,' age: 20})

db.people.update({name: 'Alice'}, {$inc: {age: 5}})

db. people.find({name: 'Alice'})

// {_id: 789, name: 'Alice,' age: 25}
```

MongoDB provides the capability to create numerous indexes for a collection, enabling efficient data retrieval. It is possible to index every single attribute of paperwork and a variety of attributes. This pertains to characteristics present in sub-documents, including attributes that are nested within other attributes) (Hikitih et al., 2021).

As previously mentioned, the arrangement of an item is not predetermined by the assembly. Because indices are generated on a per-collection basis, it is possible for certain documents throughout a collection to lack a particular attribute, despite the presence of an index for the said attribute. In MongoDB, papers of this nature are regarded as possessing a characteristic of a null value. The presence of highly diverse paperwork within a collection result in a substantial increase in overhead. Hence, MongoDB presents an alternative indexing mechanism, namely sparse indexing. In cases where an index has become sparse, it disregards any documents within a collection that lack the indexed characteristic. This feature enables improved performance and decreased storage overhead by eliminating the need for creating and upholding "empty" indexes (Indrawan, 2012).

According to relational database systems, it is well-established that while indexes enhance the efficiency of reading operations, they also increase the cost of writing operations. Each time a document undergoes creation, modification, or deletion, it is necessary to update the corresponding indexes. Therefore, particularly in scenarios with a high volume of writing, generating an excessive number of indexes could potentially have a notable adverse impact on the system's overall efficiency (Guo & Onstein, 2020).

7.5.1. Scalability

MongoDB cannot manage inter-collection references, necessitating that every client-initiated read or write operation be restricted to a single collection. Vertical expansion of applications that involve numerous smaller numbers may be accomplished by distributing the collections across multiple machines.

Nevertheless, the process of vertical scaling becomes increasingly intricate when managing vast quantities of documents that are stored within a singular collection. The MongoDB platform provides a sharding mechanism that enables the distribution of collections across multiple nodes in a manner forthcoming to the application. To execute this task, it is necessary to specify the number of fragments to be utilized and a designated shard key (Gessert et al., 2017).

For a collection to be shared, its papers must possess a shared key characteristic. Utilizing a fragmented key facilitates the partitioning of a collection through numerous segments. A chunk refers to a distinct portion of a given collection that contains a set of documents. The set of paperwork is defined by the values that comprise the fragmented key falling throughout a specific range (Mahmood et al., 2015).

Since the attribute is designated as the shard key, a collection comprising n chunks (ci)i = 1.n will include all documents alongside principles v for attribute a within each chunk ci, where mini ≤ v < maxi. Determining the fragment key varies for every chunk. Specifically, those over mini and maxi is a system-driven process to ensure equitable distribution of every record across accessible shards. Upon exceeding a predetermined threshold, the network undergoes a process of chunk division and redistribution to maintain equitable load distribution across all shards (Diogo et al., 2019).

The efficacy of reading and writing on a sharded gathering is heavily contingent upon selecting an appropriate shard key. When an attribute is utilized as a shard key and has a uniform value across most paperwork, it results in the corresponding chunk containing those files being impervious to splitting. As per reference, it is not possible to evenly distribute the assortment uniformly among all shards. If the individuals in a collection are predominantly compared to the same country, utilizing a characteristic such as "home country" as a shard key would not be optimal. In this scenario, MongoDB could not establish a uniformly distributed splitting (Xiang et al., 2010).

7.5.2. Consistency

MongoDB provides excellent consistency on individual entities when there is just a single server managing all the reading and writing demands across every shard. This implies that the atomicity property applies to all reading and writing actions performed on individual papers and that any FIND activities involving only a single record are ensured to accurately reflect the most current state of the database (Abramova & Bernardino, 2013).

Furthermore, it is possible to set a choice in MongoDB's FIND activities that permit reading from secondary sources. If replication to occur is employed, a copied node, also known as an enslaved person, has the potential to respond to the inquiry. Thus, the accessibility of the information within it can be enhanced. However, this trade-off entails a compromise in uniformity, as stipulated within the CAP theorem. Due to the possibility of the copied node retaining obsolete data about the entity in question, the only form of uniformity that can be ensured is future consistency (Manoj, 2014).

SUMMARY

The relational database structure is a highly adaptable storage solution that can be applied to various issues, owing to its intricate array of employees and integrity regulations. Furthermore, relational transactions, which possess ACID properties, provide robust assurances regarding consistency. In contrast, NoSQL storage options generally strive to offer streamlined yet highly effective resolutions for particular issues. The primary objective of numerous NoSQL databases is to offer exceptional scalability. To prioritize the accessible nature of a system, it may be necessary to ease the strong uniformity guarantees typically associated with relational systems. Consequently, the concept of eventually remaining consistent is derived.

MongoDB, a document-oriented database, has been extensively discussed among the vast NoSQL systems. In contrast to relational systems that operate within rigid data structures, document stores facilitate the storage of diverse objects cohesively, provided they conform to a uniform data format. Document archives cannot typically accommodate intricate relationships among stored entities. A potential solution to this issue could involve accepting denormalized data, which entails the storage of interconnected data redundantly. In contrast to certain NoSQL systems, such as CouchDB, that impose restrictions on data searching and necessitate using MapReduce for handling information, MongoDB provides a versatile API that employs a criteria syntax similar to JSON. However, it is worth noting that the flexibility offered by relational systems through the SQL programming language has yet to be surpassed.

No single NoSQL system can serve as a universal storage solution or supplant a system with a relational the selection of an appropriate system is necessary to address the given task effectively. When expedient data retrieval is required and querying through a solitary key is satisfactory, KeyValue stores prove to be a commendable option. Wide column stores enable the creation of more intricate key structures. A database based on graphs is most suitable for storing objects that are highly interconnected yet simple and for queries that pertain to the structure of relationships. On the contrary, querying interactions in document-oriented structures may be more complex. Document stores enable the storage of complexly structured objects in a scalable manner and provide effective mechanisms for querying such structures.

REVIEW QUESTIONS

1. What are the fundamental differences between NoSQL databases and relational databases?
2. Explain the ACID properties and their role in relational databases.
3. Discuss the concept of scalability in the context of NoSQL databases.
4. What are the different types of NoSQL systems, and how do they differ in their data models?
5. Define eventual consistency and its significance in distributed systems.

MULTIPLE CHOICE QUESTIONS

1. What is a primary characteristic of NoSQL databases?

a. They strictly adhere to the relational model.
b. They are exclusively used in small-scale applications.
c. They provide flexible schemas.
d. They require predefined schemas.

2. Which of the following is a typical use case for NoSQL databases?

a. Online transaction processing (OLTP)
b. Complex joins and transactions
c. Storing and processing unstructured data
d. Structured querying using SQL language

3. Which of the following NoSQL databases is column-oriented?

a. MongoDB
b. Couchbase
c. Cassandra
d. HBase

4. What is the primary advantage of using a document-oriented NoSQL database like MongoDB?

a. Strong consistency guarantees
b. Fixed schema design
c. Horizontal scalability
d. Limited support for large datasets

5. Which of the following consistency models is commonly associated with NoSQL databases?

a. ACID
b. BASE
c. CAP
d. CRUD

Answers to Multiple Choice Questions

1. (c); 2. (c); 3. (d); 4. (c); 5. (b);

REFERENCES

1. Abramova, V., & Bernardino, J., (2013). NoSQL databases: MongoDB vs Cassandra. In: Proceedings of the International C* Conference on Computer Science and Software Engineering (Vol. 1, No. 1, pp. 14–22).

2. Chang, B. R., Tsai, H. F., Wang, Y. A., & Chen, C. Y., (2015). Realization of secondary indexing to NoSQL database with intelligent adaptation. In: 2015 Conference on Technologies and Applications of Artificial Intelligence (TAAI) (pp. 449–452). IEEE.
3. Chauhan, A., (2019). A review on various aspects of MongoDB databases. International Journal of Engineering Research & Technology (IJERT), 8(5), 90–92.
4. Condie, T., Conway, N., Alvaro, P., Hellerstein, J. M., Elmeleegy, K., & Sears, R., (2010). MapReduce online. In: NSDI (Vol. 10, No. 4, p. 20).
5. Dean, J., & Ghemawat, S., (2008). MapReduce: Simplified data processing on large clusters. Communications of the ACM, 51(1), 107–113.
6. Diogo, M., Cabral, B., & Bernardino, J., (2019). Consistency models of NoSQL databases. Future Internet, 11(2), 43.
7. Gao, X., & Qiu, J., (2010). Scalable inverted indexing on NoSQL table storage. A Class, 1(1), 1–20.
8. George, S., (2013). NoSQL–not only SQL. International Journal of Enterprise Computing and Business Systems, 2(2), 1–20.
9. Gessert, F., Wingerath, W., Friedrich, S., & Ritter, N., (2017). NoSQL database systems: A survey and decision guidance. Computer Science-Research and Development, 32, 353–365.
10. Gudivada, V. N., Rao, D., & Raghavan, V. V., (2014). NoSQL systems for big data management. In: 2014 IEEE World Congress on Services (Vol. 1, No. 1, pp. 190–197).
11. Guo, D., & Onstein, E., (2020). State-of-the-art geospatial information processing in NoSQL databases. ISPRS International Journal of Geo-Information, 9(5), 331.
12. Győrödi, C., Győrödi, R., Pecherle, G., & Olah, A., (2015). A comparative study: MongoDB vs. MySQL. In: 2015 13th International Conference on Engineering of Modern Electric Systems (EMES) (Vol. 1, No. 1, pp. 1–6).
13. Han, J., Haihong, E., Le, G., & Du, J., (2011). Survey on NoSQL database. In: 2011 6th International Conference on Pervasive Computing and Applications (pp. 363–366). IEEE.
14. Haseeb, A., & Pattun, G., (2017). A review on NoSQL: Applications and challenges. International Journal of Advanced Research in Computer Science, 8(1), 1–20.
15. Hashem, I. A. T., Anuar, N. B., Gani, A., Yaqoob, I., Xia, F., & Khan, S. U., (2016). MapReduce: Review and open challenges. Scientometrics, 109, 389–422.
16. Indrawan-Santiago, M., (2012). Database research: Are we at a crossroad? Reflection on NoSQL. In: 2012 15th International Conference on Network-Based Information Systems (pp. 45–51). IEEE.
17. Karloff, H., Suri, S., & Vassilvitskii, S., (2010). A model of computation for MapReduce. In: Proceedings of the Twenty-First Annual ACM-SIAM Symposium on Discrete Algorithms (pp. 938–948). Society for Industrial and Applied Mathematics.
18. Leavitt, N., (2010). Will NoSQL databases live up to their promise? Computer, 43(2), 12–14.

19. Lee, K. H., Lee, Y. J., Choi, H., Chung, Y. D., & Moon, B., (2012). Parallel data processing with MapReduce: A survey. ACM SIGMOD Record, 40(4), 11–20.
20. Lee, Y. W., Pipino, L., Strong, D. M., & Wang, R. Y., (2004). Process-embedded data integrity. Journal of Database Management (JDM), 15(1), 87–103.
21. Mahmood, K., Risch, T., & Zhu, M., (2015). Utilizing a NoSQL data store for scalable log analysis. In: Proceedings of the 19th International Database Engineering & Applications Symposium (Vol. 1, No. 1, pp. 49–55).
22. Manoj, V., (2014). Comparative study of NoSQL document, column store databases and evaluation of Cassandra. International Journal of Database Management Systems, 6(4), 11.
23. Moniruzzaman, A. B. M., & Hossain, S. A., (2013). NoSQL Database: New Era of Databases for Big Data Analytics-Classification, Characteristics and Comparison. arXiv preprint arXiv:1307.0191.
24. Nayak, A., Poriya, A., & Poojary, D., (2013). Type of NOSQL databases and its comparison with relational databases. International Journal of Applied Information Systems, 5(4), 16–19.
25. Okman, L., Gal-Oz, N., Gonen, Y., Gudes, E., & Abramov, J., (2011). Security issues in NoSQL databases. In: 2011IEEE 10th International Conference on Trust, Security and Privacy in Computing and Communications (Vol. 1, No. 1, pp. 541–547).
26. Reddy, H. B. S., Reddy, R. R. S., Jonnalagadda, R., Singh, P., & Gogineni, A., (2022). Analysis of the unexplored security issues common to all types of NoSQL databases. Asian Journal of Research in Computer Science, 14(1), 1–12.
27. Schindler, J., (2012). I/O characteristics of NoSQL databases. Proceedings of the VLDB Endowment, 5(12), 2020, 2021.
28. Schindler, J., (2013). Profiling and analyzing the I/O performance of NoSQL DBs. In: Proceedings of the ACM SIGMETRICS/International Conference on Measurement and Modeling of Computer Systems (Vol. 1, No. 1, pp. 389–390).
29. Sicari, S., Rizzardi, A., & Coen-Porisini, A., (2022). Security & privacy issues and challenges in NoSQL databases. Computer Networks, 1(1), 108828.
30. Stonebraker, M., (2010). SQL databases v. NoSQL databases. Communications of the ACM, 53(4), 10–11.
31. Strauch, C., Sites, U. L. S., & Kriha, W., (2011). NoSQL databases. Lecture Notes, Stuttgart Media University, 20(24), 79.
32. Swaminathan, S. N., & Elmasri, R., (2016). Quantitative analysis of scalable NoSQL databases. In: 2016 IEEE International Congress on Big Data (BigData Congress) (Vol. 1, No. 1, pp. 323–326).
33. Tudorica, B. G., & Bucur, C., (2011). A comparison between several NoSQL databases with comments and notes. In: 2011 RoEduNet International Conference: Networking in Education and Research (10th edn., Vol. 1, No. 1, pp. 1–5).
34. Vogels, W., (2009). Eventually consistent. Communications of the ACM, 52(1), 40–44.
35. Wei-Ping, Z., Ming-Xin, L. I., & Huan, C., (2011). Using MongoDB to implement

textbook management system instead of MySQL. In: 2011 IEEE 3rd International Conference on Communication Software and Networks (Vol. 1, No. 1, pp. 303–305).

36. Xiang, P., Hou, R., & Zhou, Z., (2010). Cache and consistency in NOSQL. In: 2010 3rd International Conference on Computer Science and Information Technology (Vol. 6, pp. 117–120).

37. Yu, Q., & Zhou, J., (2022). Consistent and efficient batch operations for NoSQL databases with hybrid timestamp. In: Network and Parallel Computing: 19th IFIP WG 10.3 International Conference, NPC 2022, Jinan, China, Proceedings (Vol. 1, No. 1, pp. 340–351). Cham: Springer Nature Switzerland.

38. Нікітін, В., Крилов, Є., Корнага, Я., & Анікін, В. (2021). Combined indexing method in NoSQL databases. Адаптивні Системи Автоматичного Управління, 1(38), 3–9.

CHAPTER 8

Cloud Databases and Big Data

LEARNING OBJECTIVES

After studying this chapter, you will be able to:

- Understand the concept of cloud databases and their advantages over traditional on-premises databases.
- Explore the architecture and key components of cloud databases, including storage, compute, and networking layers.
- Learn about different types of cloud database services, such as Infrastructure as a Service (IaaS), Platform as a Service (PaaS), and Database as a Service (DBaaS).
- Gain insights into the challenges and considerations associated with migrating to and managing cloud databases, including security, scalability, and performance optimization.
- Explore the fundamentals of big data, including its characteristics (volume, velocity, variety, and veracity) and the technologies and techniques used for storing, processing, and analyzing large datasets.

"Cloud databases are the catalysts that empower organizations to turn the vast sea of Big Data into actionable insights, unleashing the true potential of data-driven decision-making."

INTRODUCTORY EXAMPLE

Imagine you're the manager of a large e-commerce platform, and you're facing a common challenge in the retail industry: understanding customer behavior and preferences to improve sales and customer satisfaction. You have a vast amount of data at your disposal, including customer purchase history, website clickstream data, social media interactions, and more. This data is incredibly valuable, but it's also overwhelming in its volume and complexity.

This is where Big Data applications come into play. By harnessing the power of these advanced tools and technologies, you can analyze and gain insights from this massive dataset in ways that were previously impossible. Here's how:

1. Enhanced Customer Insights: Big Data applications allow you to dive deep into your customer data. You can segment customers based on their preferences, track their browsing behavior in real-time, and even predict their future purchases. This level of insight enables you to tailor your product recommendations and marketing campaigns to each individual's unique interests.
2. Optimized Inventory Management: With Big Data analytics, you can forecast demand more accurately and optimize your inventory accordingly. By identifying trends and seasonality in your sales data, you can reduce overstocking and understocking issues, leading to cost savings and improved customer satisfaction.
3. Fraud Detection: Big Data applications excel in detecting fraudulent activities. They can analyze transactions in real-time, flagging suspicious patterns and potentially fraudulent behavior. This proactive approach not only protects your business from financial losses but also enhances the trust of your customers.
4. Competitive Advantage: By staying ahead of the competition, you can be more agile and responsive to market changes. Big Data applications can monitor your competitors' pricing, product launches, and customer sentiment, allowing you to make informed strategic decisions.
5. Real-Time Personalization: When a customer visits your website, you can use Big Data applications to personalize their experience instantly. You can recommend products based on their browsing history, display relevant content, and even adjust pricing dynamically. This level of personalization enhances user engagement and conversion rates.

In this example, we can see how Big Data applications enable you to transform the overwhelming amount of data into actionable insights, ultimately leading to improved decision-making, increased revenue, and a competitive edge in the market. These advantages make Big Data applications a crucial asset for businesses across various industries.

UNIT INTRODUCTION

Big Data refers to a methodology for analyzing data that is made possible by advancements in technology and architecture. This methodology is characterized by the ability to capture, store, and analyze data at high velocities. According to scholarly sources, the range of data sources has expanded beyond the conventional corporate database to encompass diverse forms of information such as email, output from mobile devices, data generated by sensors, and output from social media. Contemporary data encompasses not only structured records stored in databases, but also unstructured data that lacks standardized formatting (Awiti et al., 2020).

The processing and analysis of Big Data necessitates a significant allocation of storage capacity. Although the cost of storage has been decreasing, small and medium-sized enterprises may still encounter financial challenges in utilizing big data due to the required resources. A commonly employed infrastructure for the storage and analysis of big data involves the utilization of crowded network-attached storage (NAS). The establishment of a crowded NAS infrastructure necessitates the arrangement of multiple NAS "pods," each of which consists of multiple storage gadgets that are linked to a NAS device. The NAS appliances are subsequently interconnected to facilitate extensive data sharing along with searching (Albrecht & Naumann, 2008) (Figure 8.1).

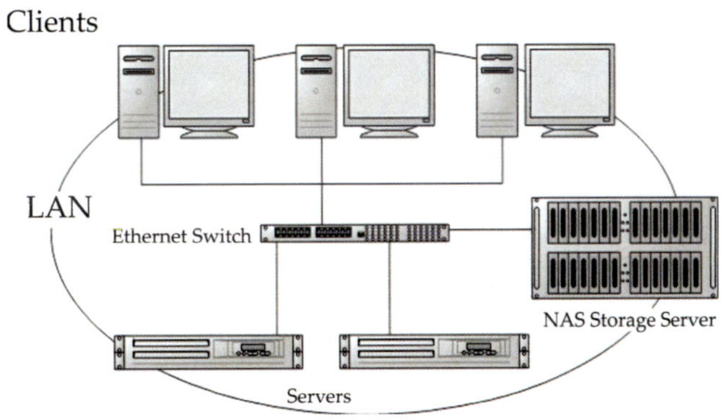

Figure 8.1. Network-attached storage (NAS).

The approach of service-oriented computation called cloud computing achieved remarkable success and brought about a significant transformation in the abstraction and utilization of computing infrastructure. The three most widely recognized cloud paradigms can be Infrastructure to be a Service, Platforms to be a Service, as well as Software be a Service. The aforementioned concept can be further expanded to encompass a database in the form of a service (DBaaS) or storage space-as-a-service (STaaS).

Cloud computing has become a widely accepted paradigm for deploying innovative applications that had been previously not affordable in traditional business infrastructure settings. This is due to several enabling features like flexibility, pay-per-use, minimal upfront investments, minimal time to markets, as well as the transfer of potential hazards. Database management systems that can be scaled to accommodate update-intensive apps and decision-support tools are crucial components of cloud infrastructure. For over 30 years, the field of database analysis has aimed to achieve scalable as well as dispersed data management. Considerable scholarly attention has been devoted to the development of scalable systems that can accommodate the two: update-intensive tasks and ad-hoc analysis tasks. The preliminary designs encompass the utilization of databases that are distributed for tasks that require frequent updates, as well as parallel database structures for workloads that involve analysis. The development of parallel databases progressed from prototype systems to extensive commercial systems. However, distributed database platforms did not achieve significant success and weren't commercialized. Instead, diverse ad-hoc methods were employed to facilitate scaling (Bao et al., 2007).

The emergence of Key-Value outlets can be attributed to alterations within the data accessibility patterns of apps and the necessity to expand to numerous commodity machines. This has resulted in the development of a new category of systems that are being extensively embraced by diverse enterprises. The MapReduce framework and which is open-source execution Hadoop have been extensively adopted in businesses as well as universities for data analysis purposes. Proposals have been put forth to enhance the usability as well as efficiency of Hadoop-based mechanisms (Galici et al., 2020) (Figure 8.2).

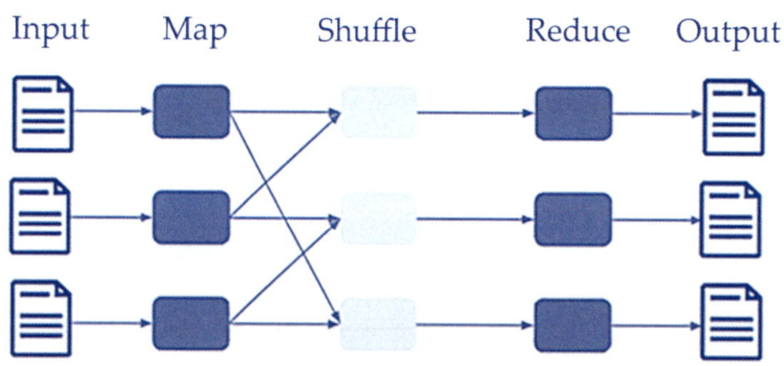

Figure 8.2. Schematic of MapReduce framework.

Conversely, data centers have been employed for the purpose of managing vast quantities of data. The existing warehouses and their associated solutions are inadequate in terms of providing timely responses to cope with the increasing volumes of data. There are two approaches to data processing: batch analytics on large volumes or real-time transactions on small data sets. Given the updated specifications, it is imperative to guarantee a prompt and efficient response, either in real-time or nearly real-time, for vast quantities of data. The four dimensions of big data, namely the amount, speed, variety, as well as veracity, pose significant challenges to conventional data warehousing systems in terms of data management along with analytics. The term "big data" refers to data sets that surpass the processing capabilities of traditional database systems. The aforementioned statement suggests that the quantity of data is excessive, and/or the data values undergo rapid changes, and/or it fails to conform to the established principles of traditional database management systems, such as consistency. Professionals in the field of information and technology management must possess novel competencies that enable them to proficiently model along with prepare data for assessment. Additionally, they must possess a deep understanding of the problem at hand to effectively execute analytics. Due to the vast size and dynamic nature of data, a substantial amount of memory and central processing unit resources are required. These resources can be obtained through the utilization of distributed processors as well as storage space in cloud environments (Lee & Park, 2021).

The utilization of cloud computing over data storage seems a feasible alternative for small and medium enterprises that are contemplating the implementation of Big Data analytical methodologies. Cloud computing refers to the provision of computing resources by an external entity, which can be accessed on-demand through a network.

This approach typically requires minimal management effort from the business. Cloud computing encompasses various architectures as well as deployment models that can be integrated with diverse technologies along with design methodologies. Small and medium-sized business proprietors who lack the financial resources to implement clustered NAS technologies may explore various cloud computing algorithms to fulfill their big data requirements. It is imperative for small as well as medium-sized enterprise proprietors to contemplate the appropriate cloud computing solution to sustain their competitiveness and profitability (Rodriguez-Muro et al., 2012).

8.1. BIG DATA

Learning Objectives

At the end of this section, readers will be able to:

- Define the concept of Big Data and its significance in modern data-driven industries.
- Explain the key characteristics of Big Data, including volume, velocity, variety, veracity, and value.
- Discuss the challenges and limitations associated with managing and analyzing Big Data.

The term "Big Data" is utilized to describe the inadequacy of conventional data frameworks in effectively managing contemporary data collections. The need for a novel architecture to attain efficiencies is driven by certain characteristics. These include the amount and diversity of data available from diverse domains or forms, which pertain to the data itself set at rest. Additionally, the data-in-motion features such as velocity, the degree of flow, as well as variability (primarily denoting a change within velocity) also play a crucial role. Diverse attributes give rise to distinct architectures or varying sequences of data lifecycle processes that are necessary to attain the required efficiencies. Several alternative terms (frequently commencing with the word 'V') are utilized, however, a subset of these pertain to analytics rather than big data structures (Silva et al., 2016) (Figure 8.3).

Figure 8.3. Illustration of big data.

The emergence of the big data framework is characterized by the need to prioritize managing all kinds of data as a crucial factor in the development of system architecture, particularly when dealing with large volumes of data that are either at rest or constantly in motion. The big data framework entails a fundamental transformation in data system structures, moving away from monolithic structures that rely on vertical scaling (i.e., more powerful processors or disks) and towards horizontally scaled structures that incorporate a loosely integrated collection of resources. Approximately two decades ago, a transition took place within the modeling community whereby scientific simulations started utilizing massively parallel processing (MPP) networks. By employing diverse arrangements of segregating the code as well as data among autonomous processors, researchers in computational science succeeded in significantly enhancing their simulation capacities (Uddin & Gupta, 2014). The aforementioned has resulted in several intricacies in domains such as communication of messages, transfer of data, delay in uniformity across resources, distribution of workload, and operational inadequacies while anticipating the completion of tasks by other resources. Similarly, the big data framework embodies a comparable transformation, employing distinct mechanisms to disseminate code and data among loosely-coupled resources to facilitate the requisite scaling in data management that corresponds to the scaling within the data.

The primary objective of the storage and retrieval of substantial volumes of data has been to conduct a study that generates supplementary insights into the data. Historically, data analysis usually took place on a randomly selected subset of the dataset (Bakshi, 2012).

8.1.1. Big Data Engineering

Big Data Technology refers to the utilization of storage as well as data manipulation technology that make use of a set of horizontally connected resources in order to attain performance scalability which is almost linear. The increasing significance of data types that aren't amenable to effective handling within a conventional relational model has propelled the development of novel engineering techniques within the data layers. The requirement for expandable accessibility in both organized and unorganized data has resulted in the development of software centered on name-value/key-value pairs or just columnar (big table), document-centric, along with graph (that includes triple-store) models (Chacko et al., 2015).

8.1.2. Non-Relational Model

Non-Relational Simulations pertain to logic-based models, including records, graphs, key-value, as well as additional models, which are utilized to facilitate more effective storage and retrieval of non-tabular databases.

8.1.3. NoSQL

NoSQL, also known as "no SQL" or just "not only SQL," pertains to data storage and interfaces that do not adhere to rigid relational methodologies (Davoudian et al., 2018) (Figure 8.4).

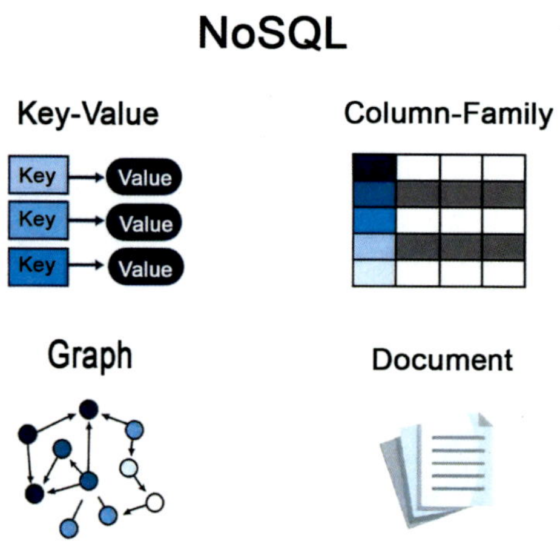

Figure 8.4. Elements of NOSQL.

8.1.4. Big Data Models

The term "Big Data Models" pertains to conceptual data models, including both relational as well as non-relational models, as well as the processing along with computation models such as batch, streaming, as well as transactional models. These models are utilized for the purpose of storing and manipulating data within horizontally developed resources (Sharma et al., 2014).

8.1.5. Schema-On-Read

Big data that follows a schema-on-read approach is frequently stored within an unprocessed state according to the method of production. The schema required for arranging and frequently refining the data is identified and modified during the querying process. The structuring of data for supporting particular algorithms or just processing structures is crucial for the effective operation of numerous analytics (Janković et al., 2018).

8.1.6. Big Data Analytics

The field of Big Data Analysis has undergone swift development with respect to its functionality as well as the fundamental programming paradigm. Analytical functions facilitate the integration of parallel-derived results from distributed segments of one or multiple data sources (Tsai et al., 2015).

8.1.7. Big Data Paradigm

The big data framework is characterized by the deployment of data systems that are horizontally distributed throughout independent resources, which enables the scalability required for the effective processing of large-scale data sets.

The emergence of the Big Data Framework has enabled the performance of analytical operations on the complete data set or possibly on an ongoing flow of data within real-time. The process of analysis has the potential to incorporate diverse data sources originating from various entities. An illustrative inquiry pertains to the correlation that exists among insect-borne ailments, temperature, precipitation, as well as variations in foliage. In order to address this inquiry, a comprehensive analysis would necessitate the integration of data pertaining to disease incidence along with geographic distribution, meteorological data, as well as aerial imagery (Sun et al., 2018).

It is anticipated that there will be further advancements in the techniques employed to attain optimal scalability across various resources. However, the current shift towards the utilization of several horizontally-coupled facilities for processing or data systems, commonly referred to as "crowdsourcing," can be likened to a paradigm shift. This shift is expected to be a singular event unless another paradigm shift arises in the future. This is similar to the previous paradigm shift observed in the simulated community.

The technical improvements associated with the Big Data framework have additional implications. The modifications are not solely confined to rational data retention but also encompass the concurrent dissemination of data as well as code within the tangible file system, along with direct interrogations directed toward this retention (Patgiri & Ahmed, 2016).

The alteration in cognitive processes results in modifications to the conventional data life cycle. The entire data lifecycle can be delineated into four distinct stages, namely, collection, preparation, evaluation, as well as action. Big data utilization scenarios can be classified based on the attributes of data sets in a stationary or mobile state and with regard to the duration of the complete data lifecycle. The features of a collection of data have varying impacts on the processes involved in the data lifecycle. One such impact is observed in the stage of the lifecycle where the data is stored in a persistent manner. In the conventional relational paradigm, the data undergoes preparation procedures such as extract-transform-load as well as a cleansing before being stored. In scenarios where there is a need for rapid data processing, the information is first subjected to preparation and analysis to enable timely alerting. Subsequently, the data or its aggregates are stored persistently. In a scenario involving voluminous data, it is common practice to store the data in its original form, prior to undergoing any preparatory procedures aimed at refining and structuring the data. The ongoing existence of data within its raw form implies that the application of an arrangement or representation of the data occurs exclusively during data retrieval, which is commonly referred to as schema on read (Strang & Sun, 2017).

One of the outcomes of big data building is commonly known as "processing relocation from data to processing," which involves shifting the computation of data toward the location where the data is stored, rather than transferring the data to a separate processing location. The suggestion is that the volume of data is excessively large to be retrieved and transferred to an alternative resource for examination. Consequently, the analysis software is disseminated to the data-storing resources, and solely the outcomes are consolidated on a distinct resource. Given that data transfer rates are often constrained by I/O bandwidth, an alternative strategy would be to integrate query and filtering programs directly into the tangible storage medium (Kressbach, 2021).

The concept of Big Data primarily involves the expansion of data storage and analysis capabilities throughout horizontally-scaled resources. This bears resemblance to the approach taken by the compute-intensive modeling community in the past, where enormously parallel processing was adopted. Historically, traditional parallel computing programs employed a wide range of syncing and communication mechanisms and established varied communication structures. Presently, compared to the past, the size of data sets has grown significantly, reaching Petabyte as well as Exabyte levels. As a result, distributed computation frameworks have emerged, providing patterns such as map-reduce, which offer a dependable high-level, commercially feasible computing model based on commodities computing hardware, dynamic schedulers of resources, as well as synchronization methods.

Big Data refers to a collection of data sets that possess certain characteristics, including size, speed, variety, variability, as well as veracity, which make it difficult to analyze via current or developed technologies and methods. This challenge is particularly relevant within a particular area of concern and at a specific point in time; additionally, the ultimate goal is to determine value from the data (Jeansoulin, 2016).

The aforementioned definition serves to differentiate Big Data from conventional transactional analyzing as well as business intelligence, besides implying a diverse range of potential applications that encompass these domains. The primary objective of Big Data analysis is to extract distinctive value that is reliable, owing to the dependability of the underlying data. This is achieved by utilizing sophisticated analytical techniques on the entire dataset, irrespective of its magnitude. The act of parsing these objective aids in structuring the discourse on the significance of implementing Big Data applications.

- The utilization of the complete corpus of pertinent data, instead of limited samples or subsets, across all scales of operations. The objective is to integrate decision-support time horizons, encompassing the past, present, as well as future, by utilizing statistically obtained insights from extensive data sets across all these dimensions.
- The acquisition of reliable data is crucial for obtaining accurate insights. This can be achieved through either consolidating or purifying deep data to establish a single form of reality or via utilizing statistical techniques to extract reliable information from large amounts of unrefined data (Hitzler & Janowicz, 2013).
- The utilization of sophisticated analytical techniques and tools to extract insights and knowledge from data is referred to as sophisticated analytics. The utilization of diverse analytical and mining methodologies to extract insights via data patterns, including "long tail" evaluations, micro-segmentations, as well as others, can lead to expedited insights. However, such techniques may not be viable when limited by smaller amounts, slower speeds, narrower variations, as well as undetermined veracities.

An intricate inquiry pertains to the defining characteristics of "Big Data" and the threshold at which a dataset can be classified as such. The response to the question is inconclusive and contingent upon various factors. One aspect of this matter pertains to the relativity of the term "Big," given the increasing density of computation as well as storage capabilities, which includes the availability of greater capacity in more compact and effective form factors. As a result, what is currently deemed as "Big" may not retain the same designation in the future? The term "big data" is applied to datasets that exhibit improved company efficiency when processed using new scalable buildings, as compared to traditional architectures. Stated differently, the conventional relational database platform is incapable of attaining the said functionality (Kitchin, 2014).

The concept of big data primarily centers on the perspective that data is considered large due to the necessity for scalable frameworks to manage it. As a result, improved architectures with enhanced scalability have emerged to address the demands of big data (Pajić et al., 2018).

8.2. CLOUD COMPUTING

Learning Objectives

At the end of this section, readers will be able to:

- Explain the fundamental concepts and principles of cloud computing, including the key components and service models.
- Discuss the advantages and disadvantages of adopting cloud computing for businesses and organizations.
- Describe the various deployment models of cloud computing and compare their characteristics, such as public, private, hybrid, and multi-cloud environments.

Cloud computing is a technology that provides a range of computing services, including storage devices, databases, networks, software, analytics, as well as intelligence, through the internet. This technology is designed to facilitate faster innovation, offer flexible resources, enable heavy computation, support parallel computation, as well as offer economies of scale. The abstraction of computing, storage, as well as network facilities to tasks as required, along with access to a plethora of prebuilt services, enables organizations to focus on their core business. The document presents a comprehensive overview of the distinct services provided by individual computing layers, along with a comparative analysis of their dissimilarities (Dillon et al., 2010).

The assortment of services for cloud computing that are currently accessible is extensive, however, the majority of them can be categorized into either of the groups that follow (Armbrust et al., 2010):

8.2.1. SaaS: Software-as-a-Service

The SaaS sector is the most extensive cloud market and frequently employed business alternative in cloud computing services. Software-as-a-service (SaaS) is a software delivery model that enables the provision of applications to end-users via the Internet. SaaS apps are managed by external providers, and clients access their interfaces via web browsers. Due to the fact that a majority of SaaS applications operate directly through a web browser, there is no requirement for the end-user to download or set up any software. SaaS vendors assume responsibility for managing applications, execution, data, middleware, operating systems, virtualization, storage facilities, servers, as well as networking. This comprehensive approach facilitates streamlined maintenance as well as assistance for enterprises (Godse & Mulik, 2009).

8.2.2. PaaS: Platform-as-a-Service

The (PaaS) model facilitates the delivery of software as well as hardware via the internet, enabling developers to construct tailored applications. Platform-as-a-service (PaaS) facilitates the expeditious, uncomplicated, and economic development, testing, as well as installation of applications. This particular model enables businesses to develop and construct applications that are seamlessly integrated into Platform-as-a-Service (PaaS) software parts, while the management of the operating system, cloud computing, servers, data storage, network, as well as the PaaS software actually is handled by either enterprise operations or third-party providers. The aforementioned applications exhibit cloud characteristics, rendering them both highly available as well as scalable (Giessmann et al., 2012) (Figure 8.5).

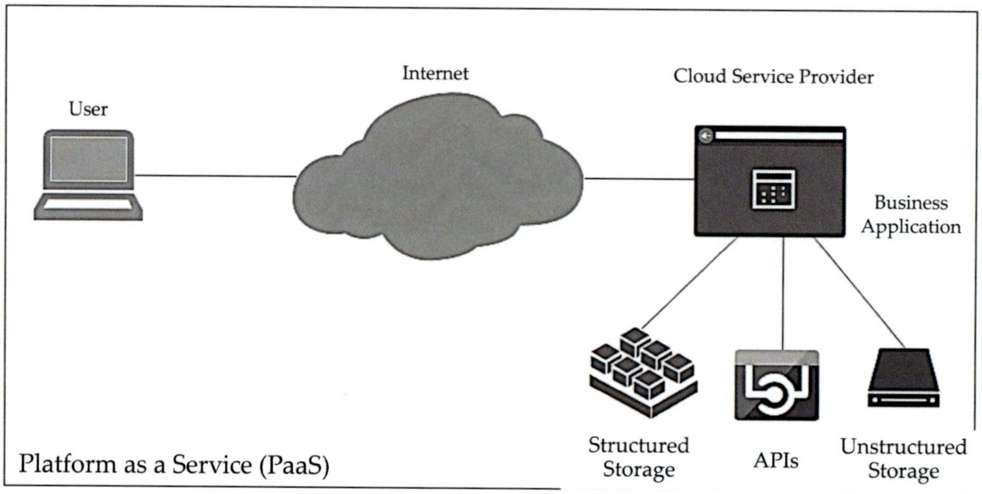

Figure 8.5. Platform-as-a-service (PaaS).

8.2.3. IaaS: Infrastructure-as-a-Service

IaaS refers to a cloud computing model where a third-party provider hosts virtualized computing resources over the internet. These resources can include servers, storage, networking, and other computing infrastructure components. Customers can then access and use these resources on a pay-per-use basis, allowing them to scale their infrastructure up or down as needed without having to invest in and maintain physical hardware. The cloud computing paradigm offers a self-service platform that enables organizations to obtain, monitor, and supervise remote data center infrastructures, including servers, storage devices, and networking services, via the use of virtualization technology. The responsibility of managing data, apps, runtime, middleware, as well as OS falls upon the users of infrastructure-as-a-service (IaaS), while the providers are still accountable for managing virtualization, computers, hard drive retrieval, and networking. Infrastructure-as-a-service (IaaS) offers comparable functionalities to traditional data centers, while eliminating the need for physical maintenance (Manvi & Shyam, 2014).

8.3. CLOUD DATABASE PROVIDERS: AWS, AZURE, GOOGLE CLOUD

Learning Objectives

At the end of this section, readers will be able to:

- Compare the key features and services offered by AWS, Azure, and Google Cloud in the context of cloud database solutions.
- Describe the benefits and limitations of using AWS, Azure, and Google Cloud as cloud database providers.
- Analyze the pricing models and cost structures of cloud database services on AWS, Azure, and Google Cloud, and how they impact decision-making.

Cloud database suppliers are entities that provide cloud-oriented database solutions to both corporate and individual clients. The company offers managed database services that enable users to securely store, efficiently manage, and easily retrieve their data in a cloud-based environment. The three primary providers of cloud databases are Amazon's Web Services, Azure from Microsoft, as well as Google Cloud. This exposition will comprehensively examine each of these service providers, expounding on their provisions, characteristics, and benefits (Kaushik et al., 2021).

8.3.1. Amazon Web Services (AWS)

Amazon.com provides a comprehensive cloud-based computing platform known as Amazon Web Services (AWS). Amazon Web Services (AWS) offers a range of database services that are tailored to meet diverse requirements. Several noteworthy database services are available by Amazon Web Services:

- Amazon RDS serves as a controlled database service offering support for multiple relational database platforms, including but not limited to PostgreSQL, MySQL, SQL Server, Oracle, as well as MariaDB. The software automates various database administration tasks that are typically time-consuming, including hardware provisioning, updating, backups, as well as failover. This enables users to direct their attention towards their applications (Hashemipour & Ali, 2020).

- Amazon DynamoDB serves as a NoSQL database service that is fully managed and provided by AWS. The system exhibits high scalability and is specifically engineered to effectively manage substantial amounts of data while maintaining minimal latency. DynamoDB is a fitting choice for applications that necessitate adaptable, efficient, and expandable database functionalities.
- Amazon Aurora represents a cloud-based relational database key designed specifically for cloud computing. This solution provides comparable efficiency and accessibility to that commercial-grade files while being significantly more cost-effective. Aurora has the capability to function seamlessly with both MySQL as well as PostgreSQL, thereby augmenting its proficiency and expandability (Mathew & Varia, 2014).
- Amazon DocumentDB acts as a NoSQL record database service that has been fully managed and has compatibility with MongoDB. The technology in question presents the capacity for scalability, resilience, and availability, rendering it a fitting option for applications that prioritize document-oriented functionality.
- Amazon Web Services (AWS) offers a diverse array of database services, including but not limited to Amazon Redshift, which is used for data storage, Amazon Neptune over databases with graphs, as well as Amazon ElastiCache over in-memory caching (Cook, 2018).

8.3.2. Microsoft Azure

The Microsoft Azure system is a solution for cloud computing offered by Microsoft. Azure provides a variety of database services that are tailored to accommodate diverse data types as well as workloads. Several notable database services offered by Azure are:

- Azure SQL database seems a relational database assistance that is managed and constructed on the foundation of SQL Server by Microsoft. The product provides elevated levels of efficiency, expandability, and protection. The Azure Microsoft SQL Database platform offers a range of capabilities such as automated tuning, integrated intelligence, and adaptable deployment alternatives (Lang et al., 2015).
- Cosmos DB from Azure has become a database assistance that is distributed globally and supports multiple models. The system provides support for a variety of data models, such as key-value, record, column family, as well as time-series. Cosmos DB is a database management system that offers features such as automatic scaling, reliability, as well as low latency. These capabilities make it a fitting choice for applications that are distributed globally.
- Azure Database over MySQL, as well as Azure Database over PostgreSQL, as well as Azure Database over PostgreSQL, are cloud-based services that provide completely managed databases to MySQL as well as PostgreSQL, respectively. The aforementioned features encompass high availability, computerized backups, as well as intelligent optimization of performance.
- In addition to its primary offerings, Azure provides supplementary database

services including Azure Synapse Analytics, which specializes in data storage, Azure Cache over Redis, which facilitates caching, along with Azure Database over MariaDB (Das et al., 2019).

8.3.3. Google Cloud

Google Cloud has become a cloud-based computing system provided by the technology giant, Google. Google Cloud offers a variety of database services that cater to a wide range of needs. Prominent database services offered by Google Cloud consist of:

- Cloud SQL Services is a type of managed relationship-based database service with the capability to support both MySQL as well as PostgreSQL. The product provides automated backup functionality, robust availability features, and effortless scalability options. Cloud SQL is a suitable option for applications that necessitate conventional relational database functionalities.
- Cloud Spanner seems a relational database assistance that is firmly consistent, horizontally adaptable, as well as globally distributed. The system offers transactions using ACID spanning multiple regions as well as features automated scaling as well as data synchronization capabilities. Cloud Spanner serves as a highly appropriate solution for apps that are critical to the success of an organization and necessitate global reach and robust consistency (Bisong & Bisong, 2019).
- Cloud Firestore serves as a document-oriented NoSQL database assistance. The software offers instantaneous synchronization, offline functionality, and automated scalability. Firestore is a viable option for mobile and web-based applications that require instantaneous updates and the ability to function without an internet connection.

In addition to its primary offerings, Google Cloud provides supplementary database solutions such as BigQuery, which facilitates data warehousing, Cloud Bigtable, which enables efficient NoSQL, as well as Memorystore over Redis, which supports caching (Shah & Dubaria, 2019).

8.3.4. Advantages of Cloud Database Providers

- The capacity of cloud database suppliers enables users to adjust the size of their databases to meet their specific requirements. The attribute of scalability obviates the necessity for initial capital expenditure on hardware as well as empowers enterprises to proficiently manage fluctuating workloads (Avram, 2014).
- Cloud databases have been designed to exhibit high availability by incorporating inherent redundancy and automated failover mechanisms. This guarantees the persistence of data accessibility in the face of potential hardware or network malfunctions.
- Cloud database suppliers provide management services, which encompass a range of administrative duties including software updates, restores, and overall

performance optimization. This enables users to allocate their time as well as finances more efficiently toward their primary business operations (Ahmadi & Aslani, 2018).

- Cloud database vendors offer a global reach by means of data centers situated across various regions, which allows customers to store as well as imitate their data for enhanced performance along with data redundancy.
- Cloud database practitioners employ stringent security protocols to safeguard data against unauthorized access as well as ensure adherence to industry norms and regulatory requirements. The provided security measures include encryption both at rest as well as during transit, authentication for users, along with access controls according to assigned roles.

In general, AWS, Azure, as well as Google Cloud offer extensive and dependable cloud-based database solutions, enabling enterprises to harness the benefits of cloud computing for their file storage and administration requirements (Abadi, 2009).

8.4. RELATIONSHIP BETWEEN THE CLOUD AND BIG DATA

Learning Objectives

At the end of this section, readers will be able to:

- • Explain the fundamental concepts of cloud computing and how it relates to the storage and processing of big data.
- • Discuss the advantages and disadvantages of using cloud-based solutions for big data analytics and storage.
- • Analyze the scalability and elasticity features of cloud platforms in the context of handling large volumes of big data.

The domains of Big Data along with Cloud Computing exhibit a strong interdependence. The concept of big data centers on the extraction of value, whereas cloud computing is centered around self-service models that are scalable, flexible, on-demand, along with pay-per-use. The analysis of big data necessitates significant on-demand computational capabilities along with dispersed storage. Cloud computing offers a seamless solution by providing elastic, incorporated computer resources, as well as the necessary storage and computational power to facilitate the analysis of big data. Cloud computing provides distributed processing capabilities that enable scalability as well as expansion via the use of virtual machines, thereby addressing the needs of rapidly increasing data volumes. The proliferation of analytical websites has arisen to meet the needs of users, particularly those of data-intensive enterprises, by furnishing contextualized analyzes of their stored data. The emergence of big data has led to the provision of cost-effective big data systems by service providers including Amazon, Microsoft, as well as Google. These systems are designed to capture data as well as incorporate analytics for offering proactive along with contextual experiences (Zanoon et al., 2017).

The utilization of cloud computing infrastructure represents a novel and highly effective method for delivering information technology services. The cloud computing environment comprises multiple providers as well as consumer terminals. The aforementioned encompasses a variety of computing devices and software, as well as services that are either pay-per-use or dependent on subscriptions, which are available online as well as within real-time. Big data resources are utilized for data collection, which is subsequently kept and analyzed in the cloud. Cloud computing offers readily available facilities and amenities that facilitate the uninterrupted management of data. The prevalent big data analytics designs include software-as-a-service (SaaS), platform-as-a-service (PaaS), and infrastructure-as-a-service (IaaS). Cloud-based analytics as well as Analytics just like a Service have emerged as contemporary solutions that cater to the needs of customers on a demand basis. Analytics-as-a-service (AaaS) is a cloud-based subscription model that offers data analysis tools and procedures.

This approach provides a rapid and scalable method for integrating data in partially structured, unstructured, as well as structured formats, as well as transforming and analyzing them (Bahrami & Singhal, 2015).

Virtualization refers to the technique of generating a software-based or virtual depiction of network connections, operating systems, servers, storage, along with virtual desktops. The process involves the establishment of a simulated computing environment within a pre-existing server, which enables the execution of preferred software applications while ensuring that the server's additional features and services remain unaffected and available to other consumers. The practice of sharing a solitary physical instance for an item or application among numerous consumers and companies is commonly referred to as a method. This is accomplished through the allocation of a symbolic identifier to a tangible storage entity and the provision of a reference to that tangible resource upon request. The process of virtualization allows for the consolidation of numerous workloads, which are executed on various physical servers, and then transferred onto distinct virtual computers that are accommodated on a solitary physical server. Reducing the quantity of physical servers can lead to a decrease in data center intricacy, as well as a reduction in both capital as well as administrative expenses. This approach results in decreased resource utilization along with enhanced power efficiency in comparison to a setup involving multiple nodes. Virtual machines possess a high degree of flexibility and portability, thereby facilitating the transfer of workloads to alternative server hardware in the event of unforeseen downtime, equipment malfunction, or maintenance of applications. The utilization of computerized big data applications such as Hadoop offers advantages that are not attainable through physical structures in areas such as usage of resources, expenses, as well as data management. Online data encompasses a diverse array of data sources as well as enhances the accessibility of data across heterogeneous environments. Moreover, it facilitates the transmission of data at a rapid pace across the network, thereby expediting data processing (Hashem et al., 2015).

Preserving confidentiality and safeguarding the integrity of information constitute a crucial facet of big data. The hosting and processing of data on outside infrastructure as well as services within cloud computing presents a significant challenge with regard to security and confidentiality. The greater the magnitude, diversity, and accuracy of large-scale data, the more significant the potential hazards related to its confidentiality and protection. The utilization of mobile health technology has significantly transformed the delivery of healthcare services across various domains (Sandhu, 2021). The availability of diverse healthcare mobile apps has facilitated individuals in preserving their standard of living, physical well-being, medicinal guidance, and diagnosis. The transmission of data across mobile internet may present a significant risk to the privacy of information in the absence of adequate network security measures or in the event of unauthorized access. In order to instill confidence in users and ensure the protection of their data, it is imperative to uphold a range of new laws, confidentiality guidelines, regulations, safeguards, regulatory requirements, as well as service level commitments between suppliers and buyers. The safeguarding of big data within the cloud has become a crucial concern due to the necessity of shielding the data from malevolent external entities. Additionally, the secure management of vast storage capacity by cloud service providers becomes of utmost importance (Marx, 2013).

The correlation within big data, as well as computing via the cloud adheres to the input-processing-output paradigm. The data input comprises voluminous data procured from diverse sources including smart devices like cellular phones, which may be structured, or partially structured in nature. The copious amount of data is subjected to a cleansing process and subsequently maintained in Hadoop or just other data repositories. The data that has been stored is subsequently subjected to cloud computing methods and devices in order to facilitate the provision of services. The computation steps encompass all the necessary tasks involved in converting the entered data. The output refers to the numerical or graphical representation that is obtained subsequent to the processing of data for the purposes of analyzing and displaying it (Zheng et al., 2013).

The (IoT) represents a shared characteristic across Cloud computing as well as big data. The voluminous data produced by Internet of Things (IoT) devices necessitates real-time analysis. Cloud service providers facilitate the transmission of data through the internet or leased lines and subsequently store it within data repositories. Cloud computing methodologies and instruments are subsequently employed to process and scrutinize the voluminous data housed in the cloud. It offers a means for information to traverse, be stored, and undergo analysis. Cloud computing offers a shared infrastructure for the integration of the Internet of Things (IoT) as well as big data. The domains of cloud computing, the Internet of Things (IoT), as well as Big Data, exhibit a mutually reinforcing relationship (Khan et al., 2015) (Figure 8.6).

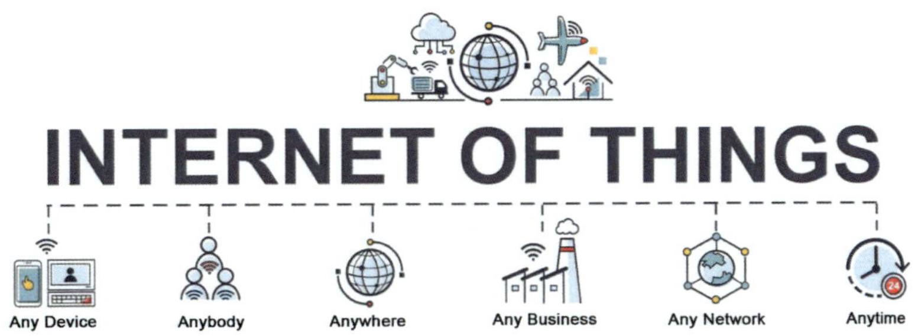

Figure 8.6. Internet of things.

8.5. SOLUTIONS AND METHODOLOGIES FOR DATA STORAGE

Learning Objectives

At the end of this section, readers will be able to:

- Explain the key principles and concepts of data storage solutions and methodologies.
- Discuss various data storage technologies and their respective advantages and limitations.
- Explore data storage architectures, including centralized, distributed, and cloud-based storage systems.

Various solutions have been proposed to address the storage and retrieval of vast quantities of data required by Big Data, with some of these solutions currently being implemented in Cloud computing. Internet-scale storage systems, like the Google Document System, endeavor to furnish the durability, expandability, and dependability that specific Internet services necessitate. Several alternative solutions offer object-store functionalities that enable the replication of files across various geographical locations to enhance redundancy, scaling, and data accessibility. Several cloud storage offerings are available, such as Amazon Simple Storage Service (S3), Nirvanix Dropbox, OpenStack Swift, as well as Microsoft Azure Binary Big Object (Blob) data storage. While these solutions may offer the necessary scalability as well as redundancy for numerous Cloud apps, they may not always satisfy the requirements for concurrency as well as efficiency in specific analytics applications (Jaseena & David, 2014).

Data location is a crucial factor in ensuring optimal performance over Big Data analytics apps. The reason for this is that the extensive amount of data implicated in the analytics renders it impractical to transmit the data for processing. In conventional systems, the favored approach involves executing CPU-intensive computations on an average to medium-scale data set. This is due to the fact that the data transmit-to-processing time ratio is relatively low, making it practical for transferring data to computer units. However, within the realm of Big Data, this methodology of relocating data to calculation nodes would result in a significant proportion of time being allocated to the transmission of data as opposed to processing time. Therefore, an alternative methodology is favored, whereby the computational process is relocated to the location of the data. The method of investigating data locality has been previously examined in scientific processes as well as Information Grids (Catthoor, 1999).

Within the realm of Big Data analysis, the MapReduce paradigm offers a compelling framework that leverages data locality to enhance application performance. Hadoop, a freely available implementation based on the MapReduce framework, facilitates the formation of clusters that employ the HDFS, to divide and duplicate data sets across nodes, thereby enhancing the likelihood of their consumption by mappers. HDFS mitigates the effects of failures by duplicating datasets to a customizable quantity of nodes, while also capitalizing on the concurrence of numerous nodes. The development of a platform for analysis for processing Facebook's extensive data sets is being documented by.

The platform employs the Scribe tool to consolidate logs generated by Web servers, subsequently exporting these into Hadoop Distributed File System (HDFS) archives. The analytics tasks are executed by a Hive-Hadoop group. The platform incorporates replication and compression methodologies, as well as columnar compression about Hive7, in order to efficiently store vast quantities of data (Lo et al., 2019).

Despite the prevalence of unorganized data in contemporary times, relational databases remain the preferred storage option for organizations seeking to manage information pertaining to customers, business operations, goods, and other relevant domains. As data stored in conventional DBMS grows older, it is transferred to information warehouses for the purpose of analysis and occasional retrieval.

The suitability of models like MapReduce for analyzing relational data is generally limited. Hybrid solutions are being developed to integrate MapReduce functionality into the data analyzing as well as query operations of DBMS, as documented in reference. The authors of present a design for databases that enables analytics through the use of SQL as well as MapReduce coding, while also facilitating the integration of diverse data sources within a DBMS. Several vendors for analytics and information mining options are adopting a strategy of deploying processing tasks in proximity to the information's storage location, leveraging models that include MapReduce.

This approach aims to reduce redundancies in preparing the data, archiving, and processing. The processing and analytical capabilities associated with data are increasingly shifting in the direction of Enterprise Data Warehouses (EDWs) or being implemented in data hubs that allow efficient utilization across diverse data sets (Kumar et al., 2018).

A discernible pattern in the realm of Cloud computing involves the growing adoption of NoSQL databases which are the favored approach for information storage and retrieval. The NoSQL database management system employs a non-relational approach to storing data. According to Leavitt, unrelated models, including object-oriented, ordered, and graphed databases, have already been in existence for over half a century. However, in recent times, this approach has garnered increased attention with the emergence of models that include key-store, column-oriented, as well as document-based outlets.

Levitt attributes the increase in interest to improved performance, capability to manage unstructured data, and compatibility with distributed environments.

The authors of conducted an in-depth examination of NoSQL databases, highlighting their strengths and weaknesses in the context of Cloud computing. The classification of NoSQL structures within the survey is based on how well they are able to handle distinct groups of CAP (consistency, accessibility, partitioning). The research study additionally investigates the supported data model of the NoSQL database systems under examination (Ranky, 2006).

8.6. DATA PROCESSING AND RESOURCE MANAGEMENT

Learning Objectives

At the end of this section, readers will be able to:

- Explain the fundamental principles of data processing, including data collection, transformation, and storage techniques.
- Discuss the importance of resource management in data processing, highlighting key concepts such as scalability, load balancing, and fault tolerance.
- Describe various data processing tools and technologies, such as batch processing, real-time processing, and stream processing, and their respective use cases.

In attempting to comprehend the notion of Big Data, one cannot evade the usage of terms that include "Map Reduce" as well as "Hadoop."

8.6.1. Hadoop

Hadoop comprises a Java-based coding framework that facilitates the computation of extensive datasets in the context of distributed computing and is available at no cost. This is a component of the Apache initiative that is financially supported via the Apache Software Foundation. The Hadoop cluster is organized in a Master/Slave architecture. Hadoop facilitates the processing of voluminous data sets across a network of servers, enabling the execution of apps on systems comprising numerous nodes as well as involving extensive storage capacity in the order of several terabytes. The utilization of a file system that is distributed within the Hadoop framework facilitates expeditious transmission of data as well as enables the system to maintain its standard functionality in the event of certain node failures. The aforementioned methodology mitigates the likelihood of a complete system breakdown, even in scenarios where a substantial quantity of node failures occurs. The Hadoop framework facilitates a technological solution that possesses the desirable attributes of scalability, cost-effectiveness, flexibility, and fault tolerance. The Hadoop Guidelines are utilized by prominent corporations such as Google, Amazon, as well as IBM, among others, to facilitate their applications that entail substantial quantities of data. The Hadoop framework comprises two primary sub-projects, namely MapReduce as well as (HDFS) (Luckow et al., 2016).

8.6.2. MapReduce

The Hadoop MapReduce platform is utilized for developing applications that can efficiently handle massive data sets in a parallel manner across clusters of low-cost hardware resources while ensuring reliability and fault tolerance. The Map Reduce procedure initially partitions the data into discrete segments, which are subsequently subjected to parallel processing by Map tasks. Subsequently, the reducing tasks receive the results in the form of maps that have been sorted according to the structure. Typically, the data entered, and the results of the task are stored within a file system. It is responsible for managing the scheduling, tracking, and re-execution of failed tasks (Wang et al., 2013).

8.6.3. Hadoop Distributed File System (HDFS)

The Hadoop Distributed File System seems a distributed file system that provides data storage across all nodes within a Hadoop cluster. The process involves the integration of file systems present on individual nodes into a unified file system of significant magnitude. The High-Performance Distributed File System (HDFS) enhances reliability by implementing data replication across various sources to mitigate the impact of node failures (Borthakur, 2007) (Figure 8.7).

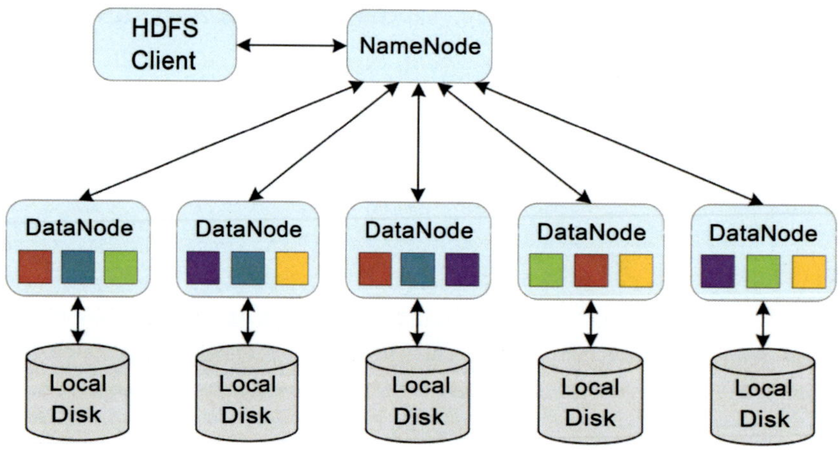

Figure 8.7. Schematic of high-performance distributed file system (HDFS).

8.7. ADVANTAGES OF BIG DATA APPLICATIONS

Learning Objectives

At the end of this section, readers will be able to:

- Explain the key advantages of utilizing Big Data applications in improving business decision-making processes.
- Discuss how Big Data applications can enhance predictive analytics and forecasting accuracy in various industries.
- Explore the benefits of scalability and cost-effectiveness offered by Big Data applications for data storage and processing.

The term "big data application" pertains to distributed apps that operate on vast data sets. The task of exploring and analyzing data has become a challenging issue across various industries in the era of big data. The processing of vast and intricate datasets poses a challenge for conventional data processing apps, necessitating the creation of big data apps. The Google MapReduce platform as well as Apache Hadoop have become popular software systems for managing large-scale data applications that often produce substantial volumes of intermediary data. The two primary domains of big data utilization are manufacturing activities as well as Bioinformatics (Oussous et al., 2018).

The utilization of big data within the production sector offers a framework for promoting transparency. This technology has the potential to address uncertainties that arise from issues including erratic component functionality and accessibility. The theoretical framework for automated production in big data apps commences via the collection of data, which may encompass different kinds of sensory information, including but not limited to pressure, tremors, acoustics, electrical current, voltage, as well as controller data. The amalgamation of sensory information and historical records constitutes large-scale data within the realm of production. The aforementioned amalgamation produces a substantial amount of data, commonly referred to as big data, which serves as the primary input for predictive techniques as well as preventative measures, including prognostics as well as medical management.

Hadoop has a significant application in the field of Bioinformatics, particularly in the areas of genome sequencing as well as other biological areas. Hadoop is utilized in the field of bioinformatics, which involves extensive analysis of vast amounts of data. The integration of computer clusters along with web-based interfaces via an accelerated shared computing structure is a characteristic feature of cloud computing (Muhammad et al., 2020).

SUMMARY

This chapter explores ETL (Extract, Transform, Load) processing with SQL in the context of Big Data. It discusses the significance of Big Data models and their flexibility in handling structured, semi-structured, and unstructured data. The chapter also delves into cloud computing, including different service models and popular cloud database providers like AWS, Azure, and Google Cloud. It highlights the relationship between the cloud and Big Data, as well as solutions and methodologies for data storage and processing. The chapter concludes with an examination of the advantages, challenges, and business applications of Big Data, emphasizing the importance of good architectural design, analytical methods, and in-memory analytics.

REVIEW QUESTIONS

1. What are the different types of data models used in Big Data processing?
2. Name three major cloud database providers and their advantages.
3. How does ETL processing with SQL contribute to data transformation and integration?
4. Explain the concept of schema-on-read and its significance in Big Data analytics.
5. What are the three categories of cloud computing services?
6. Describe the Hadoop framework and its role in data processing.
7. How does MapReduce facilitate distributed data processing?

MULTIPLE CHOICE QUESTIONS

1. Which of the following best describes a cloud database?

a. A database stored on physical servers within an organization's premises.

b. A database accessed and managed over the internet, hosted by a cloud service provider.

c. A database that can only be accessed using specialized software installed on local machines.

d. A database designed specifically for storing multimedia files such as images and videos.

2. What is the primary advantage of using a cloud database?

a. Lower security compared to traditional on-premises databases.

b. Limited scalability and storage capacity.

c. Reduced infrastructure costs and increased flexibility.

d. Higher latency and slower data retrieval speeds.

3. Which term refers to the process of analyzing large and complex datasets to uncover patterns, trends, and insights?

a. Data warehousing

b. Data mining

c. Data normalization

d. Data replication

4. What is the main challenge associated with big data?

a. Limited storage options

b. Lack of data variety

c. Difficulty in processing and analyzing large volumes of data

d. Low data velocity

5. Which technology is commonly used to store and process big data in distributed environments?

a. Relational databases

b. NoSQL databases

c. Mainframe computers

d. Desktop PCs

Answers to Multiple Choice Questions

1. (b); 2. (c); 3. (b); 4. (c); 5. (b);

REFERENCES

1. Abadi, D. J., (2009). Data management in the cloud: Limitations and opportunities. IEEE Data Eng. Bull., 32(1), 3–12.
2. Bahrami, M., & Singhal, M., (2015). The role of cloud computing architecture in big data. Information Granularity, Big Data, and Computational Intelligence, 5, 275–295.
3. Bakshi, K., (2012). Considerations for big data: Architecture and approach. In: 2012 IEEE Aerospace Conference (Vol. 1, pp. 1–7). IEEE.
4. Bamiah, S. N., Brohi, S. N., & Rad, B. B., (2018). Big data technology in education: Advantages, implementations, and challenges. Journal of Engineering Science and Technology, 13(2018), 229–241.
5. Bao, Y., Song, J., Leng, F., Wang, D., & Yu, G., (2007). Study and implementation of a new SQL-based ETL approach. Wuhan University Journal of Natural Sciences, 12(5), 804–808.
6. Bisong, E., & Bisong, E., (2019). An overview of google cloud platform services. Building Machine Learning and Deep Learning Models on Google Cloud Platform: A Comprehensive Guide for Beginners, 4, 7–10.

7. Borthakur, D., (2007). The Hadoop distributed file system: Architecture and design. Hadoop Project Website, 11(2007), 21.
8. Catthoor, F., (1999). Energy-delay efficient data storage and transfer architectures and methodologies: Current solutions and remaining problems. Journal of VLSI Signal Processing Systems for Signal, Image, and Video Technology, 21, 219–231.
9. Fothergill, B. T., Knight, W., Stahl, B. C., & Ulnicane, I., (2019). Responsible data governance of neuroscience big data. Frontiers in Neuroinformatics, 13, 28.
10. Galici, R., Ordile, L., Marchesi, M., Pinna, A., & Tonelli, R., (2020). Applying the ETL process to blockchain data. prospect and findings. Information, 11(4), 204.
11. Garber, L., (2012). Using in-memory analytics to quickly crunch big data. Computer, 45(10), 16–18.
12. Giessmann, A., & Stanoevska-Slabeva, K., (2012). Business models of platform as a service (PaaS) providers: Current state and future directions. JITTA: Journal of Information Technology Theory and Application, 13(4), 31.
13. Godse, M., & Mulik, S., (2009). An approach for selecting software-as-a-service (SaaS) product. In: 2009 IEEE International Conference on Cloud Computing (Vol. 2, pp. 155–158). IEEE.
14. Hashem, I. A. T., Yaqoob, I., Anuar, N. B., Mokhtar, S., Gani, A., & Khan, S. U., (2015). The rise of "big data" on cloud computing: Review and open research issues. Information Systems, 47, 98–115.
15. Hashemipour, S., & Ali, M., (2020). Amazon web services (AWS)–an overview of the on-demand cloud computing platform. In: Emerging Technologies in Computing: Third EAI International Conference, iCETiC 2020, London, UK, Proceedings 3 (Vol. 3, pp. 40–47). Springer International Publishing.
16. Hitzler, P., & Janowicz, K., (2013). Linked data, big data, and the 4th paradigm. Semantic Web, 4(3), 233–235.
17. Hu, F., Yang, C., Schnase, J. L., Duffy, D. Q., Xu, M., Bowen, M. K., & Song, W., (2018). ClimateSpark: An in-memory distributed computing framework for big climate data analytics. Computers & Geosciences, 115, 154–166.
18. Janković, S., Mladenović, S., Mladenović, D., Vesković, S., & Glavić, D., (2018). Schema on read modeling approach as a basis of big data analytics integration in EIS. Enterprise Information Systems, 12(8, 9), 1180–1201.
19. Jaseena, K. U., & David, J. M., (2014). Issues, challenges, and solutions: Big data mining. CS & IT-CSCP, 4(13), 131–140.
20. Jeansoulin, R., (2016). Review of forty years of technological changes in geomatics toward the big data paradigm. ISPRS International Journal of Geo-Information, 5(9), 155.
21. Jin, X., Wah, B. W., Cheng, X., & Wang, Y., (2015). Significance and challenges of big data research. Big Data Research, 2(2), 59–64.
22. Kaisler, S., Armour, F., Espinosa, J. A., & Money, W., (2013). Big data: Issues and challenges moving forward. In: 2013 46th Hawaii International Conference on System Sciences (Vol. 1, pp. 995–1004).

23. Katal, A., Wazid, M., & Goudar, R. H., (2013). Big data: Issues, challenges, tools, and good practices. In: 2013 Sixth International Conference on Contemporary Computing (IC3) (Vol. 1, pp. 404–409). IEEE.
24. Kaushik, P., Rao, A. M., Singh, D. P., Vashisht, S., & Gupta, S., (2021). Cloud computing and comparison based on service and performance between amazon AWS, Microsoft azure, and google cloud. In: 2021 International Conference on Technological Advancements and Innovations (ICTAI) (Vol. 1, pp. 268–273). IEEE.
25. Khan, Z., Anjum, A., Soomro, K., & Tahir, M. A., (2015). Towards cloud based big data analytics for smart future cities. Journal of Cloud Computing, 4(1), 1–11.
26. Kim, H. Y., & Cho, J. S., (2018). Data governance framework for big data implementation with NPS case analysis in Korea. Journal of Business and Retail Management Research, 12(3), 98–100.
27. Kimura, A., Yokozawa, T., & Ozaki, H., (2021). Clarifying the biomechanical concept of coordination through comparison with coordination in motor control. Frontiers in Sports and Active Living, 3, 753062.
28. Kitchin, R., (2014). Big data, new epistemologies, and paradigm shifts. Big Data & Society, 1(1), 8481–8489.
29. Kressbach, M., (2021). Period hacks: Menstruating in the big data paradigm. Television & New Media, 22(3), 241–261.
30. Kumar, P. R., Raj, P. H., & Jelciana, P., (2018). Exploring data security issues and solutions in cloud computing. Procedia Computer Science, 125, 691–697.
31. Lang, W., Bertsch, F., DeWitt, D. J., & Ellis, N., (2015). Microsoft azure SQL database telemetry. In: Proceedings of the Sixth ACM Symposium on Cloud Computing (Vol. 2, pp. 189–194).
32. Lee, S., & Park, S., (2021). Performance analysis of big data ETL process over CPU-GPU heterogeneous architectures. In: 2021 IEEE 37th International Conference on Data Engineering Workshops (ICDEW) (Vol. 2, pp. 42–47). IEEE.
33. Li, S., Dragicevic, S., Castro, F. A., Sester, M., Winter, S., Coltekin, A., & Cheng, T., (2016). Geospatial big data handling theory and methods: A review and research challenges. ISPRS Journal of Photogrammetry and Remote Sensing, 115, 119–133.
34. Lo, S. K., Liu, Y., Chia, S. Y., Xu, X., Lu, Q., Zhu, L., & Ning, H., (2019). Analysis of blockchain solutions for IoT: A systematic literature review. IEEE Access, 7, 58822–58835.
35. Luckow, A., Paraskevakos, I., Chantzialexiou, G., & Jha, S., (2016). Hadoop on HPC: Integrating Hadoop and pilot-based dynamic resource management. In: 2016 IEEE International Parallel and Distributed Processing Symposium Workshops (IPDPSW) (Vol. 2, pp. 1607–1616). IEEE.
36. Madhavan, K., & Richey, M. C., (2016). Problems in big data analytics in learning. Journal of Engineering Education, 105(1), 6–14.
37. Manvi, S. S., & Shyam, G. K., (2014). Resource management for infrastructure as a service (IaaS) in cloud computing: A survey. Journal of Network and Computer Applications, 41, 424–440.

38. Marx, V., (2013). The big challenges of big data. Nature, 498(7453), 255–260.

39. Mathew, S., & Varia, J., (2014). Overview of amazon web services. Amazon Whitepapers, 105, 1–22.

40. Moreno, J., Serrano, M. A., & Fernández-Medina, E., (2016). Main issues in big data security. Future Internet, 8(3), 44.

41. Muhammad, R. N., Tasmin, R., & Aziati, A. N., (2020). Sustainable competitive advantage of big data analytics in higher education sector: An overview. In: Journal of Physics: Conference Series (Vol. 1529, p. 042100). IOP Publishing.

42. Oussous, A., Benjelloun, F. Z., Lahcen, A. A., & Belfkih, S., (2018). Big data technologies: A survey. Journal of King Saud University-Computer and Information Sciences, 30(4), 431–448.

43. Pajić, V., Govedarica, M., & Amović, M., (2018). Model of point cloud data management system in big data paradigm. ISPRS International Journal of Geo-Information, 7(7), 265.

44. Patgiri, R., & Ahmed, A., (2016). Big data: The v's of the game changer paradigm. In: 2016 IEEE 18th International Conference on High Performance Computing and Communications; IEEE 14th International Conference on Smart City; IEEE 2nd International Conference on Data Science and Systems (HPCC/SmartCity/DSS) (Vol. 1, pp. 17–24). IEEE.

45. Patil, H. K., & Seshadri, R., (2014). Big data security and privacy issues in healthcare. In: 2014 IEEE International Congress on Big Data (Vol. 1, pp. 762–765). IEEE.

46. Rajaniemi, M., (2003). Nokia mobile phones' development of business logistics and customer support. In: Information Technology Enabled Global Customer Service (Vol. 1, pp. 249–257). IGI Global.

47. Ranky, P. G., (2006). An introduction to radio frequency identification (RFID) methods and solutions. Assembly Automation, 26(1), 28–33.

48. Rodriguez-Muro, M., Hardi, J., & Calvanese, D., (2012). Quest: Efficient SPARQL-to-SQL for RDF and OWL. Proceedings of the ISWC 2012 Posters & Demonstrations Track: ISWC 2012 Posters & Demos, Collected Abstracts, 914, 53–56.

49. Salleh, K. A., & Janczewski, L., (2016). Technological, organizational, and environmental security and privacy issues of big data: A literature review. Procedia Computer Science, 100, 19–28.

50. Sandhu, A. K., (2021). Big data with cloud computing: Discussions and challenges. Big Data Mining and Analytics, 5(1), 32–40.

51. Scalici, S. P., Carry, Sr. W., Donnell, E., Rado, Z., & Hartmann, M. R., (2014). Red bus lane treatment evaluation. In: T&DI Congress 2014: Planes, Trains, and Automobiles (Vol. 1, pp. 132–141).

52. Shah, J., & Dubaria, D., (2019). Building modern clouds: Using docker, Kubernetes & Google cloud platform. In: 2019 IEEE 9th Annual Computing and Communication Workshop and Conference (CCWC) (Vol. 2, pp. 0184–0189). IEEE.

53. Sharma, S., Tim, U. S., Wong, J., Gadia, S., & Sharma, S., (2014). A brief review on leading big data models. Data Science Journal, 13, 138–157.

54. Silva, Y. N., Almeida, I., & Queiroz, M., (2016). SQL: From traditional databases to big data. In: Proceedings of the 47th ACM Technical Symposium on Computing Science Education (Vol. 1, pp. 413–418).
55. Sivarajah, U., Kamal, M. M., Irani, Z., & Weerakkody, V., (2017). Critical analysis of big data challenges and analytical methods. Journal of Business Research, 70, 263–286.
56. Smith, M., Szongott, C., Henne, B., & Von, V. G., (2012). Big data privacy issues in public social media. In: 2012 6th IEEE International Conference on Digital Ecosystems and Technologies (DEST) (Vol. 1, pp. 1–6). IEEE.
57. Stephens, Z. D., Lee, S. Y., Faghri, F., Campbell, R. H., Zhai, C., Efron, M. J., & Robinson, G. E., (2015). Big data: Astronomical or genomical? PLoS Biology, 13(7), e1002195.
58. Strang, K. D., & Sun, Z., (2017). Big data paradigm: What is the status of privacy and security? Annals of Data Science, 4, 1–17.
59. Sun, Z., Strang, K. D., & Pambel, F., (2018). Privacy and security in the big data paradigm. Journal of Computer Information Systems, 4(1), 45–49.
60. Tallon, P. P., (2013). Corporate governance of big data: Perspectives on value, risk, and cost. Computer, 46(6), 32–38.
61. Toshniwal, R., Dastidar, K. G., & Nath, A., (2015). Big data security issues and challenges. International Journal of Innovative Research in Advanced Engineering (IJIRAE), 2(2), 12–16.
62. Tsai, C. W., Lai, C. F., Chao, H. C., & Vasilakos, A. V., (2015). Big data analytics: A survey. Journal of Big Data, 2(1), 1–32.
63. Tsou, M. H., (2015). Research challenges and opportunities in mapping social media and big data. Cartography and Geographic Information Science, 42(1), 70–74.
64. Uddin, M. F., & Gupta, N., (2014). Seven V's of big data understanding big data to extract value. In: Proceedings of the 2014 Zone 1 Conference of the American Society for Engineering Education (Vol. 1, pp. 1–5). IEEE.
65. Villars, R. L., Olofson, C. W., & Eastwood, M., (2011). Big Data: What it is and Why You Should Care (Vol. 14, pp. 1–14). White paper, IDC.
66. Wang, L., Tao, J., Ranjan, R., Marten, H., Streit, A., Chen, J., & Chen, D., (2013). G-Hadoop: MapReduce across distributed data centers for data-intensive computing. Future Generation Computer Systems, 29(3), 739–750.
67. Wassouf, W. N., Alkhatib, R., Salloum, K., & Balloul, S., (2020). Predictive analytics using big data for increased customer loyalty: Syriatel Telecom Company case study. Journal of Big Data, 7, 1–24.
68. Wisesa, O., Adriansyah, A., & Khalaf, O. I., (2020). Prediction analysis for business to business (B2B) sales of telecommunication services using machine learning techniques. Majlesi Journal of Electrical Engineering, 14(4), 145–153.
69. Yang, L., Li, J., Elisa, N., Prickett, T., & Chao, F., (2019). Towards big data governance in cybersecurity. Data-Enabled Discovery and Applications, 3, 1–12.

70. Yu, M., Yang, C., & Li, Y., (2018). Big data in natural disaster management: A review. Geosciences, 8(5), 165.

71. Zanoon, N., Al-Haj, A., & Khwaldeh, S. M., (2017). Cloud computing and big data is there a relation between the two: A study. International Journal of Applied Engineering Research, 12(17), 6970–6982.

72. Zheng, Z., Zhu, J., & Lyu, M. R., (2013). Service-generated big data and big data-as-a-service: An overview. In: 2013 IEEE International Congress on Big Data (Vol. 1, pp. 403–410). IEEE.

73. Zuech, R., Khoshgoftaar, T. M., & Wald, R., (2015). Intrusion detection and big heterogeneous data: A survey. Journal of Big Data, 2(1), 1–41.

Index

D

FSC
www.fsc.org
MIX
Papier | Fördert gute Waldnutzung
FSC® C083411

Kolibri 360 GmbH
Ferdinand-Jühlke-Straße 7
99095 Erfurt, Deutschland
produktsicherheit@kolibri360.de